At the Margins

At the Margins

Four Years in South Asia and West Africa

Roger H. Guichard, Jr

WIPF & STOCK · Eugene, Oregon

AT THE MARGINS
Four Years in South Asia and West Africa

Copyright © 2017 Roger H. Guichard, Jr. All rights reserved. Except for brief quotations in critical publications or reviews, no part of this book may be reproduced in any manner without prior written permission from the publisher. Write: Permissions, Wipf and Stock Publishers, 199 W. 8th Ave., Suite 3, Eugene, OR 97401.

Wipf & Stock
An Imprint of Wipf and Stock Publishers
199 W. 8th Ave., Suite 3
Eugene, OR 97401

www.wipfandstock.com

PAPERBACK ISBN: 978-1-5326-1856-7
HARDCOVER ISBN: 978-1-4982-4424-4
EBOOK ISBN: 978-1-4982-4423-7

Manufactured in the U.S.A.   AUGUST 14, 2020

Maps are reproduced under license from Shutterstock.

For Martha, without whose spur
none of the following would have happened.

Contents

Illustrations | *ix*
Maps | *xi*
Preface | *xiii*

1	Peshawar and Quetta	1
2	The Mine Dog Center	12
3	Bismullah	21
4	Darra Adham Khel	25
5	Central Asia	32
6	The Khojak Pass	63
7	The Prison	73
8	The Ambassador	80
9	Mohammed	87
10	Norman Sicily	92
11	The Mosque	119
12	The Roof of the World	125
13	The Sale	138
14	Central Asia Revisited	143
15	Bakistan	178
16	Paris Interregnum	185
17	Cherif	189

18	Demilunes and Looney Tunes	194
19	The Project	199
20	The Bulletin	204
21	Foreign Service Nationals	209
22	Thanksgiving	217
23	The Milk Run	227

Glossary of Foreign Terms | 235

Illustrations

1	The trim, along the Grand Trunk	1
2	Cane juice vendor, Peshawar	2
3	The Khyber Pass, NWFP	4
4	Taxi, Quetta	5
5	The uniform, Peshawar	6
6	Dog and Handler, Mine Dog Center	15
7	Handler, Mine Dog Center	17
8	Shotguns, Darra	27
9	Karl Marx, Tashkent	36
10	Melons, Tashkent	37
11	Fruit market, Tashkent	37
12	Babushka, Tashkent	38
13	Restoration, Bokhara	42
14	Arslan Khan, Bokhara	42
15	Islam on the move, Bokhara	43
16	The generations, Samarkand	51
17	Turkman, Samarkand	52
18	The domes, Samarkand	52
19	Gala, Samarkand	53
20	Rajistan Samarkand	54
21	Vestibule, Samarkand	55

22	Camel transport, Quetta	67
23	Ghulam Ahmad Khan, Quetta	70
24	Martha, Shish Mahal, Lahore	80
25	The Movies, Delhi	82
26	Tourist, Red Fort, Delhi	84
27	Qutb Minar, Delhi	85
28	Qutb Minar detail, Delhi	86
29	Mohammed, Islamabad	87
30	Carabinieri, Palermo	99
31	Palermo Cathedral, Sicily	100
32	Orange domes, Palermo	101
33	Cefalu Cathedral, Sicily	110
34	C5, Islamabad	118
35	Rice paddies, Karakoram Highway	126
36	Karakorum Highway, northern territories	130
37	Khalta Minar, Khiva	155
38	Spetsnaz, Almata	163
39	May Day, Almata	165
40	Woman, Santigui, Niger	201
41	Driver, Santigui	202
42	Kids, Santigui	203
43	Planting rice, Kolo, Niamey	223
44	Rice paddy, Kolo, Niamey	224
45	Piroques, Niger river	225
46	The yard, Niamey	226

Maps

1. Islamic Republic of Pakistan | xvi
2. Uzbekistan | 31
3. Sahara and the Sahel | 184

Preface

AT THE MARGINS TELLS the story of living and working in the Afghan program in Pakistan for three years in the early 1990s followed by fourteen months in Niger in West Africa. The title comes from the fact that South Asia and West Africa represent relative extremes in the geographical reach of Islam. It is the second book in a series chronicling my twenty-five years in the Muslim World. The first, *Masr, an Egyptian Miscellany*, was published by Wipf & Stock in 2015.

I came to Pakistan in 1991 after ten years in the Arab world. For most of that time Arab eyes were fixed on the Indian subcontinent because of the Russian occupation of Afghanistan. Saudi Arabia in the 1980s had been a hotbed of resistance to the Soviets and exhibits in Jidda displayed grisly photographs of civilian mine victims and memorabilia taken from the corpses of Russian soldiers. Collectively the Arab world, along with America, were the greatest supporters of *jihad* in Afghanistan, although the integration of Arab volunteers into the resistance in Pashtun areas was not without friction.

But the Indian subcontinent was not entirely unfamiliar territory. My undergraduate background was in English literature, but it had been exposure not only to novelists and poets, but also to Victorian prose essayists: Hazlitt, Darwin, Huxley, Mill, Morris, Arnold, Burton, Palgrave, and Bell. For some of them experience of India was direct: Richard Burton and Gifford Palgrave were posted to the west coast early in their military careers and John Stewart Mill, arguably the greatest English-speaking philosopher of the nineteenth century, was for years a servant of the "Company of Merchants of London trading into the East Indies." For others, the connection was more distant.

However, for all of them empire—and India—was a constant, if unspoken, preoccupation throughout the century during which it achieved its greatest geographical extent. If nothing else there was the "Sepoy Rebellion" in 1857 that was as traumatic for mid-nineteenth century Britain as the attack on the twin towers was for the United States in the early twenty-first. The reaction was nearly as fierce. The events of 1857 may have put an end to the Company, but not to empire, and twenty years later Queen Victoria would assume the honorific "Empress of India." It would be another seven decades before the ties with India were finally severed.

So, in a sense, India—writ large—seemed as much part of my background as Arabia. And Pakistan remained "India" in my mind, if by that was meant a part of the larger subcontinent. Even today there remained vestiges of the Raj, if only in the English spoken by the natives of the two countries. And the major languages traditionally spoken in the subcontinent were still there: Urdu, with its sister Hindi, as the everyday language of the people, Arabic as the language of religion, and Farsi as a remnant of Persian influence at the Moghul court. Although Arabic is not widely spoken in the subcontinent, long familiarity with its structure, not to mention its influence on the lexicons of languages that *are* spoken there, provided me with a ready entrée into the thinking of the people of the region.

A word about methodology is in order. Rather than a chronological or more conventional arrangement, this book—like *Masr*—consists of a series of themed essays that are intended to shed light on a particular aspect of the countries in question. The light is often indirect, reflecting the human side of the story. I believe that this provides a more nuanced view of a part of the world that is often portrayed only in primary colors. The inhabitants of Pakistan, Afghanistan, and Niger are allowed to speak for themselves. They do not represent a monolith. Along with Muslim societies elsewhere they struggle with the challenges to a deeply-rooted religion in an increasingly secular world.

This has generated a drumbeat of bad news from a region extending from West Africa through the Levant to the Indian subcontinent and Central Asia. But there has always existed an undercurrent of decency and reason, often expressed *sotto voce*, and I have tried to capture some of those murmurs. While the essays exhibit little of a typical scholarly approach, they are informed with facts and citations woven into the narratives. They constitute a firsthand record of incidents and impressions as they occurred, unfiltered through any prism of later knowledge. I believe that the witness the essays offer, the record of an important period in history, is as pertinent today as the day they were written.

The pieces that follow, some long and some short, chronicle a period working in Pakistan on the Afghan program for a private American company that acted as a kind of factotum for USAID. With the chaos that accompanied the Soviet withdrawal, Afghanistan was deemed too dangerous for an official American presence. So, we pulled the strings—if it could be said that anyone truly pulled the strings in that country—remotely from Islamabad, Peshawar, and Quetta. In that respect, the old relationship between India and Afghanistan still prevailed.

Niger may seem an odd pairing with Afghanistan, but the assignments were of a piece: large-scale commodities and infrastructure assistance for impoverished, overwhelmingly Muslim countries in the throes of man-made and natural disasters. According to a 2011 Pew Research Center listing, Afghanistan was 99.8 percent Muslim, Niger was 98.3 percent, and Pakistan was relatively cosmopolitan at 96.4 percent. The countries occupied almost polar extremes in the African and Eurasian landmass, Niger in West Africa and Afghanistan and Pakistan in Southwest Asia. All were early converts to Islam and had long histories of Islamic learning. There the similarities seemed to end.

But the Sahel, of which Niger mostly consists, has become a battle ground of late. In 2017 the United States is spending millions on a drone base in Agadez in northern Niger as part of its effort to monitor Islamic State insurgents in a broad swath of Africa from Senegal to Chad. In the last decade of the twentieth century, Niger was largely immune to the bacillus of Islamism. But the spread was inexorable and the familiar issues of corruption, rapid population growth, inequality, and diminished opportunities have combined with religious zealotry to spark violent eruptions against the existing order. It would be immodest to claim that in 1995 we saw it coming, but the ingredients were already there. We should not be surprised at the spread.

1

Peshawar and Quetta

I OFTEN TRAVELED TO Peshawar and Quetta on business and they were a welcome change from the quiet of Islamabad. Peshawar was in the NWFP, or the Northwest Frontier Province, and a round-trip ticket on Pakistan International Airways, or PIA, cost 525 rupees, or about nineteen dollars. It was cheaper to fly than to drive. But the flights were unpredictable and mechanical problems, delays, or simply the weather made getting into or out of Peshawar a bit of a lottery. The drive down the Grand Trunk took about three hours and it was notorious. The road was poorly maintained and there were times when you could almost smell the paint on a passing flying-coach, so close were the encounters. Readers of *Kim* would recognize the Grand Trunk, "such a river of life as nowhere exists in the entire world," according to Kipling. It ran some 1,500 miles from Calcutta to Kabul, along whose teeming length Indians had lived and worked for thousands of years. There were some interesting sights to see along the way, including the sixteenth-century caravanserai and the always-impressive confluence of the Kabul and the Indus at Attock. The Kabul was muddy and brown and the Indus a light blue after its passage through the northern reaches. There were

The trim, along the Grand Trunk

even white caps on the Indus, so cold and rapidly did it flow. After joining the rivers flowed on together, the two colors side by side until they fused beyond Akbar's fort.

But the flight was an adventure in itself. Direct, it took about forty-five minutes. The "equipment" was a propeller plane like the Twin Otters that flew from Jidda to Yanbu. A prop plane always seemed to gather itself before taking off. As the propellers revved, like a rubber band being wound tighter and tighter on a model plane, it would seem to shudder in anticipation of the effort it would soon make, producing such violent vibrations that we were afraid it would damage itself. Then it would hurtle down the runway and climb quickly up the sky. A jet seemed to overpower the air. But a prop plane was forced to work with it and, together, they kept it aloft. The descent, coming in low over the Vale of Peshawar with its peach orchards and little patchwork plots planted in wheat or maize, was equally dramatic. We walked from the aircraft to the terminal building.

A Mitsubishi Pajero was always waiting, and on this morning in September of 1992 I was going directly to the Mine Dog Center or MDC. The driver was an Afghan, a Pashtun, but he was from Kabul and had no particular tribe. He had long, downwardly-sloping eyebrows and huge, luminous black eyes. Combined with his black beard and thin, sad face he looked like an icon of a Byzantine Christ. The cassette player was turned up high and "Why do you want to dream for me?" sounded monotonously, over and over again. I asked the driver who it was and he said Michael Jackson. When I asked him if he liked Michael Jackson, he just smiled his sad smile as if to say: "What kind of a question is *that*?"

Cane juice vendor, Peshawar

The city itself was made up of several districts, from the old *Qissa Khawani*, or storytellers, bazaar behind the Sikh fort, to the large cantonment area in the center of the city with its crumbling barracks and wide, tree-lined avenues. The cantonment was built for the British army, long gone, although the Pakistani army had stepped in seamlessly to fill the gap. Peshawar was still a military town and the main part of the city was dominated by the barracks the British left behind. The trees in the cantonment area were old and they included many large *shishams*, three feet in diameter, that had been spared the saw. It was this tree from which the fine Pakistani hardwood furniture was made. The latest addition in Peshawar had been University Town, called after another institution introduced by the British. Everyone said they were crazy to build a university there since it was in the tribal area. But it had survived, was now called Islamia College, and had the red-brick look and little turreted pavilions that characterized the architecture of northern India. The city had eventually grown up around it and, during the war against the Soviets University Town was home to scores of institutions like the Swedish Committee for Afghanistan, the Saudi Red Crescent Society, and the ICRC, or Red Cross, hospital. Its dusty little streets were full of the expatriates that came with the institutions. The Afghans also used the streets to work off their interminable feuds and newspapers regularly told the stories of Afghans ambushed in their Pajeros in University Town's back alleys.

The place to stay in Peshawar was the Pearl Continental Hotel. Once it had been Dean's, which had an imperial past like Raffles in Singapore or Shepheard's in Cairo. Dean's was still there, but was now decidedly down-at-the-heels and, aside from the high ceilings, large sitting rooms, and furniture that looked like it had been there from the beginning, there was little to recall its storied past. Now, it was the Pearl that catered to everyone who was anyone in Peshawar, or just passing through on their way to Afghanistan. They could be Americans working for an NGO or journalists on their way to Kabul. There had even been a recent sighting of Arthur Kent, the "Scud Stud" of CNN and Gulf War fame. The conversations in the dining room were always interesting. Groups of influential Pashtuns—sleek, prosperous-looking men with their signature bellies—always seemed to be there in the evening. We would see their pictures in the *Frontier Post* the next morning under captions like "NWFP Notables Meet in Peshawar."

Meals at the Pearl were good as long as you ate the buffets and the local food, the pilavs, curries, and *ghoshts*. At breakfast, in the full light of day, the dining room looked shabbier than it had the night before and the table linen was soiled. The breakfast buffet consisted of unappetizing western dishes: watery scrambled eggs, heavy croissants, bland little chicken sausages, and baked beans that looked like they had just come out of the can. But the local fare was good: spicy chickpeas, a chicken and green pepper stir-fry, chicken livers, the ever-present curry, and fried *nan*. There was also an omelet cook but his white uniform, although pressed, was dirty and his bare ankles protruded from a pair of scuffed shoes. He cooked eggs to order and watching him was a study in the pecking order in the developing world. He attended to the westerners relatively efficiently, the quiet, odd-looking Englishmen, Americans in T-shirts and ball caps, and Frenchmen who seemed to think that the entire room was interested in their conversation. But he made the

Chinese work for their eggs, pretending not to understand or simply ignoring their requests.

The early mornings in Peshawar were always a compound of odd odors. In the summer, it had the same heavy air as Cairo, redolent of dust, diesel fumes, human exudations, spices, and something else that you couldn't quite put your finger on. The hotel smelled like a hotel anywhere in the Third World, and the corridors reeked of a petroleum-based industrial cleanser. As the city awakened the cars, trucks, and auto-rickshaws began to fill the air with their thick emissions, although there were still many horse-drawn *tongas* in the streets. The horses added their own fragrance to the mix. The toxic combination usually made me sick to my stomach, and I always had a slight headache in Peshawar.

The Khyber Pass, NWFP

But it wasn't bad once you were out in it. On a clear day, the Hindu Kush was visible to the west. Kabul, through the Khyber Pass, wasn't much farther away than Islamabad. And Peshawar hummed with the activities of thousands of people—Pakistanis, Afghans, and foreigners—most of them involved directly or indirectly in the civil war that increasingly centered on Kabul. That lent a specious sense of adventure to the most mundane activities.

Quetta was in Baluchistan, two hours away from Islamabad by air and there was no real alternative to flying. A Serena Hotel, one in the chain owned by the Agha Khan, had recently opened and it was attractive and comfortable. The mud-brick walls gave it the look of the Baluch fortress it was meant to resemble. Being more remote, Quetta was even wilder than Peshawar. In the morning, the collection of armed bodyguards and Pajeros outside the Serena always lent it an air of heightened expectancy, of men on their way to something slightly dangerous or a little bit illegal.

The city lay on the easternmost extension of the Iranian plateau and there was always something Iranian about it. The curio shops had the look and a particularly Iranian smell about them, and the proprietors were a reminder of Richard Burton's remark that the only people who *ought* to wear beards were the Persians. Iranian goods filled the *suqs* in Quetta and Punjabis always returned to Islamabad with Iranian blankets. Westerners generally bought pistachios, the best being the *Rafsanjan* brand. Also, like Iran, Quetta was famous for its fruit trees. The dun-colored earth didn't look rich. But provided with water it would grow almost anything and the area was famous for its apples, apricots, peaches, pears, cherries, mulberries, and almonds. Like Denver, Quetta was almost a mile high and the mountains that ringed the city, rising starkly out of the plain, added another 5,000 feet to the view. They also made the approach by air a long, gradual process as the plane circled, depending on the direction of the wind, maneuvering to place itself in the center of the bowl that held the city.

It had also been an army or cantonment town, the westernmost outpost of the Indian empire, and since the late-nineteenth century a military establishment of some importance. The cantonment still dominated the city and the staff college still trained an international student body. A tour of the little museum attached to the college was a step back into the imperial past. It included, among other things, the Victoria Cross won by Lieutenant W. H. P. Hamilton in the second Afghan War in 1878 and an entire section devoted to another alumnus, Bernard Law Montgomery.

Quetta always seemed like something out of the American west in the nineteenth century, dusty, dirty, and full of armed men. We generally ate in a little restaurant that had the decor of a Virginia City cathouse, all lurid reds and pinks. Introduction to business in the city was at the Habib Bank where a guard with a sawed-off shotgun and crisscrossed with bandoliers, lounged at a desk inside the front door. It was like something out of *One*

Taxi, Quetta

Eyed Jacks. There were periodic shoot-outs on the main street, which was a *mujahideen* hangout, and truckloads of men with Kalashnikovs cruised the drag in the evening. But the Baluchis didn't need to import the violence. They were as tough as the Afghans and had their own scores to settle. I was about to say that Quetta was a wild little town. But it was full of refugees from Afghanistan and, with over a million people, it was as populous as San Francisco and Oakland combined.

The uniform, Peshawar

These frontier areas were tough places, full of tough people. It was true both in the NWFP and Baluchistan where most of the refugees had settled. In Quetta, there were more *Koochis*, or Afghan nomads, whose traditional migrations would have brought them there anyway. They lived in encampments on the great alluvial fan that lay west of the city, towards Chaman. They camped on the loose gray scree that, for millennia, had poured through gaps in the mountains that ringed the plateau. Something about the spaciousness and scale of the setting made the settlements seem clean and orderly. There were also large numbers of *Hazaras* from Ghazni who had come under different pressures in a different time, and lived in their own quarter of the city.

Around Peshawar, it was the squalid mud settlements built by the Pashtun villagers that were the rule. They were warrens and from the outside appeared impenetrable. When the refugees returned to Afghanistan they dismantled everything, down to the doorjambs and window frames. The mud walls would eventually melt back to their original state. After the victory of the Taliban and the fall of Najibullah in 1992, the road to the Khyber Pass was full of Bedford high-walls loaded with families and their possessions, little kids perched on the top with the women, goats, sheep, and dogs. But after the latest round of fighting in Kabul, the flow had stopped and even reversed itself.

In a meeting the Commissioner for Refugee Affairs in the NWFP talked at some length about the refugee problem. He thought that most people wanted to return to Afghanistan, with the exception of a few who would prefer Europe, Australia, or "your country," as he put it. They liked the climate of Afghanistan, even with the cold in the winter. The winters in

Kabul were bitter, but the temperature in the summer was not much above thirty degrees centigrade. What was needed was only a little security which was, unfortunately, not available. People were still going back at the rate of 200 families—each of six to seven people—a day. The situation was also bad in Pakistan where the ministry couldn't do much to help, so many people had little choice but to return.

All the ancillary facilities quickly grew up around the settlements. There were lean-tos housing fruit and vegetable sellers, automobile repair shops, tire vendors, bakers, and butchers. We were used to having someone do the dirty work for us, but here they butchered their own animals. Even the largest had to be killed in the *hilal*, or Islamic fashion, and cutting a bullock's throat was not an easy job. The volume of blood and offal in an animal of that size was considerable and on a cold, wet day the combination with the mud made it slippery underfoot. As if the life of the refugees weren't already difficult enough, the Pakistani authorities periodically decided that some of the settlements were encroaching on a right-of-way and bulldozed them. It was on the winter days that life seemed hardest. It could be bitterly cold, particularly at the 5,000 feet of Quetta. People rode if they were lucky but more often they walked, wraithlike in their shawls. Their *shalwar* pants were tucked up around their knees, and mud caked their bare ankles. In the frequent temperature inversions characteristic of the high plateau, the air quality could be abysmal. It was not helped by the emissions of thousands of auto rickshaws.

The rhythms of family life were difficult in the camps. They were nuclear families, and an unwed or single mother would be unthinkable. If pregnant, she would not carry the child to term as honor killings were still the custom in far more developed Muslim countries. If widowed, someone from the husband's family would traditionally step forward, although with the mortality of Afghan males during the war, that was now problematic. Absent the war, men were relatively robust and, having survived childhood, they could expect to live to about sixty. But the demands of reproduction, childbirth, and labor as beasts of burden exacted a heavy toll on the women. They were especially vulnerable and the vulnerability was exemplified in Quetta one day by the sight of a man pushing his wife to one of the special hospitals for women in a wheelbarrow.

In the early 1990s, the north of Afghanistan was relatively quiet and Abdul Rashid Dostum had played his cards very cleverly. He was now talking with Gulbudin Hekmatyar, but the fact that he was an ethnic Uzbek who had fought against the *mujahideen* for years made him suspect in their eyes. Hekmatyar, a Pashtun, was still the visionary. The country was full of Afghani bank notes, printed in Russia for "the government" in Kabul. After funding from ISI and the CIA dried up, the commanders still needed money—like divorced women—to allow them to live in the fashion to which they had become accustomed. The money arrived in flights from Moscow that stopped, first, in Mazar-i-Sharif, where Dostum took his cut. Afterwards, the Tajik Ahmad Shah Masoud took his share. Masoud used the money to buy the allegiance of many Pashtun and ex-Hizb-i-Islami (Hekmatyar's party) people, whose loyalty was, however, never very firm. There was the danger of a north-south partition of the country with Dostum taking the north. This would have ramifications for the NWFP and the tribal areas in Pakistan, Pashtunistan to some. While Bosnia and Somalia had temporarily captured the world's attention, Afghanistan remained an unsettled factor. It would eventually be sorted out by the Afghans themselves, as was their wont.

Afghanistan was one of the poorest countries in the world, lumped together with the likes of Niger and Cambodia. But the Afghans were enterprising and there was something about their attitude that called for optimism. They were not the hopelessly poor that aid had made incapable of helping themselves. In fact, the definition of an Afghan was almost the definition of an entrepreneur. One of the problems with the return of refugees was that most of the public transportation in Peshawar disappeared with them. Almost all of the German buses, most of them left-hand drive, were owned by Afghans. Before the coming of the communists, enterprising men went to Germany and drove the buses overland to Afghanistan. Public transportation had been one pocket of relative cleanliness and efficiency in the country. The roads, built by the Americans in the south and the Russians in the north, were good and the bus service had been excellent.

The same was true of the heavy trucks. In Saudi Arabia, there was really only *one* truck. There, the bulbous, round-nosed Mercedes was the vehicle of choice and almost the only one seen. In Pakistan, it was the British Bedford, which looked like an old Chevrolet. The Japanese Hino was now manufactured in Pakistan under the name "HinoPak," and they were beginning to cut into Bedford's market. But they had a long way to go. Over several years of trips up and down the Grand Trunk between Islamabad and Peshawar I counted an average of sixty-five Bedfords in every hundred ten-wheelers.

Bedfords were also used as part of the supply network for the *mujahideen* during the war against the Soviets. After the arms had been bought—largely with American and Saudi money—and delivered either by sea to Karachi or by air to Islamabad, they would be sent to the Ojri warehouse in

Rawalpindi before further distribution. That was before a massive explosion at the facility on April 10, 1988, a month before the beginning of the Soviet withdrawal from Afghanistan. Pakistan being Pakistan, suspicion fell on a wide range of bad actors, from local militants to the strongman Muhammad Zia-ul-Haq himself, allegedly covering up irregularities in the disposition of stingers or the simple lining of official pockets from the sale of weapons on the black market. The results of an official inquiry into the accident—if indeed it was an accident—were never published.

From Ojri the weapons were sent in inconspicuous convoys of Bedford high-walls, maybe ten a day, to Peshawar. Armed men would escort them, but the trucks were evenly spaced along the Grand Trunk and appeared no different from the hundreds of others that used the road on the daily basis. In Peshawar, the arms were distributed to the seven parties. A rule was that arms were never given to commanders, only to the parties. At the height of the war against the Soviets, it was not uncommon to see the living room in a villa in University Town piled high with RPG rounds or Kalashnikovs. The war against the Soviets may have ended, but an internal struggle for control was now underway.

The trucks were owned by ISI, the Pakistani Inter-Services Intelligence agency that ran the war from the Pakistani side. They still had the trucking arm, and we occasionally used them for commercial shipments into Afghanistan. Their connections were useful, although a shipment of American wheat in ISI trucks on their way to Kandahar had recently been hijacked near Spin Boldak. Most Bedfords, however, were privately owned. A truck involved a large capital outlay and even under Nawaz Sharif's scheme a man would need three lakhs of rupees to buy a truck. A lakh was 100,000 and at twenty-five rupees to the dollar, that would be about $12,000. It was a lot of money for a man who made about a hundred dollars a month as a driver. The "lakh" and the "crore"—a hundred lakhs, or ten million rupees—were still widely used in Pakistan. I remembered asking one of our drivers how many kilometers were on the odometer of his Pajero and he had said, without thinking, "over a lakh." The owner of a construction company told me that he had projects worth over three crores in progress. His eyes glazed over momentarily while he did the mental arithmetic, saying that this was over thirty million rupees. I was glad he did it as it was always a struggle. An invoice in the office might look something like "RS 2,42,18,425." That represented 2 crores, 42 lakhs, 18 thousands, 4 hundreds, and 25 units of rupees.

The money to finance a truck would probably not be borrowed, which could involve usurious rates of interest. Interest was widely charged, whatever was said about the inadmissibility of *riba* in Islam. The costs of maintenance and repair were probably also high. If nothing else, a ten-wheeler had ten tires, each of which cost several hundred dollars. So, many of the trucks in Pakistan were probably owned by "influentials," and only driven by what in the United States we would call independent truckers. That also seemed to be the case with the new Suzuki cabs, another of Nawaz Sharif's schemes designed to aid the development of small business in Pakistan. The complaint in the newspapers was that most of the cabs were owned by influentials and the small businessman was nothing more than a driver. In the NWFP it was the Afghans who owned most of the trucks. They had their own influentials and there were many who made money out of the war, western aid, and the poppy trade. So, maybe individual Afghan entrepreneurs were not as many as they appeared on the surface. But they were enterprising nonetheless, and individuals certainly owned the small buses and auto rickshaws. A commercial dealing with one of them was an education in shrewdness.

Peshawar and Quetta had been changed permanently by the long, ongoing conflict across the border. It wasn't just Afghanistan that had been affected by the war. The Pakistanis complained of a drug and Kalashnikov culture in the NWFP and Baluchistan, although many prominent Pakistanis were its beneficiaries. In the process of bloodying the Soviets we had helped to create that culture. We were now preparing to close the USAID mission and walk away again. We had done so before, after Zia-ul-Haq had Zulfikar Ali Bhutto judicially murdered in 1979. We came back after the Soviet invasion eight months later. And now after the Soviet withdrawal we were about to fold up our tents and leave again. We justified the move on the basis of the Pressler amendment that had attempted since its passage by Congress in 1985 to deal with an alleged Pakistani nuclear program. The law required a yearly finding that Pakistan was not in the business of acquiring a nuclear weapon and presidents Reagan and George H.W. Bush, with larger fish to fry in the subcontinent, had provided the necessary certification. But after the Russian withdrawal from Afghanistan in May of 1989 the immediate threat seemed to have passed and we were prepared to lean once more on the Pakistanis.

A short epilogue will bring the tale of Peshawar and Quetta more up to date. Both cities experienced an increase in violent incidents as the Taliban reasserted themselves after American attention drifted with the attack on Iraq in 2003. In Peshawar, the Pearl Continental was the target of a suicide car bombing in June of 2009, leading to a score of deaths and heavy structural damage. The attack was attributed to local militants. Like the owners of the Marriott in Islamabad, the target of a massive truck bomb the previous

September, the Pearl ownership reacted with defiance. The hotel officially reopened on January 1, 2010, and it continues to offer service to an international clientele. Quetta was the setting for multiple attacks against Shi'ite Hazara who had taken refuge in the city after a series of massacres in their native central Afghanistan. There was hardly a year in the first decade of the twenty-first century when there was not an outrage against the Hazaras who not only were different from their Sunni neighbors but *looked* different, with the epicanthic fold that immediately identified them as Central Asian. In the blowback of the American effort in Afghanistan, Quetta also became a refuge for high-level Taliban and it was rumored that Mullah Omar, their one-eyed leader, lived openly in the city.

2

The Mine Dog Center

THE MINE DOG CENTER was an outgrowth of the old Animal Holding Facility, or AHF, in Pabbi, near Peshawar in the Northwest Frontier Province of Pakistan. The AHF was established to train pack animals to carry non-lethal supplies into Afghanistan—commodities like rice, wheat, and *dal chana* or lentils. Over 1,800 mules were trained and, you might say, graduated from the AHF in the 1980s and early 90s. Supplies for the *mujahideen* were also carried by human porters, horses, and donkeys. But mules were a major part of the effort, prized for their hardiness and carrying capacity, although the American Missouri mules were not as hardy as the local animals. The facility was a carryover of the cowboys-and-Indians philosophy that prevailed in the early years of the American assistance to the Afghans in their war against the Soviets and it was run by old cold-warriors, rough and ready men who didn't much care how they got the job done. Did some of the mules eventually wind up carrying RPG rounds or Kalashnikovs to Hekmatyar or Masoud? They probably did, but that didn't hurt anyone's feelings at the AHF.

The CIA has a reputation in this part of the world for omniscience and omnipresence, and stories of how so-and-so was an operative circulated among people in the Afghan program in Islamabad. They probably should have been treated with a healthy degree of skepticism. But there may have been some truth to the stories in a place like Peshawar. The difference between Islamabad and Peshawar was the difference between a staid bureaucratic city and a wide-open frontier town. It was the same as between, for example, Boston and Virginia City in the United States in the nineteenth century. Some of the program officers were old cold-warriors for whom sending arms to the Afghans was the kind of quasi-legal enterprise they had always preferred. And the NWFP was home to drug barons and arms dealers, the sort of place where the law was only something to be evaded. This chapter of the story was now being closed and as the old warriors left, their passing was mourned in wakes at the American Club in Peshawar where all testimonials were consumed, of course, in liquid form.

With the end of war against the Soviets and the mule program winding down the veterinarian at the AHF conceived the idea of using the facility to train dogs for demining, arguably the most important factor in returning Afghanistan to normalcy. He had a connection with the Royal Thai army that had used dogs to clear mines on the Cambodian border. The connection eventually bore fruit and the American government agreed to fund a pilot program: the Thais would provide fourteen dogs and handlers, and Americans would train the Afghans in the techniques of canine mine-detecting. The original fourteen dogs were German shepherds, the animals that were particularly prized for their intelligence. There were still a few of the original dogs left and they seemed relatively placid, maybe because of their age. Or maybe it was because they represented, in a genetic sense, an older breed with all the unpredictability and aggressiveness of the newer animals bred out of them. The AHF may have been established for mules and the Americans had paid for bridles, packsaddles, and equine stomach pumps. But all of this could be changed and the staff at the facility set to work with a will.

Language was, at first, a problem. The dogs may have been German but they understood commands only in Thai. So, the Afghans had to give commands like "heel" and "good boy" in that language. But it was more than just commands. A handler had to become intimate with his dog, caring for it, feeding it, and making routine medical examinations. All of this had to be done in a foreign language. Later, when the dogs from Holland began to arrive, the handlers had to learn commands in Dutch. The situation was even more confusing because the chief trainer, an American air force veteran of German stock born in Brazil, spoke Portuguese as his native tongue. And the original veterinarian's wife was Italian, so all the signs in the facility—over the dispensary, the kitchen, and the dining room—were in that language. The Afghans must have been very confused. But they were probably used to it, each of them already speaking Pashtu or Dari, along with a little Urdu and a smattering of English.

By early 1992 the dog program was in full swing and most of the mules were gone. With a ready sense of improvisation, the staff had converted the stables into kennels and the facility buzzed with activity. It was like something out of Aesop or Thurber, or *The Bremen Town Musicians*. As a visitor arrived, a secretary bird strutted across the drive. In the caste system rigidly observed on the grounds, she remained separate from the geese that waddled in a flock farther down the walkway. They, in turn, kept themselves apart from the turkeys that occupied the lawn area on either side of the esplanade. The female turkeys always seemed to be in the family way and there were many chicks. The turkeys were eaten at Christmas and Easter as well as on the Muslim feasts, the *eids*.

There were only two mules left. Eventually they were sold, the funds accruing to the account of the United States government. But the manure they produced had been gathered over the years and sold, the money put into a kind s slush fund. That allowed the handlers to buy a dish antenna that allowed them to watch western programs and we could only imagine the widening of their eyes at MTV and some particularly lewd performance by Madonna or Prince. MTV was probably the most recognizable American export the world over.

The dogs were now the focus of the program and they were kept in a long row of kennels in the back of the facility. The kennels, each four feet on a side and maybe five feet high, were arranged on either side of a three-foot wide walkway that separated the rows. Each contained a dog with the name lettered in English characters on the cage: "Simba," or "Cora," "Rambo," or "Rambo II." The females would typically stand still and eye us with a kind of eager anticipation. But the males would be in a frenzied state, all of them feeding on the communal frenzy. Some jumped, trying to bite the mesh on the ceiling of the cage. Others snarled and tried to get at us through the bars in the front. Still others ran in tight, concentric circles in the confined space, broken by occasional snaps and leaps at the top of the cage..

The chief trainer was giving a tour. There are some people who instinctively understand animals, and Dan was one of them. He was an air force veteran who had worked with dogs all his life, and he gave us a homey little history of each animal as we walked between the cages. This female was sweet-tempered and that male needed a firm hand. The latter was a huge, shaggy, low-slung German shepherd who glowered at us through the bars. They would find a huge, shaggy, low-slung Afghan who, in Dan's words, would "kick his butt a little." Indeed.

Most of the dogs now were Belgian Malanois shepherds, used widely in Europe for explosives and narcotics detection. The Malanois was an old breed, although it had only been recognized as such by the American Kennel Club since the 1930s. Dan said they would run circles around a German shepherd. The average Malanois was leaner and stood taller at the shoulder than a shepherd. Depending on the amount of shepherd in the mix, they would be redder or blacker in color. But they all seemed to have the black muzzle and tips of the ears of the other breed. The dogs were bought for the most part in Holland and either given preliminary training in explosives recognition in the United States, or brought directly to Pakistan. This latest batch were all "green" dogs, lacking the US component of the training.

There was a Malanois network and Dan would periodically go to Amsterdam to buy dogs. His suppliers would advertise and if the dogs met the profile of age and physical condition and were for sale, he would buy them. But all the dogs didn't come from Holland. There was one German shepherd that had been brought in from Russia. He was the one that needed the firm hand. But speaking of Afghans, if by that was meant the famous breed kept by royalty in the country, I only saw one dog of that description in several years in the Afghan program. He was owned by a Pakistani in E-7, the most upscale of the neighborhoods in Islamabad. We would periodically see him being walked and with his slender body, long beautiful coat, and fine muzzle he looked like an aristocrat. David, the resident Afghan aristocrat on the project, said that they had once been raised by the wealthy in Kabul. But there was much difference between this dog and the proletarians at the Mine Dog Center as there was between David and the handlers.

The greatest difficulty with dogs in Afghanistan was religious. The dog is unclean in Islam and the mere touching of an animal requires a pious Muslim to wash thoroughly before he prays. So, at first, it was difficult for the handlers. But they eventually found ways around the problem. In the first place, they were mostly rural men and rural Afghans always had dogs. They were not pets in the American sense, residents of the house and almost members of the family. But the Afghans always kept dogs to help with the sheep and keep the wolves away. More importantly, the men needed the money and they were able to subordinate their religious scruples. The first test for a prospective handler was on the walkway between the cages where he would offer his hand through the bars to one of the dogs. It was a very effective way of separating the men from the boys.

Dog and Handler, Mine Dog Center

The dog would take the hand in its mouth, but generally wouldn't bite unless there was a sudden movement by the man. Actually, bites were commonplace in the program and, unless an animal was a chronic biter, they were treated routinely.

Afterwards the handler literally had to bond with the dog. He became his friend and confidant, and together they would stay out of trouble. They would be deployed for sixty days at a time and the handler was responsible for keeping the dog fit and alert during that period. Four hours a day was about the limit of a dog's working time. There was considerable danger and we bought life insurance for the handlers. But the greatest danger was to the dogs. Several dogs had been killed in the field, but it was rare for a handler to be killed. The handlers were usually affiliated with one of the seven parties who constituted the resistance in Afghanistan, and came to us on the recommendation of someone else in the program. In Pakistan, they said that nothing was done without *sifarish*, or connections, and the same was true of Afghanistan. We often saw letters of recommendation for handlers on Hizb-i-Islami stationery, attesting to a man's fine Islamic character.

Most of the trainers were Americans, typically young men who had worked with dogs in the military. They displayed the bravado that came with the territory. Like most Americans they got along well with the Afghans in a rough, backslapping sort of way. But that only went so far, and when the training sessions began they became *Mr.* Terry or *Mr.* Paul. The training was very systematic and each team consisting of dog and handler was evaluated on a daily basis against a regular menu of threats they would encounter in the field: the different odors of TNT, metal, and plastic; tripwires, anti-personnel mines, and anti-tank mines planted on roads. During the training the male dogs seemed difficult to control. The females were more focused and workmanlike.

In action, the dog was deployed on a long, retractable leash over a series of six-foot swaths of ground. A dog's nose was extremely keen, said to be many thousand times more sensitive than that of a human. However, the conditions were important and too much wind, an area that had recently been burned, or simply the cold could degrade its performance. A dog could find metal fragments, unexploded ordinance, trip wires before activating them, and antipersonnel mines. A dog was light enough that it wouldn't set off an antipersonnel mine unless it stepped directly on it. In addition, it could smell a plastic mine that a metal-detector would miss. The Russian antitank mines—drums a foot in diameter and eight inches thick—were plastic, and the dogs were often the only means of finding them. Once the dog had checked a road, the truck with the handler had to drive over the cleared portion, and that made for *very* careful work. Dan said that a dog was about 90 percent effective, about the same as most mechanical means. But, like people, they had good days and bad days and they weren't perfect.

By far the most common alert in the field was on metal fragments. That was what made demining so time-consuming. Every alert had to be investigated, whether it was an antitank mine or just a piece of shrapnel. The dog was trained to find the mine and then sit, marking its location. Then, a deminer—not the dog handler—would pinpoint the mine, unearth it, and defuse or explode it. That was the most dangerous part of the work and there had been several deminers killed early in the program with terrible wounds to the head and face. They generally lay on their stomachs while they dealt with the mine. The United Nations was now buying them helmets with shields. To keep the dogs interested, a system of rewards had been developed. When a dog had alerted on something suspicious it was allowed to fetch a rubber ball. The balls were a specialty item imported from the United States. The handler kept it in a pouch on his belt and the dogs *loved* those balls. The handler often had to manhandle the dog to get it back, wrenching the choke collar and inserting his hand into the animal's mouth to forcibly extract it. The ball came back covered with saliva and that had to be the most difficult part for a pious Muslim.

The handlers were a tough bunch. When a large flatbed truck disgorged its twenty dogs and their handlers there was some question as to which were more formidable looking. A handler was typically a young Afghan with a beard—an incipient beard, a scanty beard, or the kind of lush growth that was a characteristic of the country—but always a beard. He would be dressed in athletic shoes, camouflage fatigues, and a *Chitrali* cap. The men came in several shapes, sizes, and colors. Some were dark with that Semitic blue-black hair. Others were light, with sandy hair and beards and looked like Europeans. One was a former wrestler with the signature look of wrestlers everywhere, square jaw, bridgeless nose, and tiny gnarled ears.

Exposure to the handlers was exposure to the rough democracy of Afghanistan. Everyone shook a visitor's hand with the same courtly gesture, a slight bow and the laying of the left hand along the inside of the right forearm.

Handler, Mine Dog Center

There was no cringing or hanging-back. The program had been Afghanized, with good reason. They originally had a Punjabi second-in-command who alternately fawned over his superiors and abused those beneath him. That was not the Afghan way. In spite of their common religion, the Afghans had never gotten along very well with the Punjabis. The British noticed the difference, and some civil servants chose careers on the Northwest Frontier among the more-manly Pashtuns. They were instinctively reacting against dealings with "the wily Hindu." After partition, the British thought that an Indian army would be no match for the Pakistanis since the latter were made up of the more martial races. So, it was a considerable shock to Pakistani self-esteem when at the end of the war that created Bangladesh they were forced to surrender to three Indian generals, a Hindu, a Sikh, and a Jew.

Not much had changed since the middle of the nineteenth century when Mohan Lal Esq., a Europeanized Kashmiri from Delhi, accompanied Alexander Burnes on his journey to Kabul. In his *Journal of a Tour through the Punjab, Afghanistan, Turkestan and Part of Persia with Lt. Burnes, and Dr. Gerard* (Calcutta, 1834) Lal described the Afghans as:

> ... bold and careless, with a mixture of rudeness ... they speak Pashtu, and also Persian; quarrel for an insignificant thing, and kill each other for a trifling offence. They boast of their heroism, and think themselves the most incomparable warriors of the age. Their heart is the seat of revenge and jealousy, and humanity never touches their breasts. They cut off a man's head with as much indifference as we cut a radish.

Among themselves the Afghans still had irreconcilable feuds. We were all witness to the ongoing chaos in the country and the definition of "internecine," in *Chambers Concise 20th Century Dictionary,* seemed particularly apt in the Afghan context: " ... deadly, murderous; loosely, mutually destructive." They would tell you how it didn't matter that so-and-so was a Pashtun or a Tajik, or how such a one had a Pashtun father and a Tajik mother (although not the other way around!). But it did matter. When they told us that they were all Afghans and that they would work for a common goal, it was what they thought we wanted to hear. The reality was somewhat different.

We once sent a Hazara to the MDC to be interviewed for an accounting position. The Hazaras were a Mongol people from central Afghanistan, and the term came from the Farsi word for "thousand" since there had originally been about that many of them. They had the classic Eurasian look with fair skin and a slight epicanthic fold. To an Afghan they were different from the Turkmen who sold carpets in Friday Bazaar in Islamabad, or the

Uzbeks who sold fried potatoes in the street. To us, they all looked the same. They were also Shia. The majority of Afghans, both Pashtun and Tajik, were Sunni. So, I was careful to ask the Pashtun chief accountant if he would have a problem with this man's ethnicity or religion. "No," he said, "we are all Afghans." But he added "was he a Communist?" It turned out that he wasn't, although his brother had been. Such were the shoals that had to be navigated with personnel decisions. We hired the Hazara accountant.

There were anywhere from ten to twenty million mines sown in Afghanistan during the war, depending on what source you read. Clearing at least some of them would be one of the first priorities as the refugees began to return after the war. One study estimated that clearing all of the mines, even with the latest technology, would take thousands of years. But the problem could at least be managed and a rudimentary level of security provided in the more usable areas, agricultural land and the environs of cities. However, thousands of Afghan civilians continued to be injured by mines every year, enduring the suffering with their characteristic stoicism. Mines were designed not to kill but to maim. Militarily, they had a multiplier effect and, in a grisly bit of arithmetic, it was calculated that several soldiers would be occupied in treating and evacuating a single casualty. But they also affected civilians. The literature was full of pictures of children, holding up what remained of an arm or a leg, the hand or foot having just been blown off. What made it even more difficult was that the mines were still being used. The deminers were instructed by commanders in southeast Afghanistan to leave the fields alone since they were being used in the civil war that followed the war against the Soviets.

The Mine Dog program could be considered a success if the measure were only the institution-building among the Afghans. It was also the American contribution to the demining effort, by any measure the critical factor in helping the Afghans recover from war. From the initial fourteen dogs the program eventually grew to nearly a hundred animals, with their 300 handlers, paravets, drivers, and support staff. They were a smoothly functioning organization and very keen to do the right thing. The keenness came from their Afghan upper management.

If the Afghans had problems with one another, they got along very well with the dogs. And the expat trainers, who should have known, were lavish in their praise. An assessment of their effectiveness in finding mines, however, was difficult, given the jealousies of the NGOs with whom they worked and the interest of some parties in keeping the mines in place. The ban on cross-border travel by Americans meant that their work couldn't be monitored firsthand. But there was evidence of genuine, and heartfelt, testimony from other demining agencies, and from villagers who saw the dogs as the key to getting their fields back into production. The language of the letters, translated from the Pashtu or Dari, was testament to what an Afghan and Muslim operation it was. The malapropisms somehow made them more poignant:

> Your team under Abdul Qayum (set leader) . . . shoulder to shoulder have done their well-done job with the very high morale of patriotism. The demining office of Camp B appreciate the kind cooperation of the MDC teams especially the set leader Abdul Quyum and we wish him more success from Almighty Allah in the future.

Or:

> Your team under control of set leader Mr. Saidullah is doing their assigned duties successfully in Gorko and Toorkham, Nangarhar Province. However, they cooperate with our teams. ATC supervisory in Nangarhar inform you confidentially that MDC are doing their job honestly and actively and with the great joy. We are quite satisfied with them.

For all of the talk of cooperation, however, the greatest problem with the demining program, apart from the funding, was institutional rivalry. Intensely tribal, the Afghans often viewed criticism from another agency as mean-spirited. Because the dog handlers did not defuse the mines, and yet made marginally more money than the deminers, they were disliked by the latter. It was useless to argue that the dog handlers had to be surrogate parents, psychologists, and amateur veterinarians at the same time. And the marriage between the several organizations involved had never been easy. The MDC was better organized and better paid than the others. The difference grated with the other demining NGOs and the ill feeling was probably the MDC's greatest challenge. There was even talk of mines being re-sown after the dogs had cleared a field, to discredit them. Such was the envy of the dog handlers who started at 5,551 Rupees, or about $185 a month. A deminer made a little less. The expats, mostly Americans and Australians, tried to mediate. But they soon became partisans of one tribe or another and fought as tenaciously as their protégés.

In that respect, the program was a microcosm of Afghanistan itself. They will probably have reconciled their feuds at about the time the last mine is found and defused in the country.

3

Bismullah

HE WAS LYING ON the bed when we entered the room, covered by a cheap army blanket. Sefatullah asked if it was Bismullah and a man sitting by the bed nodded. These "ullahs" were characteristic of Muslim names in the Indian subcontinent and we also had Khairullah, Saidullah, Saleemullah, Habibullah, Waseemullah, Najibullah, and Kefayatullah in the program. They were almost never found in the Arab World. Sefatullah shook the bed and Bismullah sat up, looking bewildered. He appeared to be a little better than in the photographs we saw of him just after he was admitted to the hospital. He was a dog handler and he and his dog, Axil, had been clearing mines near a village in the Surkhrud district of Nangarhar province in Afghanistan. The dogs worked best in a minefield or on a road, where their acute sense of smell would alert on anything out of the ordinary. They were trained to detect plastic, metal, and explosives. But in built-up areas there seemed to be too many distractions for a dog to be effective and this incident illustrated the point. Or maybe they had just been careless.

They had been working a path between buildings when the mine went off, just as the dog found it. The blast killed Axil outright. Bismullah had been a couple of meters behind the dog, having just begun to pay him out on the long, retractable leash used to control his movements. The force of the blast was directed up and away from the mine and it sprayed Bismullah with shrapnel, rock, and bits of earth, many of the fragments hitting him in the face. But Axil took most of the force of the explosion and that probably saved Bismullah's life. He lay there for half an hour before arrangements were made for a vehicle to take him to a first-aid station in Nangarhar and then to the ICRC, or Red Cross, hospital in Peshawar. It was a two-hour drive to Peshawar, and when they admitted him, his face was still a bloody mess and he was in a great deal of pain. His left eye appeared to be gone and his face, particularly the area around the nose and mouth, was covered with cuts and abrasions. It remained to be seen whether the damage would result in permanent disfigurement.

The ICRC hospital was in University Town, the suburb of Peshawar that was the home to scores of NGOs during the height of the war against the Soviets. Its back streets and alleyways had been full of foreign institutions, although the Pakistani government was now shutting them down and this hospital would soon move across the border to Jalalabad. It was hardly a hospital in our sense of the word. A rambling, two-story building, it was more like a cheap hostel. There were several large wards and they were filled with people—patients and their families—in beds, lounging, or sitting on the floor. There was little sense of hygiene. The "linen" didn't look like it had been changed in weeks. Under each bed was a shallow plastic bowl into which the patient spat or emptied the contents of pop bottles or water jugs. In spite of the international name this was a third world hospital, where people often came to die rather than recover.

When we first learned of the accident it had come as a shock. There had never been a handler killed in the line of duty. Several dogs had set off mines like this one, and several deminers had been killed while defusing the mines the dogs found. But the program prided itself on its record with the handlers. In addition, given the close relations that prevailed in any Afghan organization, this was almost a family matter. Bismullah had been known and liked by everyone. He was a good handler. A picture of him and Axil taken before the accident showed a heavyset man with a luxuriant beard, the mustaches clipped in the Sunni fashion. Among other things the blast had done was to reduce the beard to tatters.

We bought life insurance for the handlers, drivers, and staff who were regularly deployed across the border to Afghanistan. The premiums for over 200 staff were a considerable outlay, but no one begrudged the expense. The policy was whole life and it covered accidents everywhere, not just in Afghanistan. And there were provisions for partial payment, for the loss of a leg or an arm. Also covered were loss of an eye, loss of an eye with disfigurement, and loss of sight. It looked like Bismullah would qualify for the second category. The photographs showed him to be badly swollen although the swelling seemed to have subsided a little.

He sat up and greeted us with the traditional Afghan handshake, the left hand laid along the inside of the right forearm. The man sitting beside him was his brother and, a few minutes later, a son of about twenty arrived.

We shook hands all around again. At first the fear was that he would lose both eyes. But his right eye seemed fine and he was alert as we talked. Sefatullah was translating for us. Bismullah described the pain he had begun to feel behind the damaged eye. They had given him a few pills that morning but nothing else. His nose was black and looked like a part had been sliced off. He explained with a gesture that they had plugged the nostrils because of bleeding. The rest of his face and lips were covered with black scabs and I wondered if afterwards he would look like he'd had smallpox.

Then he rolled up his *shalwar* pants and showed us his legs. Both calves and the insides of both thighs were peppered with small black scabs. They actually looked like peppercorns. But all this was considered superficial. What was not superficial was the damage to his left eye. There was talk of a lacerated cornea. The eye was shut and pus oozed from between the lids. He daubed at the eye with a dirty red cloth, occasionally applying it to his good eye as well.

Bismullah was surprisingly good-humored when we suggested that we didn't want to tire him. His son was looking expectantly at me, but I think it was just the natural deference shown by Afghans to foreigners. I asked Bismullah how old he was and he said forty. Sefatullah laid a hand on his arm and said that he couldn't be *that* old, and he grinned crookedly back at us. Sefatullah was speaking Dari and I caught an occasional word. Bismullah was a Tajik, like many of the handlers. Sefatullah was a Pashtun-Tajik mix and he spoke both languages. He was leading the discussion, explaining to me what he was saying to Bismullah. We decided not to mention the insurance, one of the reasons for my visit. It didn't seem necessary as we could begin the claim process without him.

I later saw Bismullah after he left the hospital. He was blind in the left eye and the insurance carrier had quickly settled for the loss of an eye without disfigurement, a 30 percent payout of the full amount. But the claim was resubmitted for an additional 10 percent. There was obvious damage to the external part of his eye. The lid was partly gone, revealing a staring eyeball that was red and angry in the area that had once been white. The cornea was covered with an opaque film. The combination was not pleasant to look at. He had taken the 150,000 Rupees—about $5,000—in cash, in spite of the recommendation that he open a bank account, and had given the money to his brother-in-law for safekeeping. The brother-in-law had a business in Peshawar. In these unsettled times land was going for a million Afghanis per *jerib* but he wanted to buy before prices went up again. At forty rupees per Afghani, and four *jeribs* to the acre, it meant that the insurance money would buy about an acre and a half of land. Bismullah said he would use it for a vineyard.

There was another claimant in the dog program and I saw him at about the same time. He had damaged a ring finger in Afghanistan and the finger became infected. It had been amputated, along with a part of the attached metacarpal, by a German surgeon at the Afghan Trauma Clinic in Peshawar. The work had been done so skillfully that, when he showed me his hand, I couldn't tell where the missing digit had been. The baby finger had been drawn in to cover the gap, but there was no scar or other evidence of the missing digit. It was beautiful. He would probably get 7 percent. We paid over $80,000 a year in insurance premiums and it was money well spent.

Sefatullah completed the interview and the tender way he dealt with this man was touching, and I was proud of these Afghans and their stoicism in the face of pain, and of the gentle, manly way they sometimes dealt with one another. They were hard and tough, but this was a side of their character that wasn't often seen.

Afterwards I spoke with both the Pakistani duty nurse and the expat head nurse and neither seemed particularly interested in Bismullah. It wasn't hard to see why. The hospital was full of men with injuries that were far worse than his. There were three other patients in the room with him, all young and all amputees. One boy in particular stood out. He was sitting on the bed and rocking back and forth with a curious, nodding motion. His head had been shaved and visible through the brown stubble was a long, semicircular scar that began in the center of his skull and disappeared beneath a bandage that wound around the upper part of his face. The odd thing was that the scar looked white and old, evidence of a previous wound. One eye and ear were heavily bandaged and he periodically touched his mouth with his remaining hand, while emitting a long sucking sound as if drawing in air through his clenched teeth. The other arm was gone about halfway between the wrist and the elbow.

The head nurse told us that Bismullah would be discharged in a few days and then would be transferred to the care of the Afghan Eye Hospital. Anwar, the Afghan driver who had gone in with us, probably put it best. Bismullah was a lucky man, he said. He could see, hear, and talk, and his arms and legs worked. Anwar had a point.

4

Darra Adham Khel

DARRA ADHAM KHEL WAS the little town in the border area between Pakistan and Afghanistan where firearms had been manufactured for generations. It was in the Federally Administered Tribal Area, or FATA, and required official permission to enter. The Pakistanis inherited many things from the British, some of which they maintained intact and one of them was their administration of the tribal areas. The FATA was not a regular part of Pakistan and tribal law, not Pakistani law, applied. It was administered not by a governor, but by a political officer. A sign at the border prohibited entry by foreigners without permission. So Khoshal, our man in Peshawar and a retired air force brigadier, made the arrangements. As insurance, he brought along one of his friends, the retired chief of police of the area. But we weren't stopped at any of the checkpoints along the way. Khoshal said with a giggle that since the *road* was not part of the tribal area, they had no right to stop us anyway.

But evidence of the sensitivity of the authorities in the FATA was the pass issued to foreigners for permission to enter the area. The stipulations were explicit:

1. The foreigners will enter the agency through the specified route i.e. in case of Kyber via Jamrud in case of Bajur Via Timorg area muda route, in South Waziristan agency via Jandola, and Mohmand Agency via Yakka Ghund etc;
2. Foreigners should contact the political Authorities in the entry points and take levy/Khassnadar personnel for security coverage.
3. The foreigners should not travel before sunrise or after Sun-set;

4. The foreigners while on tour in the Agency should contact the Political Authorities in both at the time of arrival and departure.
5. That the foreigners are not allowed to take photography of prohibited areas.

We followed the road to Kohat, not to the Khyber Pass, and the drive took about forty-five minutes from Peshawar. The Kohat road eventually ended in Karachi, a thousand kilometers to the south, and repair gangs were busy improving it as part of the new Indus highway. We understood this was for strategic reasons, but if it were to be a major artery it badly needed improvement. The drive was the typical roller derby in rural Pakistan: Bedford high-walls loaded with everything from gravel to sheet steel, flying coaches crammed with people, inside and out, little Suzuki cabs, Pajeros, bicycles, donkey carts, and flocks of sheep. All were dodging, passing, and jockeying for position on the little two-lane road. And all, with the exception of the donkeys and the sheep, were going too fast.

Khoshal explained that the area between Peshawar and Darra had been unsettled—probably in both senses of the word—in the past. Now, as the pressure of population pushed out from Peshawar, the land was being reclaimed. Fields on either side of the road were planted, mostly in winter wheat. Large walled compounds had grown up as well, built by the newly wealthy. Most of the wealth came from the drug or arms trade. After fifteen-minutes we passed the Bada Bedr air base, once isolated, from which Francis Gary Powers took off on his fateful U-2 flight over the Soviet Union.

We reached the frontier shortly afterwards and passed into the tribal area. A man at the police post tried to flag us down, but the driver either didn't see the signal or just ignored him, because the big car purred on. It was a Nissan Patrol and we had taken one like it on the bad road to the Kagan Valley in the lower Himalayas the year before. It had a wide wheelbase and didn't have much pick-up, but it was powerful and reliable and without the four-wheel drive we wouldn't have gotten far on that previous trip. It had also been reassuring to have that much extra car around us in the event of an accident.

The landscape now changed to mirror the change in sociology. The cultivation disappeared, replaced by low hills covered by scrub and an occasional thorn tree. In the distance were several large, barren-looking mountains. The important question in the FATA was a man's tribal affiliation and the people in this area were Pashtuns, Adham Khel Afridis. The name conjured up a different kind of human being and they probably were. Churchill described an action on the frontier where he had come face to face with many of these "savages," and they were fierce and heavily armed.

The women were as formidable as the men and, after an action, would come out to disembowel the wounded enemy in the field. But they didn't look like savages and were lighter than Punjabis. In fact, the farther north in Afghanistan you went, the lighter they became and some were blond haired and blue eyed. Many of them looked like Europeans. We periodically sent people across the border to check on the security situation and one had recently returned with the report that he had witnessed " . . . the gathering of thousands of Shinwari tribesmen." It sounded like something out of the Second Afghan War.

After another ten-minutes we swung around a hill and over a *wadi*—this was beginning to look more and more like parts of the Sinai—and then the little town of Darra came into view. It looked like every other town in this part of Pakistan, with its dirt main street and little storefronts, just now coming to life with men rolling up the corrugated metal shutters that were closed at night. But a difference soon became apparent: everything in the shops was lethal. We stopped about fifty yards into the town, left the driver to find a place to park and set out to see the goods. There had always been shotguns and rifles in the FATA, and many stores featured these standard weapons. There were shops with walls covered in nice looking, double-barreled shotguns, and others with old Lee-Enfields. On the frontier, every man owned a shotgun and until recently the .303-caliber Lee-Enfield had been the rifle of choice, valued for its accuracy, reliability, and stopping-power. One man—we were obvious customers—even dragged us into his shop to show us two old Enfields with external hammers and the dates 1860 and 1865 stamped on the breech.

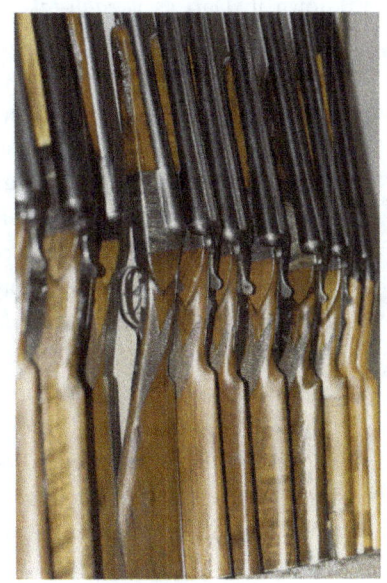

Shotguns, Darra

Trade was irrepressible in the frontier area and goods flowed everywhere, like water. It was always a little reassuring, in spite of the efforts of the regulators among us, that this normal human activity went on. As we walked down the street we saw several men unloading goods. From each of several neatly packaged bundles, looking like hikers' backpacks, protruded the snouts of four Kalashnikovs. The men were from Miramshah in North Waziristan and had carried these packs over the mountains to avoid the checkpoints. During the war against the Soviets the Kalashnikovs would probably have been captured in Afghanistan and brought here to be sold, the proceeds going to individual *mujahideen*, their only compensation since they were otherwise unpaid. Maybe the same practice still prevailed during the civil war that followed.

Most interesting were the old automatic weapons. In several of the shops were lines of Bren guns and the old air-cooled Russian assault weapons of Korean-war vintage. There didn't appear to be any M1 Garands, though. They had been used early in the resistance to the Soviets and were known in Dari as *yazdah-taka*, or the eleven-shot. But we didn't supply American weapons to the *mujahideen*, since they would have compromised our plausible deniability. The arms had been primarily Soviet-block, bought first from the Egyptians, the Israelis, and Turks, and later from China. The Chinese were the most reliable suppliers. The Stinger changed all that and, incidentally, the course of the war.

But the trade and the business of manufacturing had also changed with the war in Afghanistan. Now, there was everything you wanted: Kalashnikovs, Kalakovs—the improved Kalashnikov—light machine guns, heavy machine guns, even American M16s. We were especially interested in the last and where they had come from. In one shop, we saw many stacked against the wall. If we wanted an especially good one, that was available too. From a cheap veneer or mirrored door, behind which we were used to seeing maybe the best carpet or a special shawl, the proprietor would produce several of these black weapons, still covered with packing grease. They had come from Afghanistan, and it was anyone's guess as to how they got there.

The weapon of choice these days was, of course, the Kalashnikov. They were everywhere, the prices varying, depending on whether you wanted a Russian model, a Chinese model, or something locally made. Prices had dropped recently and you could still get a good local version for 6,000 rupees, or about $250. It used to be 25,000 rupees. A Chinese model was more expensive and a Russian, the top of the line, cost more yet. The asking price for an M16 was 16,000 rupees. Ammunition was available as well and the price for ten rounds of the Kalashnikov was eighteen rupees, or about seventy US cents. Ten rounds of the M16 went for ninety rupees, and had recently been as much as 150 rupees. It made sense. Ammunition for the American weapons was expensive and hard to get and, until that changed, there would be less demand for them.

But I was still struck with how people stroked that black gun. American goods were prized, whatever problems we may have had with our quality control. I was used to people looking at the Blazer and asking if it was really a *Chevrolet*, as if it were some sort of forbidden fruit. In fact, the Mitsubishi Pajero was a much better car, better made and certainly more comfortable. And the Pajero came in a right-hand drive version that made it suitable for Pakistan. The Kalashnikov was simpler and more reliable than the M16, which reportedly had a tendency, at least during our experience in Vietnam, to jam.

We soon became accustomed to the street scene, of people walking with weapons: single weapons, sometimes slung backwards over shoulders, multiple weapons carried by the handful, sometimes a consignment of weapons being moved to a shop. Occasionally a man would come out on the street to test fire a purchase, and the single report of a pistol or the rapid *whump whump whump* of a Kalashnikov fired at semiautomatic, would punctuate the commercial din. Outside one shop a little boy, maybe eight years old, absent-mindedly inserted a pistol into his mouth and pulled the trigger, over and over again. When he saw us, he giggled and ran inside. These were a people used to guns. In Islamabad, we were often awakened in the middle of the night by what sounded like a platoon trying to take the hill behind the house. But it was only a wedding party firing joy shots.

Down the street, a butcher worked matter-of-factly work at a haunch of beef. On his wooden stand a transparent sheet of connective tissue was draped to dry like a bed linen. Little boys darted through the crowd carrying trays of steaming tea or plates of curry. Other boys gathered pieces of wood from large piles on what passed for the sidewalk, probably to stoke the furnace in a little foundry. It was the same scene all over Pakistan, just that the business here was different. And it was a business, not a trade. Darra had always manufactured weapons, and when we saw a man fitting the breech to the welded double barrels of a shotgun, he was only doing what others before him had been doing for generations. But there was a difference, also due to the war in Afghanistan. Now, they made everything. I had heard stories of how a piece of reinforcing bar would enter at one end of the town and, after some sort of magic in a little shop, it would emerge as a machine gun at the other end. But it didn't work that way.

The manufacture of weapons here was the result of the same ingredients anywhere else: good steel, the right machine tools to work it, and skillful hands to assemble the finished product. We wandered through several shops and they were furnished with perfectly adequate lathes, drill presses, and milling machines. It was years since I had worked in a machine shop growing up, and set a lathe to make a beveled cut in a piece of straight stock. But it all looked familiar, from the piles of metal scrap, often twisted into interesting curlicues, to the pervasive odor of cutting oil. A difference seemed to be that the operators worked by a sense of feel instead of mechanical settings. The process probably differed from Remington or Winchester or Kalashnikov only in degree. There, the lathes would be computer-programmed and there would be less room for individuality and, of course, for error. These weapons were probably not as good as the originals.

But they certainly made them and they worked. All the satellite industries were there too: foundries to cast parts, bluing establishments to color them, woodworking shops to make the stocks, even places to mold the plastic parts. They were in the warrens behind the innocent-looking storefronts on the main street. It was said that most of the workers were not Pashtuns, but came from the Punjab. Many looked like Arabs, with their skullcaps and frizzy beards. That may have explained where some of the thousands of Arabs reportedly in the FATA were, and why countries like Egypt and Algeria didn't want them back.

All this took some of the mystery out of Darra. But it was still a phenomenon. If we wanted a British—or a German or a Russian—standard-issue bayonet, there was a shop for bayonets. A mild-looking man sold Kalashnikov rounds that he took from steel cases piled on the shelf behind him as if he were a pharmacist filling a prescription. There were cane guns and pen guns and plenty of pistols. We removed our shoes and entered one shop filled with lethal toys. The proprietor showed us a ballpoint pen with which he first wrote his name. Then he took out the point and filler, loaded a 6.2 mm cartridge, took us out on the street and pressed the pocket clip. It went off with a loud report and he grinned as he blew away the smoke. We could have it for 200 rupees, or about eight dollars.

The visit ended with an obligatory cup of tea in the shop of the man with the M16s. He had earlier sent his brother to show us around the town. The lethal nature of the business, after all, couldn't interfere with a man's obligations to his guests.

We didn't see any women in Darra.

5

Central Asia

CENTRAL ASIA HAD ALWAYS seemed to be among the most remote places on earth. But with the breakup of the Soviet Union, access to the region was the least of many things that once seemed impossible and suddenly were not. In Islamabad, we were only a few hundred miles from Uzbekistan and the Pakistanis were clearly in the hunt when it came to influence in the newly-independent Muslim republics. Air service from Islamabad to Tashkent began early in 1992 and only occasional concerns about the safety of Afghan air space kept Pakistan International Airways, or PIA, from its regularly scheduled Monday flight.

Pakistani travel agencies began to respond to the new market as well and were now offering package tours. Some of the early reports were not encouraging: money paid in Islamabad had not been transferred to hotels in Uzbekistan and travelers had been forced to make their own arrangements after they arrived. There were allegations of a cartel, of collusion between the travel agents and the Uzbeks, and of price gouging. But these problems seemed minor given the general inexpensiveness of accommodations and interest in the places to see. Tashkent, Bokhara, and Samarkand were names to conjure with, and a little discomfort and uncertainty seemed a small price to pay for an opportunity to see them.

So, when a friend at the American embassy mentioned that they were organizing a tour through a local travel agency I signed up. Everyone wanted the tour to go well, not least the travel agent who was looking for repeat business. PIA's service to Tashkent was suspended a week before we left, but there was always Uzbekistan Airways from Karachi and reservations had been made on both airlines just to be sure. As it turned out, the suspension was lifted a few days before our departure and we gathered in the airport in Islamabad on a Monday morning in early October, the usual two hours before flight time.

It was a good group. There were several embassy types, the political section heavily represented; two diplomats from the consulate in Lahore; a pair of army officers—an Australian and an American—from the staff college in Quetta; and the remainder a mixed bag of USAID contractors and their wives and one graduate student in the Fulbright program. None of us knew more than a few of the others. But as we made the round of introductions we found we had a great deal in common. There were only fourteen of us and we proved to be a congenial bunch. There were no prima donnas, no chronic late risers, and no complainers. As it turned out there was no serious breach of the good humor necessary to endure package trips. Maybe that was because everything happened pretty much on schedule.

The flight left on time and after a birds-eye view of Afghanistan, the country most of us were there to help but had never seen, we landed in Tashkent in the early afternoon. The Soviet Union may have collapsed but remnants lingered at the airport. At one time Aeroflot had been the largest airline in the world, measured in terms of passenger miles, and the tarmac was littered with aircraft, all of them products of the domestic manufacturing industry. Soviet Russia may have been a Third World country with nuclear arms but it had a First World aircraft industry, and these planes were evidence of their skill in making at least one complex piece of equipment. The ride to the terminal building was another story. The bus—actually a truck cab attached to the familiar airport transporter—was old and drab and seemed barely functional. The overhead handrails looked like simple 3/4 inch pipe and most were bent from the weight of too many passengers hanging on for too many miles. As we began the drive to the terminal we felt that we were being hauled rather than transported.

We entered through a back door and the building was as colorless as the bus. The materials were familiar enough: particleboard partitions with an artificial veneer, acoustic tiles in the drop ceiling, terrazzo floors. But the workmanship was poor. Miter joints were open, the painting was sloppy, and letters were missing from the signs in Russian, German, and English. It took an hour and a-half to clear customs in three very slowly moving lines. The wait was punctuated by the prayers of a group of Pakistanis and several Arabs who, from the sound of their Arabic, were Saudis. They determined the direction to Mecca, selected a leader from among the group and prayed, as usual, oblivious to their surroundings. This was probably a recent phenomenon, the terminal building in Tashkent not being used to the regular rhythms of the call to prayer.

The customs officials all looked to be ethnic Russians, fair men with light hair and wearing green uniforms. The Uzbek police, we later learned, were dressed in gray. They were methodical and clumsy. The first stop was at passport control and the man behind the glass grimly studied each document and the matching face for what seemed a comical length of time. He looked first at the passport and then the face, and then the document and then the face, before allowing us to pass through a small electronically-activated gate. We waited patiently for the heavy "thunk, thunk" of the stamp on the page that announced each successful passage.

We were then directed by a combination of grunts and gestures through a metal detector. This was odd, and the first time I had seen one on the way *out* of an airport. By this time our luggage had arrived, but it was piled in an area near the customs booths and there was a great deal of confusion as the two activities merged. Finally, all foreign currency was listed and counted by several characters in civilian clothes. We had been warned about changing money in the street, but it seemed odd in retrospect because we weren't asked to produce receipts on the way out later in the week. This process had taken far too long and we were only one Boeing 737. The airport was a relic and it would have to be improved before it could handle much more than one medium-sized aircraft at a time.

Outside we were greeted by our Intourist guide, Ludmilla, and cute little Uzbek girls with impressive bouquets of gladiolus for each of us. Then we drove the fifteen minutes to the Hotel Uzbekistan through a city that looked like it might have been somewhere in eastern Europe, not the steppes of Central Asia. Very little we saw of Tashkent in the next few days altered that first impression. The hotel was the flagship facility in this, the fourth largest city in the former Soviet Union, or FSU. It may have been sixteen stories high, but the rooms were small and Spartan with primitive plumbing and hard little beds. The bar sold Western beer and whisky at reasonable prices: for two dollars, you could get a Heineken and for three dollars a shot of Johnnie Walker Red Label from a bartender who reacted to every order as if it were an imposition, although he didn't seem to have anything else to do. In the lobby there were a few entrepreneurs, the new buzzword in the FSU, selling paintings, books, unappetizing-looking snacks, and handicrafts. Everything except the snacks was denominated in dollars. No one wanted rubles.

It seemed we had arrived just before the opening of the Asian, Latin American, and African Film Festival and everything had just received a fresh coat of paint. The poles that lined the esplanade in front of the hotel were newly painted and flying the flags of the participant nations. But the paint was splattered and many of the poles stood crookedly, in spite of crude attempts to make them stand upright. Everything we later saw of public works in Tashkent, with the exception of the subway—sidewalks, streets, pavement—seemed to be executed with about the same level of skill. Outside the hotel posters advertising the festival showed the usual collection of peoples of every hue, apparently engaged in animated conversation. But these were no longer the palmy old days of nonalignment and Soviet solidarity with the developing world. I remembered, with a little nostalgia of my own, the obvious nostalgia of Mohammed Hassaneyn Heykal describing his trips to the old Soviet Union. He was an intimate of Nasser and traveled there frequently. He tells the story of Nikolai Podgorny, the president of the Soviet Union, trying to get into bed with him during a blackout in Yalta.

However, the atmosphere of tawdriness and gloom gradually lifted. Ludmilla asked us if dinner at seven o'clock would be convenient, "Ya?!" Her questions always had a note of finality about them. It was a lively affair. The spread looked like standard eastern European fare, seen in countless National Geographic photographs of a family dinner in Tbilisi or Kiev: round loaves of bread, white cheese, sliced cucumbers, tomatoes, shredded cabbage, bits of ham, cheap caviar, butter, and bottles of mineral water and wine. This was followed by soup and a main course of meat, potatoes and rice. The dining room was huge and full of fashionably-dressed Uzbeks. About eight o'clock the band struck up and many people danced, both men and women shuffling with arms outstretched and making odd, sinuous motions with their hands. They played a few American pop songs, I think in our honor, and several of the women in the group were asked to dance by a pair of fat, raffish locals. They declined.

We had only a day and a-half in this first visit to Tashkent and our time was tightly scheduled. But the early mornings and late afternoons were usually free, when most of us went our separate ways on foot. They were also the times when Tashkent showed its best face. The socialist central planners had the good sense to leave the seasons alone and autumn in this "sharply continental" climate was beautiful. The park across the street from the hotel was full of huge oaks and chestnuts, through whose changing leaves the sunlight was diffused in a warm comfortable glow. The afternoons were especially lazy and we sat and watched the people strolling through the park.

They were an interesting mix, according to the guidebook mostly Uzbeks, Crimean Tatars, Chechens, Russians, Ukrainians, Volga Germans, Tajiks, Jews, and Koreans. Something like a hundred different minorities had settled or been forcibly resettled by the Soviets in Uzbekistan. The women were smartly dressed and there were many blonds with the kind of porcelain skin seen only in northern Europe. The standard-issue former-Soviet walker seemed to come equipped with a pair of shopping bags as if the chance to buy something at a good price—or maybe anything at all—was not to be missed. Across the park was Karl Marx Street, which was closed-off at night and filled with artists, hawkers of handicrafts, and strolling couples. The most popular food on the street seemed to be the *shawarma*, the revolving spits heavy with the aromatic meat and the pocket bread substantial. But the tour included three full meals and none of us was generally hungry.

Breakfast was usually about eight thirty ("Ya?!") and consisted of the same round loaves from the night before, fresh yogurt, cheese, processed meat, occasionally eggs, once a kind of sweet rice porridge, and tea in shallow cups. One report stated that the waitresses in the Hotel Uzbekistan were haughty, but we found them merely unpleasant. Their work already appeared to be unendurable and any extra request was out of the question. For the most part they simply ignored us.

Karl Marx, Tashkent

On the first morning in the city we decided to go shopping. In that respect, the old face of Intourist *had* changed. Democracy had its limits on a package tour with a prearranged schedule, but we had some say in what we would do. And the guides on our shopping excursions couldn't have been more open or pleasant. We freely discussed developments in the rest of the FSU, especially in Tajikistan, the fears of the minorities, the difficulty making ends meet, and any other topic that came to mind. In our free time, we went where we wanted, when we wanted and talked, where language permitted, with whomever we chose.

The market was well stocked with food, beautifully displayed. This *was* the harvest season so everything was unusually plentiful, and we *were* in a republic devoted almost entirely to agriculture. But still, after hearing stories of hardship and potential famine in the FSU that winter, we were impressed with the abundance. Central Asia had always been famous for its melons, and in the Indian subcontinent Babar was said to have missed them most of all. There were muskmelons, honeydews, cantaloupes, and watermelons, and they lay in great mounds over an area of a couple of acres. A slice cost two rubles, and they were sweet and delicious.

The fruit and vegetables were in a large roofed market, also of several acres. There were red, white, and purple grapes, pomegranates, apples—red and golden delicious seemed to predominate—lemons, figs, cherries, raspberries, and pyramids of pears. They all looked individually polished. The vegetables—red and green peppers, carrots, potatoes, cabbages, eggplants, onions, and turnips—arrived in great gunnysacks. The salad vegetables, green onions, radishes, and tomatoes, were artistically arranged. The herbs, basil and especially dill, made it aromatic.

In a separate building were two floors consisting entirely of butcher shops. The ground floor was devoted to beef and pork. Meat markets were always interesting for their differences in the butchering process. In the United States, it was automated. Slaughterhouse workers used chain saws or band saws and the final product came wrapped in plastic. In Egypt, all meat was meat, with hardly any separation into the cuts that we recognized, and butchers deftly separated the flesh from the attached bone with sharp knives. A rib cage was literally a cage when an Egyptian butcher was through with it. Here, an ax seemed to be the preferred instrument. They were not hatchets, but long-handled, the butchers using two hands and working hard at a quarter of beef. Some of the quarters were still frozen and it took a strong man to wrestle them onto the counter. But, the same man skillfully cut a pork rib into cutlets using a slightly smaller ax.

Melons, Tashkent

Upstairs there was cheese, cured pork, chickens, rabbits, and fish. The cheese was soft and white and tasting was encouraged. It seemed to be formed in odd molds, but then I realized that it was simply the shape of the plastic containers in which it came to market. There was probably more smoked pork than any other kind of meat. There were hocks and

Fruit market, Tashkent

hams, shoulders, bacon, cutlets, and slabs of the salted product. The chickens were fat and the heads, feet, internal organs, and fatty deposits were arranged in front of each bird like a floweret. A few rabbits lay on a shelf, their feet protruding beneath individual shrouds. But the salted fish was rubbery and almost inedible.

The market was a dramatic contrast with the government stores in the city. I stopped at one on an early-morning walk and it was unappetizing: canned fish, boxes of what looked like detergent, bottled cherries, juice, and more bottled cherries. And three dead chickens. They were plucked but otherwise intact and there was something indecent about their nakedness. The remnants of the silvery feathers on their necks made them look like old men who hadn't shaved.

From the market, we went to the Museum of Jewelry in the center of the city. It had been built by a famous Moscow architect for a Romanov reprobate banished by the family to Central Asia. The courtyard was full of modern sculpture, but the pieces were poorly maintained and the area was overgrown with weeds. The restored, lavishly decorated rooms were interesting but the displays of Uzbek folk jewelry soon grew monotonous. Here we saw our first babushkas, older women who sat in the rooms of these museums, inert except when someone dared to touch an exhibit. Then they were roused to a fury. Most interesting was a seventy-five-kilogram trove of gold pieces and ingots dating from the second-century BC Kushan Empire. It was kept in a vault in the basement.

Babushka, Tashkent

We returned to the hotel for lunch, which consisted of bread, cold tongue, soup with heavy noodles, a meat dish, and fruit. After lunch, we had an hour to rest. In a system that we would come to recognize as standard over the next week, the room keys were kept by a woman at a desk by the landing on each floor. She surrendered the key on presentation of a room chit. There was a computer on the desk but I saw it turned on only once in the four days we were there. When I asked, the woman scrolled through the room numbers and called up mine. There was a place for two names but nothing had been entered. She smiled sheepishly as if to say she really didn't know why the computer was there. The maids worked out of small rooms near the main landing where the supplies of thin towels and bits of soap were kept.

That afternoon we toured the city. There was a monument to the victims of the 1966 earthquake when much of the city had been leveled; the monument to the Uzbek couple who took in a multiethnic group of orphans during the Great Patriotic War; the monument in the park laid out by the citizens of Seattle, Tashkent's sister city; and the empty place where the monument to Lenin once stood. Ludmilla said that not everyone was in favor of this attempt to erase a part of the country's past. In fact, we spent the afternoon monument hopping, but this was understandable in a city so much of which had been periodically destroyed and rebuilt. The vistas were grand, as were the drab monolithic apartment blocks that lined the open spaces. Actually, they weren't monoliths because each had a slightly different decorative motif. Washing was hung out to dry on most of the little balconies and this gave the buildings a dreary look.

We skirted what was left of the old section of the city, mud-brick houses and narrow alleyways, and had the uneasy feeling that, like the old Chinese section of Singapore, it was all being swept under the rug. The impression was heightened when we stopped a few hundred yards from a fifteenth-century *madrasa* and had to work to get a better view of it. But we were wrong, and over the next several days we saw enough mud-brick houses and magnificent *madrasas* to last a lifetime. At the Museum of Applied Arts on the way back to the hotel there were nice oil paintings, authentic Turkman carpets, appliqué fabrics, miniature boxes, and local jewelry, all for sale. We also met some real entrepreneurs, not the ersatz kind we had seen in the hotel. One kid was selling coffee table books, very nicely done in Russian, Uzbek, and English, showing Bokhara, Khiva, and Samarkand. They had been printed in Eastern Europe for the old low prices and he seemed to have cornered the market on a rapidly diminishing supply. I bought one on Bokhara for five dollars, but thought I would leave Samarkand for later. "Ya want it? There's only one left and it's going to cost ya twenty-five bucks." He knew the market better than I did. There really was only one of Samarkand left, and it was the only one I ever saw.

The rest of the afternoon was free before we left for Bokhara. We decided to try the subway and found public transportation to be an oasis of color and efficiency amid the drabness. The stations were nicely decorated, each in a different motif, and very clean. The trains themselves were well kept, just a cut below BART in the San Francisco bay area, although of a different era in design. A ticket cost a ruble, making it virtually free. Only a few years previously we had valued the ruble at about a dollar-fifty and, with it, all Soviet economic statistics, including GDP and the defense budget. It showed that this cold-war competitor was spending as heavily as we were on defense. The truth emerged with the collapse of the union and the free-fall of the ruble. In the short week that we were in Uzbekistan the pressure was relentlessly downward. The bank in the hotel offered 210 rubles to the dollar the morning after we arrived and 230 that afternoon. There was talk of 300 in Moscow. But nobody wanted rubles anyway and the twenty dollars I changed that first morning lasted the entire week.

The Night Train to Bokhara

Although there had been settlements on the site since the second century BC, Tashkent was a Russian city and became important only after the Russian conquest of Central Asia in the middle of the nineteenth century. But it was the gateway to the old khanates and we were anxious to move on to them, the real reason for the trip. We had tickets on the Trans-Caspian Railway, built by the Russians to cement their hold on the region. It ran south and west to Bokhara and then on to Ashkabad in Turkmenistan, before ending at Krasnovodsk on the Caspian Sea. We would return to Tashkent, via Samarkand, by bus.

We left for the train station in the late afternoon. The station was packed and we moved through the crowds to the landing where the train was due. It arrived on time and left on time: that meant 6:30, not 6:29 or 6:31. We had an entire car to ourselves, the first on the train, and were distributed two to a four-person berth. Our fourteen had divided easily into pairs: two married couples, the two diplomats from Lahore, two political officers, two unaccompanied women, the two army officers, mates in the Australian sense, and a few single men. My roommate worked for a monitoring agency in Islamabad. He was from Pittsburgh and his Pirates ball cap—the one with the horizontal yellow stripes—always stood out in a crowd.

The car was well maintained and looked like it had been made in the west, if only because it was identical to the sleeper we had taken from Nairobi to Mombasa several years before. Everything was designed with the same economy of space as a stateroom in a ship, and everything worked: the windows, the doors, the fold-up tables, and the fold-down beds. The floors were covered with machine-made Bokhara carpets and the aisle along one side had the same carpeting, covered by a long, thin cotton runner. When we stood in the aisle outside our staterooms to talk or watch the monotonous scenery pass by, the runner was frequently caught underfoot. That seemed to annoy the porter who came up the car several times and, with huge sighs, fussily rearranged it. After a while he gave up.

We had been given box dinners before leaving the hotel and after settling ourselves and stowing the bed linens, everyone settled down to eat. Our Georgian- or Ukrainian-style dinner had been transferred into a box: bread, cold cuts, cheese, meat, tomatoes, cucumbers, hard-boiled eggs, fruit, and an expired Cadbury's chocolate bar with hazelnuts. The hazelnut, or *bunduq* in Arabic, was a specialty of Turkey and was about the size and shape of a musket ball. Generations of Ottoman musketeers were called *bunduqjis*, a fleeting thought here in old Russian Turkestan. To drink there was bottled water and wine. The water was carbonated like a natural Alka-Seltzer and it seemed to act like an Alka-Seltzer, because we ate and drank everything on the trip and no one complained of a stomach-upset or a hangover.

We dined differently. Some simply started and ate until the food was gone. Others—and these were the ones who traveled with a Swiss army knife, a water purifier, and probably their own salt-and pepper-shakers—used the fold-up table to carefully arrange everything before beginning. Dinner for them was a leisurely affair and they finished long after the rest of us. The wine was passed from stateroom to stateroom, prolonging the evening and we gathered in several of the rooms to chat. As some drifted off to bed others moved outside in the aisle to continue the conversations. We couldn't see much but it appeared that Central Asia was electrified because little lights regularly blinked back at us from the void.

The staterooms were heated and after a while the atmosphere inside the car became oppressive. So, we opened a window in the aisle and enjoyed the rush of cool air with our view. Others did too. That didn't last long. The porter made his way up the car, closing all the windows and muttering to himself. A half hour later we opened ours again and this brought out the little man once more. He strode to our end of the car, slammed the window, took out a small key and, with an air of triumph, locked it. The weather so far had been mild and I had not used the jacket I packed at the last minute, almost as an afterthought. In Bokhara, I would be very glad I had it.

One of the group made a tour of the next few cars and returned to say that all he could see were bare feet protruding from the much more crowded berths. I turned in at about eleven o'clock, but the night was not particularly restful. The clatter of the wheels, the periodic stops—always punctuated by a final lurch, followed by a grinding as the locomotive gathered speed—and the occasional sound of the whistle kept me drifting in and out of sleep for most of the night. I finally got up about four, shaved in cold water, and resumed my watch by the window. It stayed dark almost until we pulled into the station in Bokhara, and the tail of the wolf was just fading as we gathered in the cold on the platform. We waited for one pair who had missed their wake-up call, before finally stumbling out of the car, looking sleepy and a little bewildered. Ludmilla shepherded us into the bus for the ride to the hotel. We would check in and have a few minutes to freshen up before breakfast, which would be at eight thirty, "Ya?!"

Bokhara had a different look from Tashkent. Where Tashkent resembled Helsinki, Bokhara was, for want of a better comparison, Quetta, the dusty capital of Baluchistan. There wasn't much to see on the ride from the airport. The driver was the archetypical proletarian, down to his Lenin cap. The city, if that is what it really was, seemed laid out in large rectangular blocks. It looked more like an extended suburb. But there were a few high-rises visible and one of them was, of course, the Hotel Bokhara. The weather did not warm appreciably during the drive and the cold that we felt at the train station stayed with us most of the day. At first I

Restoration, Bokhara

would have described the weather as brisk, but raw would be a better word. I picked up a heavy cold in Bokhara and it lasted for the rest of the trip.

After breakfast, we set out to see the sights. The walls of old Bokhara were gone in most places, the mud-brick having simply melted away in the infrequent rains. But we knew we had left the regular blocks, heroic statuary, and low-rises of the new city when met a funeral procession winding through the narrow streets of the old city, the coffin in the bed of a truck and most of the mourners on foot. We passed several blue domes and graceful facades, and then the notorious ramparts of the citadel of Bokhara, recognizable from old photographs in accounts of the Central Asian slave trade. We passed it and the feeling grew, as in Tashkent, that we were missing something: old Turkistan was being airbrushed away for our benefit. But there would be time in the next

Arslan Khan, Bokhara

few days for all of it. Finally, the bus stopped near a mosque complex, and we found what we had come to Central Asia to see.

The twelfth- to sixteenth-century Kalyan ensemble included the Miri-Arab madrasa, the Kalyan mosque, and the Arslan Khan minaret and the guidebook rightly called it a masterpiece of Central Asian architecture. The first impression was of spaciousness and scale. It was not so colossal as some of the buildings we would later see in Samarkand. But, even so, there was no place from which the whole ensemble could be seen at the same time. The monumental facades and the thick, crudely powerful minaret from which malefactors were once thrown, were in sharp contrast to the tympanums with their thousands of tiny, individually-glazed tiles. Delicate arches framed the galleries and the cells in the madrasas.

The effect was heightened since we were the only ones there and the monuments easily swallowed our number. It was once thought that the Soviets had locked the mosques and madrasas of Central Asia and thrown away the keys, but this did not appear to be the case. Everywhere we went, whether in Tashkent, Bokhara, or Samarkand, there was evidence of restoration or reconstruction. The buildings may not have served as religious institutions under the Soviets, and many of the madrasas had been turned into workshops where local arts and crafts were practiced. But that was now changing and others, like this one, were opening again as schools. We saw many students—beardless boys in Uzbek skullcaps—padding through the precincts.

Islam on the move, Bokhara

Not everyone welcomed the change. The state had for years brought in restorers from Moscow and Leningrad and now that the mullahs were back in charge, some feared that this would end. The "troubles" in nearby Tajikistan—an understatement, with Dushanbe in ruins—had everyone worried, especially the ethnic Russians. Our guides were mostly Russian although Rahima, our local guide in Bokhara, was Uzbek. So, the opinions we heard were uttered furtively, in asides. It was not from any fear of speaking out but it seemed simply because everyone, European or Asian, seemed confused by the pace of change and didn't know what to think.

The blue of the domes was especially noticeable in Bokhara, where the predominant color in the old city was a dusty brown. There were clusters of low domes on many of the buildings, looking like the undersides of vitreous china basins. Many of the tiles in the facades had come away, revealing the same dun-colored field underneath. The Arslan Khan minaret, one of the earliest buildings in the complex, was decorated only in that the unvarying brown bricks were arranged differently in successive courses. In fact, this ensemble had a kind of austere dignity that was lacking in some of the later buildings, where the surfaces were so interlaced, inlaid, pargetted, fretted, fitted, and painted that hardly a square inch remained untouched.

We spent the rest of the morning on foot, walking among the other mosques and madrasas in the area. Many of the old arcades had been turned into shops and they resembled a kind of fifteenth-century mini-mall. There were Uzbek caps, simple and ornate, appliqué fabrics, copper ware, and the usual collection of painted boxes, dolls, and local jewelry. Crafts-men or-women were in many of the shops, patiently plying their trade. Some were not there just for our benefit, and a blacksmith and a radio repairman patiently endured our intrusion. But the shopping area was nicely done and it was the economic life's blood for the people. The only problem seemed to be that there were so few of us. An art gallery had several large rooms full of paintings for sale and the artists stood near their work and introduced themselves. There were many nice pieces. It was hard to say where they would fit in an art survey course but, being in a bit of a backwater, the artists could do what they wanted without worrying about fashion. The developing world had that kind of liberating effect.

We wandered down a dusty street to a kind of center of the town. The city had once been famous for its system of reservoirs, but the Soviets had filled in most of them because they were breeding grounds for disease. Only one large pool, maybe fifty yards long by the same wide, remained, and it occupied a prominent place between the two halves of the seventeenth-century Nadir Divan Begi madrasa. After the pervasive brown the green of the water was pleasant, as were the plane trees. The wind had died down and groups of old men sat in the sun on benches lining the water. Many wore the fur caps, long coats, and high boots characteristic of Central Asia. Several wore medals, probably from the Great Patriotic War. They were mildly interested in us and when we said we were from America one man offered "Los Angeles"? That and "California" appeared to be the most familiar names. The madrasa was unusual in that the tympanum on one side had a pair of opposed peacocks, looking out-of-place among these otherwise abstract facades. Inside, the cells served as workshops for various crafts, and we ducked through the low doorways of several. But there was a sameness about the things they were selling—painted plates and incised copper ware—and none of us bought much.

Back at the hotel lunch was the usual spread, the meal notable only for the group of Turks who stopped by our table when they learned that we were Americans. They were a delegation of businessmen looking for investment opportunities in Uzbekistan. One was a former world-class wrestler—he looked the part with his massive frame and ham-sized hands—who had two sons in graduate school in the United States. They understood Uzbek, a Turkic language, and if any foreigners looked like they belonged in Uzbekistan it was these Turks. There was much talk in Pakistan about a common cultural and religious heritage among the Muslim peoples of Central and Western Asia. But the talk included a certain amount of wishful thinking, or maybe it was collective amnesia. The colonization of the Indian subcontinent by these brethren from Central Asia had been traumatic in the extreme for the local populations, and Indians and Turks seemed as different as night and day. Earlier in the century both Enver Pasha and his dream of pan-Turan had died somewhere here in Uzbekistan.

After Uzbek, the most common language here was Russian, which appeared to be to Central Asia what English was to India. But there were also many Farsi speakers among the Tajik population and my rudimentary Dari, or Afghan Farsi, opened a few doors. However, they quickly closed. A few phrases and a good accent gave the impression that I knew the language. This often loosened a torrent of words that I was unable to handle. I had plenty of vocabulary but little practice in using it. The mental effort required to listen, assemble, select, conjugate, reassemble and speak must have been written across my face. After years of Arabic, Farsi at first seemed a breeze. It was an Indo-European language, closer to German than to Arabic and resembling English in the simplicity of its grammar. But like any language it took practice. It was like riding a bicycle. I knew where the handlebars and the pedals were, and understood that you had to balance on the two wheels. But I really hadn't ridden this one before.

It seemed that every other person we met in Bokhara was a Tajik. There was something a little ominous about this and just a hint of Tajik irredentism in Uzbekistan. They already had their own republic in neighboring Tajikistan, but that was seen by some only as an artificial exercise in state making by the Soviets. Several Uzbek cities had once been largely Tajik, and the feeling was that Samarkand was denied them only because Tajikistan didn't need a second major city. The Tajiks had cultural pretensions, believing that they and not the Iranians were the original ethnic stock and spoke the purer Farsi. Iranians made fun of Farsi speakers from farther east, as rustics speaking an antiquated language. But the Tajiks had endured the slights and nursed their sense of cultural superiority over generations.

The script was also being reexamined. It was hard to imagine that these people had changed from the Arabic to the Latin and then to the Cyrillic script over a period of ten years after the Russian revolution. The Turks changed only from the Arabic to the Latin script, but even that was among the most revolutionary changes of the twentieth century, effectively closing 400 years of Ottoman archives to all but the specialists. It was true that these Turkish and Central Asian societies had been largely illiterate and the effect of the change was not widespread. But still, each change made the society illiterate again at the stroke of a pen.

It was not clear whether the Uzbeks were seriously considering a change. But the Turks were reportedly prepared to offer incentives if they changed back to the Latin script. Of Arabic, there was very little evidence. The sign on the marquee of the Hotel Uzbekistan in Tashkent welcomed everyone to the film festival in English, Russian, and Arabic, but the Arabic characters were odd, not recognizable as any of the standard scripts. The inlaid texts on the monuments were in standard ornamental scripts. I saw nothing in *ta'liq*, although that was the script most widely used in Iran, and might have been expected in an area dominated by Persian cultural influences. A mosque had just been opened in the Hotel Uzbekistan. It was in a room off the landing on the second floor and was bare except for a red carpet. A handwritten sign in Arabic over the door said it was the mosque of Suleiman Abdel Aziz Suleiman, but no one in the hotel could tell me who he was.

The afternoon was devoted to more madrasas and, finally, the Ark or citadel. It was the heart of the old medieval city and sat on a natural promontory covering several acres. It was the one monument we saw without religious significance, and this gave it a slightly sinister look. Or maybe it was the thought of Conolly and Stoddart, kept in its verminous dungeon for months in 1841, before being taken out into the square in front of this same gate, made to dig their own graves, and then beheaded. The brief break in the overcast was just that, and we were cold and footsore by the time we returned to the hotel in the evening. Bokhara seemed even more like Quetta as the day passed, with its raw wind, swirling leaves, and sandy loam. That was not surprising since Quetta was really an extension of the Iranian plateau, having more in common geographically with Iran than with India.

Genghis Khan—or Chingaiz as he was called here—was our constant companion during the trip. There was hardly a place in Central Asia he hadn't visited, and hardly a place not leveled at one time by the Mongols. Many were razed over and over again. The destruction appeared to be utterly wanton. In his classic, *The Empire of the Steppes*, Rene´ Grousset saw this behavior as a cultural statement, a deliberate expression by a nomadic people of their contempt for sedentary peoples. To Grousset, Genghis Khan was a "gentlemen of good family," "in soul, a king." But he butchered hundreds of thousands, and attestations to his pedigree did little to lessen the evil of his passage. Ludmilla said that he and Alexander the Great were revered in the popular culture. People here still liked a strong man.

Dinner was the usual spread and afterwards several of us adjourned to the bar. The bartender was half Chinese and half Uzbek. He had a haircut like Moe of the Three Stooges and his front teeth were gold in the Uzbek fashion. But he spoke perfect, unaccented American English. On the train, we had met a girl who said her name was Elizabeth and that she was from Seattle. In spite of her fluent English and almost perfect inflection, something immediately said that she was not. There was nothing of the kind about this guy. His language, tuxedo, and general *savoir faire* convinced us that we had just met the first potential self-made millionaire in Uzbekistan.

I retired early to watch the nine o'clock news from Moscow. I couldn't understand very much, but enough to know that it was full of the day's violent events in Abkhazia and Dushanbe. None of it looked very good and it didn't take much imagination to picture armed men in athletic shoes and carrying Kalashnikovs dodging through the dusty streets of Bokhara, or in and out of the Kalyan ensemble.

We had another half-day in Bokhara before departing by bus for Samarkand. So, after breakfast we drove out to former summer residence of the Emir, a quasi-European building about five miles from the city. Like much of the work of the nineteenth century, the exterior contained a great deal of wood, now badly weathered. Inside, it had been restored and made into a museum of Uzbek dress, with several rooms displaying clothing, shoes, silver bowls, chafing dishes, and huge ceramic urns brought from China. It would have been interesting to see these last pieces loaded on Bactrian camels during their journey through Xinjiang, the Taklamakan, Kashgar and Kokan before they reached Bokhara.

The grounds were spacious and included one large enclosure full of peacocks, looking miserable and huddling together against the cold. There were a few shops, but their scanty wares and the lack of customers—we were the only ones there—gave them and their proprietors a pitiful look. One offered two pair of pantyhose, a pair of men's socks, a few packets of tea, cheap ceramic pots, and a few machine-made Uzbek caps. There was a Jean-Claude Van Damme poster on the wall and that was probably for sale too. The bookstore was full of books, most of them paperbacks, but all were in Russian or Uzbek. I was looking for an Uzbek-Tajik dictionary for an Afghan friend, but I didn't see one in the week we were in Uzbekistan.

We paid a quick visit to the Golden Thread garment factory where women were being trained in the local handicrafts. They occupied a large common room and were paid a thousand rubles per month, about four dollars at the going rate. The four dollars may not have been particularly meaningful, but the thousand rubles was, especially when a roast chicken in the market cost four hundred rubles per kilo. Dollars were wanted not to make foreign currency purchases but as a hedge against inflation. We later met a woman in the market in Samarkand with a shopping bag full of rubles and offering to change money. After a brief stop at a silk outlet, we returned to the hotel, checked out and had lunch. At about one o'clock we boarded the bus and left for Samarkand.

To Samarkand

The trip would take about five hours. Friends of Ludmilla, a mother and two teenaged children, were also going to Samarkand and we agreed to give them a lift. Each of us was given a bottle of mineral water and we settled ourselves, well-spaced, in the same bus that had carried us for the past two days. The partition behind the impassive figure of our proletarian driver was covered with stickers, among them the University of California Alumni Association and the Atlanta Hawks. A recent piece had stated that the roads in Uzbekistan were "as good as anything in rural Illinois," and we were expecting more in the way of infrastructure than we saw over the next several hours. In fact, the question as to whether Uzbekistan was, or was not, a developing country was the subject of lively debate in the group. Some maintained that it *was*, and that it was part of the Third World. Others said it was *not*. To them there was no comparing Uzbekistan with a country like Pakistan, for example, where the level of literacy and life expectancy were much lower and infant mortality much higher. On the other hand, there was no way you could call what we were seeing "developed." Perhaps it really was in the Second World, the term originally coined to describe the Soviet Union and its satellites.

The road was two-lanes, reasonably well maintained, and not heavily trafficked. The fields on either side were planted in cotton with occasional stands of corn. The soil was gray. There was nothing particularly neat or well-tended about the fields, and the crops looked spotty and stunted in places. Cotton was hard on the soil and this was a republic where seventy years of cotton monoculture had produced the ecological disaster of the

Aral Sea. The Oxus flowed into, not out of, the Aral and its diversion for irrigation had reduced the sea to a fraction of its former size. Maybe the fact that the weather was still raw, with the sky heavily overcast, made it all seem so dreary, mile after mile of gray fields with occasional herds of goats, horse-drawn carts, boys on donkeys, and small mud-brick houses.

Mud-brick was the almost unvarying building material. It had been used in the walls of old Bokhara and was still in use today. The construction was odd. Wood was used for headers and jambs but the studs were set at angles in the walls making large, irregularly-shaped openings. These openings were filled with mud-brick rubble, sometimes in regular courses, but more often not. The walls were then plastered over with mud and, if it were a barn or shed, this constituted the final skin of the structure. The plasterwork was good but the result still looked crude. If the building was a house, there was a second whitewashed coat of plaster. With the addition of a shed roof, a few vines, a garden plot, and maybe a cow, you would have the standard-issue rural dwelling in Uzbekistan.

The landscape was relentlessly rural, but gradually changed as we approached the outskirts of a city and a sight that opened the development debate again. The city was low lying and festooned with utility wires. But there, looming out of the overcast, was the unmistakable profile of the cooling towers of a power plant. It looked like it might be nuclear. We were again reminded of the odd amalgam that constituted the Soviet Union, and that alongside rural underdevelopment there would be pockets of First-World technological know-how. Chernobyl was the unspoken image in everyone's mind, as was the fact that in Pakistan we were only a few hundred miles to the south of this facility.

After about an hour we stopped for diesel. It cost twelve rubles a liter, or about two cents a gallon. The toilets were unspeakable and located, with good reason, well away from the pumps. Back on the road, we droned on for more monotonous miles, past broken irrigation canals and neglected vineyards looking like they had gone to seed. But as we approached Samarkand well-tended orchards and what looked like fruit trees began to appear. Also, there was a strange, very geometrical kind of bush or tree that lined the fields as a kind of windbreak. Two or three stems seemed to take off a foot or so above the ground, from which thick foliage grew up to a height of about eight feet. Ludmilla said they were mulberries, whose leaves were harvested every year to feed the silkworms.

At about four o'clock it began to rain and at four thirty-five appeared the first and only camels we saw in Uzbekistan. They were standing beside the road and single-humped, their fur gathered into little tufts in the rain. Now, the scenery began to improve. Fields were plowed and looked more fertile. The villages we passed were hardly pristine, but the clusters of houses had a neat and well-tended look. The cars were mostly Ladas, although we saw the occasional Niva. We had owned a Niva in Egypt. It was a four-wheel drive utility vehicle made to a Fiat design. The only change in seven years seemed to be the plastic grill. Roadside kiosks now began to appear, offering kabobs on spits, just as in the NWFP in Pakistan. The kabob was the signature food of Northwest Asia. But the feeling was different from Pakistan, if only because the men beside the road wore pants and shirts and stood to urinate. The Pakistanis squatted in their *shalwar khamis*. As we entered the outskirts of Samarkand an occasional blonde in the street suggested that we might be in a quasi-European city. When I saw a woman walking a lap dog, I knew that we were.

Samarkand

It was already dark when we arrived at the Hotel Samarkand. We waited in the lobby while Ludmilla handled the formalities. That was one advantage of traveling as a group: no worries about reservations, or making the train or a bus connection. We were given keys and went to our rooms to freshen up before dinner. The room was a little better than the one in Bokhara, which had been marginally better than the one in Tashkent. There was only a single, thick sheet on the bed but by now I had learned that it had an opening in one end and I was meant to crawl inside. The towels were, as usual, small and thin except for a long linen piece that looked like a shroud. None of us knew what it was for, because you really couldn't dry yourself with it. The towel situation had been discussed more than once and several in the party wondered why a country that produced more cotton than any other in the world couldn't make a decent bath towel. But the towel rack here was heated and it actually worked. There was the usual piece of soap, perhaps a quarter of a thin bar, but new here. Everything else was supplied by the occupant.

The dining room was the familiar cavernous space with a live band. The waiters wore tuxedos, including one who also wore an Uzbek cap pushed rakishly back on his head. By now we had tired of the ample but monotonous hotel fare and over the next few days we agreed to pay a little extra and sample a few meals on the outside. The rain had stopped and after dinner a few of us decided to walk to the Gur Emir mausoleum, a few blocks from the hotel. Tamerlane, Ulugh Beg, and several other members of the family, Central Asian tyrants all, were buried there and, in the light of an almost–full moon it was spectacular. We saw it several times over the next few days but it never matched that first impression. Back at the hotel I was tired after the bus trip and the mattress was the thickest to date. I fell asleep almost at once and slept uninterrupted through the night for the first time on the trip.

At six o'clock the next morning the city lay under a heavy fog. We were on the tenth floor but there was very little visible from the window. The hotel was eleven stories high, which I noticed since I later went up to the roof for a 360-degree view of the city. As I leaned through the guardrail to take a photograph, my reading glasses slipped out of my pocket and fell ten stories to the roof of the reception area. There was a moment of panic as I watched the descent, the glasses planing in a kind of circular motion as they dropped. But I hustled down to reception and found a bellhop who let me out a first-floor window. I found the glasses lying on their back with the lenses popped out, lying side-by-side nearby. I had only to snap them back in and they were otherwise intact.

The generations, Samarkand

A couple of us walked to the mausoleum to have another look before breakfast and we met a group of children along the way. They were Tajik and we had a halting conversation in Farsi. They wanted their pictures taken and a little girl was sent for a pen and paper so that they could give us their address. Ludmilla later translated it and said it was in very poor Russian. It started with the country and worked its way down to the name, the reverse of our practice. All the children wanted pens, a kind of currency in Northwest Asia, and one boy later followed us to the hotel where we gave him a ballpoint. But it was Russian-made and, disgusted, he rejected it.

The mausoleum was ornate, richly decorated in the Islamic style with bands of Qur'anic inscriptions and abstract patterns. The policeman on duty at the entrance let us know with a wink that he wouldn't charge us the usual twenty-five-ruble entrance fee. But we gave it to him anyway and he responded by giving me the emblem with the hammer and sickle from his cap. After a few more rubles he took us around to the back of the building where, after fumbling with a lock, he led us down a narrow staircase to crypt where the bodies lay. They knew this since the marble coffins had been opened several years before and the features of their occupants reconstructed from the shape of the skulls. We left thinking we had done a good bit of sleuthing that morning, but later in the day the whole group was given the same tour for nothing.

Turkman, Samarkand

After breakfast, we drove across town to the eleventh- to fifteenth-century Shahi Zinda mausoleum complex. It was the resting place of, among others, Kussam ibn Abbas, a cousin and intimate of the Prophet. The chronology and place seemed suspect, with this contemporary of Mohammed buried several centuries after his death and several thousand miles away from the peninsula. But Islam was probably like Christianity in that respect, with the same relic appearing simultaneously in several places. The complex was extensive. But it was also compact with none of the sense of scale of the Rajistan that, later in the day, would take away our collective breath.

The domes, Samarkand

The domes, alleyways, tiles, and inscriptions contained enough in the way of textures, shapes, and colors—and people—to occupy a photographer for days. Over the centuries several of the domes, coarse ribbed peaks, had collected a layer of soil in the groins. Seeds had germinated in the soil and the resulting grass, very noticeable in profile, gave them an anatomical look. High above us a man with a shovel was clearing away some of the dirt. I also noticed a pair of men who were going from tomb to tomb, praying with their hands uplifted in the Muslim fashion to receive the grace. But it seemed to be an unfamiliar phenomenon, if only because of their obvious self-consciousness. When Arabs prayed, they were generally oblivious to their surroundings.

By midmorning the fog had lifted and the day was very pleasant. People sat on benches and drank in the sun. Samarkand was surrounded by hills and was full of greenery. If Tashkent was Helsinki and Bokhara was Quetta, Samarkand seemed to be Istanbul, minus the Bosphorus. From ShahiZindah we made our way along the road that had actually once been a part of the Silk Road, to the Bibi Khanum mosque. It had been built, intermittently, in the early fifteenth century for Tamerlane's wife, the interruptions having to do with her suspected infidelities. The proportions were immense and, when it was completed, it had been the largest mosque in the world. It was still impressive, in spite of the fact that little of the enclosure remained. UNESCO had financed restoration over many years and the facade was covered with scaffolding. A worker half-way up the building waved to us and he looked tiny, too far away to see much more than the gesture. Most of tympanums had been reconstructed, and the light-blue tiles returned to their original state. But the interior was heavily damaged and large cracks were visible everywhere in the plaster. The wonder was that these huge structures had survived more than five centuries of seismic activity in the area.

Gala, our local guide in Samarkand, was Russian and, with her very white skin and high cheekbones, she looked the part. She was well informed and opinionated and told us many things about Islam. Some were accurate and most were unobjectionable enough, but there was just enough of the polemical about her attitude to be annoying. She was preaching to the converted—everyone being wary of resurgent Islam in Central Asia—but her tone demanded that we be skeptical. It was a little like a well-informed non-Christian, having read the New Testament, announcing with compete confidence that Christ had biological siblings because he referred to his brothers and sisters so often. It was the assurance more than the assertion that grated. From the

Gala, Samarkand

mosque, we walked a few yards to the main bazaar in Samarkand. It was a replica, on a smaller scale, of the market in Tashkent with the same fruits, vegetables, spices, and meats. There were many Farsi speakers and one man followed me around for several minutes after we discovered that we both spoke Arabic. He explained in rather formal language that he needed a visa and wanted to know if I could help. As Americans, we were welcome everywhere.

After lunch, we saw the observatory of Ulugh Beg, the fifteenth-century astronomer, nephew of Tamerlane, and one of the giants of medieval science. All that remained of the observatory was a huge stone sextant, perhaps sixty feet in diameter, used to take astronomical sightings. After centuries of neglect it had been unearthed early in the twentieth century and lay in a deep, semicircular trough. The divisions were fine enough to allow measurements to within a few seconds of accuracy. His star tables were well known in Europe and they were used by, among others, Carsten Niebuhr as a source document in his *Travels in Arabia*. I had seen a sixteenth-century Latin translation of the tables in the Bancroft Library at Berkeley.

Rajistan Samarkand

The museum attached to the observatory was well laid-out and looked interesting, although the commentary and labels were only in Russian or Uzbek. There were artists' renderings of what the observatory must have looked like, a short history of medieval astronomy, and pictures of many astronomers. Gala explained that the portraits of both Ulugh Beg and Tamerlane were based on the reconstructions done after the crypts were opened and their skulls examined. Ulugh Beg was killed because he openly proclaimed his disbelief, which probably was why he was honored by the Soviets.

The rest of the afternoon was devoted to the Rajistan, the *pièce de résistance* of Samarkand. It had been built by Tamerlane in the fourteenth century as the centerpiece of his plan to make the city the most magnificent in the world. We often forgot that these monuments were contemporaneous with a developing Europe, and that Europeans traveled to this part of the world in the sixteenth, seventeenth, and eighteenth centuries not with our sense of superiority, but with a very engaging capacity to be awed by what they saw. Samarkand, Lahore, and Delhi were marvels to be seen and reported, and only later became epitomes of Oriental, albeit corrupt, splendor. This may have been "Orientalism" at its most superficial, but it was in response to an Orient that was to be feared, not patronized.

The scale of the Rajistan, of the three madrasas and the enclosed foreground, was monumental, the equal of St. Peter's square in Rome. Humans seemed puny next to the structures. Everything in the viewfinder of the camera looked heroic. The fact that Samarkand was in a seismically active area made the survival of the buildings even more remarkable. One of the minarets *had* fallen in an earthquake in the early twentieth century, and had been rebuilt by inexperienced restorers from Leningrad. That accounted for its present, considerable tilt. One of the madrasas was also noticeably out of square and plumb, its lines seeming to run in every direction, or no direction at all. Gala said something about Islam recognizing imperfection in all that men did, and that these little blemishes had been left as reminders of our common humanity. But when you looked closely they were not little. The face of the building no longer lay in a single plane but, half way up its hundred-foot height, it was grotesquely out of plumb. Many of the horizontal members weren't level and opposing bays tilted towards the center. The whole thing looked like it had been subjected to considerable buckling and twisting, and one side seemed to have settled, perhaps in the same earthquake that had knocked down the minaret on the corner.

Vestibule, Samarkand

The interior of the central madrasa was being restored. The restoration had already taken many years and, given the sheer surface area of the decorations, it looked like it might go on for many years to come. However, some of the work had been poorly done and was itself in need of repair. Heavy, molded and gilt texts from the Qur'an had simply been painted over where the raised portions were gone. Even worse, the restorers had used silk paper on some of the surfaces, through which they had drilled small holes to allow the paper to breathe. It had curled up in many places. And there was hardly a new plaster surface that wasn't already cracked. But to be fair, these were only blemishes, and the overall impression was sumptuous. We were given an hour to see the complex, but after a while many abandoned the attempt and simply sat and drank it in. Something about the scale seemed to mock our efforts, as if haste and inquisitiveness were out of place here. As we wandered back to the bus we passed several artists doing their versions of the scene in oils. It seemed odd that most of them were older men wearing suits and ties, and we wondered whether they were repressed artists having just rediscovered their vocation, or whether they had just seen us coming. The paintings were all for sale.

The closest thing to a revolt on the tour—actually, it was a more like a mild insurrection—was over the food. We all wanted to sample the local cuisine and one of the waiters at the hotel was prepared, for eight dollars a head, to entertain us at the home of his extended family. Ludmilla laid on the bus and we gathered at about seven thirty for the ten-minute drive to the suburbs, the ride punctuated by the questions of the cynics as to whether we would be in the first or the second seating. On arrival, we were given a short tour of the grounds, of the vines and sheep pens, before removing our shoes and trooping into a large reception area. There, we seated ourselves on the floor around a long, low table for the meal. Ludmilla delivered a little lecture about how this was a typical Uzbek home but, after a day of lectures, most of us were not interested. The meal was a disappointment. It was the standard hotel fare with a little more in the way of hors d'oeuvres. The main course, a pilav with even less meat than in the hotel, was edible. But there was plenty of alcohol and when one member of the party opened a bottle of champagne with a flourish he drenched his wife seated across the table. Our host did not share in the mirth. He was probably counting the loss.

The next day, our last in Samarkand, was devoted to tying up loose ends and seeing the ruins of Afrasiab. It was the capital of the old Persian satrapy of Sogdiana and had been conquered with the rest of Transoxiana by Alexander the Great in 328 BC. The ruins occupied an area of many square miles on the outskirts of the city. It was near an extensive Muslim cemetery, but all was now a wasteland. A French-Uzbek team was excavating the site, but several miles to the north of the museum where we had gathered. We walked over the rolling yellow hills covered with sheep droppings to a little promontory where Gala delivered a lecture on the city. The look and smell of the wide-open spaces was a reminder that we were in the steppes. There wasn't much to see to the untrained eye, except for occasional mud-brick courses in the honeycombed mounds. The museum was nicely laid out with much in the way of weapons, coins, pottery, and implements. There were also several frescos that dated from the pre-Islamic period. They had been removed and mounted on three walls and the colors were surprisingly vivid. Albert von le Coq and Aurel Stein had carried away whole walls from Central Asia to the museums of Europe, but at least the frescos were now available for everyone to see.

Afterwards, we drove across town to the Samarkand equivalent of the Gum department store in Moscow. There were five floors of goods, everything from alcohol to children's clothes. It was everything we had heard about state enterprises in the FSU. The merchandise appeared to be shoddy and the staff uninterested. Unlike the private food markets there didn't seem to be an alternative to these stores for standard manufactured goods. We returned to the hotel for lunch and checkout. We said goodbye to Gala and, in place of the usual tip, I had meant to give her a pair of Guess jeans our daughter had outgrown. Gala was no babushka. But when I looked for the jeans in my unlocked suitcase they weren't there. I was sure I had packed them and just as certain that they were gone.

The fog of the first day was also gone and the weather was beautiful. We had taken a walk that morning along a wide boulevard under a canopy of shade trees, and the first impression of Samarkand as another Istanbul was reinforced. It was a pretty city and it was with a tinge of regret at leaving that we identified our luggage and boarded the bus for the return to Tashkent.

Tashkent and Home

The bus ride began with more promise than the trip those few days before from Bokhara. The weather was better and we left just after noon. By one fifteen the faint outline of the snowcapped Pamirs appeared ahead. They grew closer and more distinct until we descended a long sloping plain and then turned as the road ran parallel to the border with Tajikistan. It was the best view we had of the mountains and then they gradually began to disappear behind us. I asked the driver to stop for a photo, but he either didn't understand or didn't want to, because he finally stopped in a hollow behind a stand of trees where nothing was visible. After that, there wasn't much to see.

We followed a small river for a while, and then went past many farms, all of them looking well-tended. After another hour, we turned north and left the Tajik border behind us. There were large fields covered with what looked like alfalfa and dairy cattle that looked like Holsteins, as well as a few horses. And the omnipresent cotton. The fall colors in the occasional trees were brilliant. It all looked a little like the Sacramento valley, except for the mulberries that, with their look of careful husbandry, were our constant companions. Actually, there were no berries, just mile after mile of succulent leaves.

We crossed another river, this time the Syr Darya. The word "Syr" appeared to be Turkish, although "Darya" was Persian for a body of water. Together they were the Greek Jaxartes and technically we had left the old province of Sogdiana. It lay between the Syr Darya and Amu Darya, or

Oxus, to the west. I bought some "Sogdiana" aerosol deodorant in Bokhara, as much for the name as anything else. It cost sixteen rubles and the woman in the little shop told me, disgustedly, that it had cost only two rubles under Brezhnev. It turned out to be a room freshener, but did seem to be a blend of "Oriental" scents. I had never really understood the Greek influence in this area, and thought that it was perhaps another example of the ethnocentrism of which westerners were so often accused. But Bactrian and Sogdian coins like those we had seen in Samarkand were some of the most beautiful ever minted and they were evidence of the lasting imprint of Hellenism in Central Asia. The little museum at Taxila in Pakistan had many Buddhas with the aquiline profile and curly hair of Greek statuary. The Greeks hadn't stayed very long in the area but they left their artistic calling card.

After another hour, the rural landscape gave way to the outskirts of a city and soon we were back in good old Tashkent. We noticed again the wide streets, electric tramcars, and classical faded-yellow facades. Ludmilla said all these Central Asian cities were laid out in a nineteenth-century Russian pattern and I noticed again her difficulty in pronouncing the word "century." She always said "thentury," as in "eighteen thentury" or "nineteen thentury." The problem was with the "th" sound, impossible for some palates—or was it the tongue and the teeth—to combine with the following "c" sound.

At the Hotel Uzbekistan, there was some question as to whether our reservations were still good. The film festival was in full swing and Ludmilla thought they might have been canceled. But all was well, although the house detectives were now particularly watchful. One of them refused to let me pass without my room chit, although I was obviously a westerner. He moved me with his chest, bumping me into a corner before I convinced him I was a guest. Then he went impassively back to his place by the door. His manner, and the fact that he was not in uniform, made the incident particularly disagreeable. He was like the armed men who delivered the cash to the hotel the next morning. They were only doing their jobs, what a company like Brinks would do in the United States, but the unmarked sedan, their shabby clothes, and the pistols on their hips said something unpleasant about the potential for violence in the country.

The lobby now looked like a mini United Nations, with a hubbub of multi-hued delegates. The portrait artist was setting up his easel, around which the crowds had to part to flow. The same staff sat in the same places selling the same stuff as when we left. The notices in French and English on the bulletin board were unchanged, including the one with the month-old schedule of a conference on immunology and the word "T cell" jumped off the page. Ludmilla had told us that there was no AIDS in Uzbekistan, but that sounded like the blurb in the old tourist brochure about there being no unemployment in the republic. We recognized many faces, people who appeared at mealtime in the hotels in Bokhara and Samarkand, obviously doing the same tour as ours. There was even the Brooke Shields look-alike we first noticed in Tashkent the week before, but the resemblance faded when she smiled. You can always tell Americans by their teeth.

After dinner, most of us set out independently, but we eventually met later in the evening on Karl Marx Street, across the park from the hotel. As before, the street was closed off and full of people and exhibits. One, by a cartoonist, who showed that he was as good a businessman as an artist. For a small fee, we were admitted to his portable stall with rows of pen-and-ink drawings lining the partitions. One showed a socialist woman in the usual heroic pose with a howling child in one arm and a drunken socialist man slumped under the other. The locals seemed to enjoy the humor. The drawings, all originals, sold for ten or fifteen dollars, depending on the size.

The next morning there was time for a long walk before breakfast and I varied my usual route. The city was laid out radially and, for those used to a more regular grid, it was easy to become lost. This was a Sunday morning and they observed the western weekend in Uzbekistan, so there weren't many people in the street. After losing my way I stopped at a kiosk to ask directions. There were newspapers in Russian and Uzbek but nothing else. There was even what looked like a London tabloid with a great deal of flesh displayed. At ten o'clock we were taken to an art museum, said by Ludmilla to be one of the best in the FSU. The first few floors were of Uzbek folk art, including some spectacular robes of one of the Emirs. The next several floors featured European paintings and sculpture of the past several centuries, and the top was devoted to modern, local work. It was a treasure trove and we were allowed circulate for half-an-hour or so among the babushkas who watched over the exhibits. I had long-since learned that they were inert except when someone dared touch a picture, when they were roused to a fury.

By now I had run out of Kodak and had bought a few rolls of German film in Samarkand. But I didn't notice that it had been made in the old East Germany and it seemed that it needed special chemicals to develop. I left the rolls with a woman at the desk in the Hotel Tashkent who though she could find a place in the city to process them. The hotel lab—they advertised one-hour service—was a joint venture with a Japanese firm and they processed only western brands. When the negatives arrived in Islamabad a month later they were of very poor quality, and only repeated attempts at printing salvaged a few of the shots.

We had bought tickets to a performance of Prokofiev's "Cinderella" before we left Tashkent the first time, and now we hurried over to the Opera House for the noon matinee. Someone in the party had paid for all of us and, at one ruble a head the total came to about seven cents. The performance was excellent, although the costumes looked a little threadbare. We seemed to be as interesting as the dancers to the kids, done up in their Sunday best, the girls with huge bows and pigtails. One especially bold girl blurted out in English "What is your name?" before they all dissolved in giggles. The parents looked wary. The children were mostly European with a sprinkling of Uzbeks and an occasional Eurasian, very fair with just a hint of an epicanthic fold.

Tashkent had more and more the flavor of European Cairo. Both existed in a time warp, forced to make do with local or Eastern-Bloc goods for years. Both, in spite of the Oriental setting, had a European veneer. Egypt under Sadat had begun to emerge from the isolation, but even in the 1980s there were still pockets of the old inefficiency in places like the New Shepheard's hotel in Cairo or the Palestine in Alexandria. The public sector in both places was hopeless and everything they did collectively seemed to be of poor quality. But there was something ineffable in some of the faces you saw in the two places, of old men at Groppi's in Cairo and now at the Opera House in Tashkent. There was a gentility and culture about them, and a fatigue that seemed too deep for words. They looked like they had seen it all, and had been through far worse than the tough times that surely lay ahead.

The afternoon was free and, after the bustle of the morning, it was pleasant to sit in the park and watch the leaves fall. There was no question that this was a European world, and it would be interesting to see if the synthesis, achieved at some cost to all the communities would last under the new dispensation. It seemed to have worked, but the same was probably also said of Sarajevo. If the non-Europeans suddenly took umbrage at seventy years of European hegemony the whole thing could fall apart.

I wasn't sure it would be because of Islam. There had been bogeymen before in this part of the world and the two Afghan wars were the direct result of the Russian bogey on the northwest frontier of India. The "Great Game" had been never been more than a series of little skirmishes if the direct conflict of the great powers were the measure. The same kind of fear may exist about fundamentalist Islam in Central Asia. Ethnicity seemed to be everything in Uzbekistan and religion just another factor to be manipulated by the parties. None of the supposed major players except the Turks—not the Iranians, the Saudis, or the Pakistanis—looked like they belonged here. Fellow Muslims were often different in color and habits and these differences were often more important than their common Islam. The experience of the Arab volunteers in Afghanistan was a case in point. They were generally disliked, ostensibly for their zealotry, but also probably just for being different in an Afghanistan where the tribe was everything. I recalled the incident near Landi Kotal in the frontier area where our car was stopped by several very nasty-looking people looking for Arabs. On the drive back from the border a crowd had gathered around an Iraqi they had found and killed.

A great deal was made of the Muslim/Christian dimension in Yugoslavia. It was a factor but probably not the most important one. The Serbs may have collectively remembered 400 years of Ottoman domination, but they were asserting Serbian nationalism, not Christian chauvinism. Christian Europe was passive when faced with Sarajevo not because the Bosnians were Muslim, but because, having depended on the Americans for fifty years, they were not prepared to deal with the problem themselves.

We asked Ludmilla to arrange another special meal on this last night in Uzbekistan and for seven dollars a head she had made reservations at a famous Tashkent eatery. It was within walking-distance of the hotel and the walk sharpened our appetites. We checked our coats at the door and made our way through the main dining room, where a string quartet was playing chamber music, to a room in the back where a large table lay. The setting was very Russian and we felt we should be addressing each other as "little flower" or perhaps "dear comrade." The waiters were, as usual, in tuxedos and we started with champagne. The first of many bottles of the local red wine were opened and placed strategically around the table.

The spread was lavish. The hors d'oeuvres dominated and we spent nearly an hour playing at them. There was caviar, pate, jellied meat with horseradish, coleslaw, olives, pickles, sliced turkey, potato salad, sliced beef, salted pork, ham, cucumbers, white cheese and yellow cheese, sliced tomatoes, beets, onions, and pickled whole red peppers. It was all washed down with champagne and tart red wine. We cleansed our palates with bits of the good, round bread. Shortly after we began, the string quartet was replaced by a band and the European atmosphere evaporated. Instead of Brahms we were served up selections from the Beatles and *Abbey Road*. The main course was almost an afterthought and, by the time we had finished with the hors d'oeuvres, no one was hungry anyway. We strolled back to the hotel, past the sculpture of the drill bit in the middle of the sidewalk, half a block up the street. It looked like a real drill bit, about a foot in diameter, with the three interlocking heads, and was about three feet high. It was an odd size and an odd place to have put it.

The next morning, our last in Tashkent, we met after breakfast to do some final shopping. Ludmilla had arranged for the bus with the driver who was the only one during the week who seemed to have a sense of humor. He later took pictures of all of us standing in front of the bus with half a dozen cameras. It was a busy final half-day. We had three destinations: the market, a bookstore, and the gift shop at the Museum of Applied Arts, all in a couple of hours. We took a quick turn around the bazaar and then bought books, posters, and maps at a bookstore that might have been located in Cairo. The map was a large 1:5,000,000 roadmap of the Soviet Union with the long, southern border outlined in red. It was interesting to see the Great Game from a northern perspective. We spent our few remaining rubles in the gift shop. It was forbidden to take rubles out of the country, but no one in his right mind would exchange them for anything else. One couple bought an old Bokhara carpet, and they were concerned that they would be stopped at customs. But it passed safely.

We left for the airport at noon, missing lunch for the first time in a week. We said goodbye to Ludmilla near the gate where we had met her only a week before, but it seemed much longer. The customary tip in hard currency was probably many times the average monthly wage in Uzbekistan, but she had earned it. The departure formalities were routine, with much less security than in Pakistan. The only difficulty was in lining up to go through the single door into the customs area. We went through as a group and formed a second line that, understandably, annoyed other passengers who had been waiting for some time before we arrived. One Pakistani wearing an Uzbek cap and carrying a porcelain lamp hectored us loudly in lawyerly terms for having formed another "queue."

However, we were merely following directions and did as we were told. The Pakistani was right of course, but his manner was offensive and no one was prepared to concede the point. When the door opened, the scene became farcical, with a great deal of pushing and shoving and everyone jockeying for position. But we all made the plane. After the meticulous counting off currency on our arrival, the declarations on departure were routinely stamped. Even the grim man behind the glass in the booth seemed less forbidding. None of us really had anything to hide, but there was still a sense of escape when this final hurdle was cleared, a feeling that we had made it. There was a wait of about an hour before takeoff, which took place on time. The flight was scheduled to arrive in Islamabad at five thirty but the pilot radioed Kabul over Mazar-i-Sharif and received permission to fly over the capital. This cut a half-hour from the normal flight time. From 30,000 feet Afghanistan looked placid and orderly.

It was warm when we landed in Islamabad, that day in the city when it changes from summer to winter not yet having arrived. Autumn in Central Asia in 1993 had been pleasant but there was already a hint of winter in the air. We hoped it wouldn't be too severe.

6

The Khojak Pass

WE ALWAYS THOUGHT OF the Great Game as relic of the nineteenth century, of Russian maneuvers and British imperial obsessions, conjuring up images of *Kim* and *The Man Who Would Be King*. But the Khojak Pass showed that it belonged to the more recent past as well. When the vulnerability of British India was discussed, it had always been said that an invader would come by one of two ways: the Khyber Pass in the north or the Bolan Pass in the south. The Khyber Pass was well known, and the Epthelites, or White Huns, along with Genghis Khan, Tamerlane, and Babar had all descended to the plains of the Punjab through the Khyber. But when the fear of a Russian invasion began to preoccupy minds in India the British were equally concerned about the southerly route through the Bolan Pass and Baluchistan. The Bolan was actually easier than the Khyber. The British themselves had invaded Afghanistan twice via that route, each time in response to what was perceived as a Russian forward move in the area. In the First Afghan War, the invasion of Kabul in 1839 had been solely through Quetta and the Bolan. In the second war, they took Kandahar from their base in Quetta in 1878 and it was from there that they salvaged what little they could after the inevitable disaster in Kabul. Quetta had been the most westerly outpost in the Indian Empire. The base was designed to cover the southern route into India, although the city itself was not of great military value.

But lost in all of this was the fact that there was a third pass, the Khojak, that was just as important as the other two. In fact, it was the first line of defense in the south. Before an enemy reached the Bolan—over 200 miles from Afghanistan as the crow flies—he first had to cross the Khojak Pass into Baluchistan. The fortifications showed that the British intended to contest this passage as well. Some of the works in the Khojak dated not from the nineteenth but from the twentieth century and the early part of the Second World War after the Germans and Russians concluded their nonaggression pact.

Nineteen airfields had been rapidly built in the Quetta area in 1939 in the early part of the war and the tank traps on the western face of the pass dated from that period as well. But after Hitler invaded Russia, the concern evaporated and there must have been a huge sigh of relief in Delhi or Simla. After partition, however, Pakistan joined both CENTO and SEATO and everyone returned to the obsession with Russia. Again, it was Soviet ambitions in Afghanistan and, ultimately, the NWFP and Baluchistan, that were of concern.

American interest in the area was a result of the wars in Afghanistan. The mine-dog program deployed dogs and handlers from Quetta into the southeastern part of the country, although they didn't have much success in finding mines there. The civil war was still in progress in 1993 and the minefields that ringed Kandahar were left untouched. The commanders told our people to leave them alone. In addition, we shipped food and other commodities into Kandahar. A shipment of 2,000 tons of PL-480 (or "Food for Peace") wheat had recently gone across the border, all but sixty-four tons having reached the city. The missing sixty-four tons had been hijacked, even though all of it was transported in ISI trucks provided by earlier American aid. The ISI, or Inter-Services Intelligence agency, ran the war from the Pakistani side and its fingerprints were everywhere.

There had been a recent book, *The Bear Trap*, by an ISI brigadier general who described, in great detail, how *he* had evaluated and engaged *his* enemy, and conceived a strategy to defeat *him*. Language that personalized conflict was the staple of generals throughout history, but there was probably no one who really directed the war against the Soviets or controlled the *mujahideen*. Most of the arms financed by the Americans and Saudis were either diverted by the ISI or hidden away in anticipation of the civil war, the one that was now taking place. But the book was interesting, if only for its description of the routine logistics networks that were used to ship the arms. They were the same networks we used to bring non-lethal supplies into Pakistan and Afghanistan. In many cases, we even used the same shippers. It was not a military operation although Earl, our man in Quetta, was a retired US Army Special Forces officer.

Kandahar, the closest major city in southeastern Afghanistan, had suffered heavily in the past year and Quetta was full of real and bogus Afghan NGOs, all looking for a handout. There was no question that people were suffering in the Kandahar area. We had seen a video taken in the city in February of 1992 and, aside from the general overall appearance—with the same people, the same shops, and the same little three-wheeled tuk-tuks as in the streets as in Peshawar or Quetta—what was noticeable was the number of undamaged buildings, many of them of impressive size. We understood that most of them were now gone, and everyone was afraid that another round of fighting would complete the destruction of what little remained. It was said that many people had left the city and they were now living in the surrounding villages.

But even with the general mayhem, or maybe because of it, NGOs had sprouted up everywhere. All you needed was a letterhead and a rudimentary command of English to approach the donors for food or medical supplies, air conditioners or vehicles. We had recently received a letter from one, thanking us for aid. It began:

> With highly spiritual express our sincere deeply thanks regarding the 3,292 items cloths . . . for our districts residence.

It was a form letter, with a space for the items left blank and the number written in ballpoint pen. The letter ended in the same fractured English with the same hopelessly confused syntax:

> Hence it is statable that some contributions should rescue our people from this critical situation which in present time as be encountered more sincerely friends for your Aid/plan in the future in the area.

It was not cynicism to see self-interest behind the platitudes of the pirates who presented themselves to USAID. With our help, they reviewed the applications and extracted a promise from the grantee that commodities would be used properly. That meant they wouldn't be diverted to personal use and would not be sold. But we knew that some of the stuff eventually was misappropriated or peddled. It was the same problem everywhere with western aid agencies in the developing world and smooth operators were attracted to them like bees to nectar. There was even a question as to whether the Afghans needed the aid at all. They were merchants and manipulators of the first water and our assistance may just have meant that a few clever people were better off than they might otherwise have been.

One kind of assistance *was* badly needed, however, and that was medical. The ICRC, or Red Cross, hospital in Quetta was still treating war wounded even though the facility in Peshawar had been closed and moved across the border to Jalalabad. I spoke with an orthopedic surgeon and several nurses and they all had their hands full. In hospitals in the United

States or Europe there would have been neurosurgeons, plastic surgeons, dermatologists, and other specialists. Here, they had to do their best with limited staff. It was not uncommon to treat a patient who had lost a limb to a mine several days before they saw him. He would have traveled two days by donkey litter to the ICRC first-aid station in Chaman, then arrived at the hospital in Quetta by taxi. They didn't generally see women, although they were also victims of the mines. They were in *purdah* and most simply died in their homes or what passed for homes in their devastated country.

One problem mentioned by the head nurse was the need for extended post-operative care for children. Even though a limb had been amputated, the remaining bone in a child continued to grow. When the pain associated with growth became too great the children were brought back for corrective surgery. It wasn't an obvious complication to a layman. They were an international group. One nurse had been in Somalia prior to this assignment, and on the Cambodian border before that. The chief surgeon was British, the anesthesiologist a Dane, two of the nurses were Japanese, two were Danish, and the head nurse was Norwegian. We generally met them at parties where the drinking was heavy and the behavior uninhibited. Surprisingly, for a group in the medical profession in the late twentieth century, almost all of them smoked heavily.

We had over 2,000 tons of diamonium phosphate, or DAP, stored at Chaman and we periodically went there to inspect the warehouse and office. The fertilizer was intended for Afghan farmers, but some of it had reportedly made its way into poppy-growing areas and there was a temporary ban on distribution. Three expat narcotics agents had been kidnapped just across the border the previous month, and a pair of women from Save the Children had their vehicle stolen and themselves brutalized a couple of weeks before on the same road. But the trip was relatively routine, although we took a couple of levies from the Frontier Constabulary with us. This was standard procedure in the frontier areas and we often took the same precautions on trips to the Khyber Pass. Earl's vehicle was a brand-new Mitsubishi Pajero and he did his best to keep it inconspicuous, mainly by not washing it. But it proved to be too great a temptation and the vehicle was later taken at gunpoint in Quetta itself not far from the office. It was never seen again.

Quetta was over 5,000 feet in elevation and at seven o'clock in the morning it was cool. The day before, I had been in Lahore where it was 110 degrees, very humid with a great deal of dust in the air. Quetta was always a relief and after we passed the city limits the slight pollution that hung over the populated area disappeared. The city lay in a kind of bowl and the surrounding mountains were stark and treeless. What little vegetation that existed had been cut down to feed the brick factories. But there were patches of man-made greenery, and we passed through several areas planted in apples, apricots, and mulberries. In Central Asia, the mulberries were cultivated for their leaves, to feed the silkworms, but here the berries were harvested. They were black and white in color and they looked and tasted like our blackberries, although they were smaller. In the city, there were mulberry trees with trunks a foot or more in diameter and the evening air was heavy with their fragrance. Here, they were irrigated from large earthen cisterns that lined the road. As we passed boys were climbing out of the green water and plunging back in again.

After an hour, we reached a large refugee camp. In spite of talk about the return of the refugees, there were still hundreds of thousands in Pakistan. Kandahar was still unsettled and many Afghans had built businesses here. Their children were in school in Pakistan and even if peace returned overnight, the decision to return to Afghanistan would be a difficult one. At about nine o'clock we reached Killa Abdullah and the base of the Khojak Pass. It looked like a southern version of the Khyber. This, the eastern side, was a gradual climb to the summit, and we passed through revetments, camps, and railroad tracks that disappeared into a tunnel. The tracks would reappear on the other side of the summit, about three miles away. The serpentine climb took another ten minutes before we arrived at Shelabagh, or the summit, at 7,457 feet, and we stopped for a look. The western side was far more rugged and covered by tank traps

Camel transport, Quetta

and pillboxes. There wasn't a tree to be seen. Chaman was just visible in the morning haze, about fifteen miles away. After Chaman the plains of Afghanistan stretched away to Spin Boldak and eventually to Kandahar.

The descent on the western side took longer, and we wound through a bleak gray landscape before reaching the bottom. After that, the road became a dirt track and we bounced into Chaman covered with dust, our internal organs severely shaken. We went directly to the warehouse where our man, Sherali, met us. The rural Afghans had a characteristic odor, not that unpleasant, but very noticeable. It probably came for wearing the same clothes for weeks at a time without bathing. The outfit was a dark *shalwar* and *khamis*, the loose trousers and matching tunic that constituted the national dress of both nations; a waistcoat—they still used the old word for the vest; one of several styles of turban; and high-heeled shoes without socks. The Afghans said that a man's glory was his beard and some of the beards were spectacular.

Chaman was just like Quetta, only wilder looking. There were many unveiled women in the streets, unusual enough to be noticeable. We inspected the DAP in the warehouse and then drove to the border crossing, where a kind of no-man's land stretched the 200 yards between the Afghan and Pakistani checkpoints. Traffic moved freely. There were donkey carts carrying black-market fuel into Afghanistan before returning empty, tractors loaded with wood, pick-up trucks with armed men, and a considerable flow of people on foot. This was the official crossing. From the roof of the border post we watched the smugglers pass on an alternate route, a quarter of a mile away. Everyone knew what was going on but they passed, unmolested, in a steady stream.

After this we returned to the office where we had a Coke and indulged the desultory conversation that constituted the workday in places like Chaman. The office was furnished with a desk, a few metal chairs, and a telephone. The walls were papered in maps with the text in Farsi. One showed Pakistan, Afghanistan, and, to the north, an area designated as "Muslim lands under the control of Russia." The landlord had arranged for lunch at a government rest house on the outskirts of town. So, just before noon, we left for the rendezvous in our Pajeros. The Mitsubishi Pajero was to Pakistan what the Mercedes was to rest of the developing world, the vehicle of prestige and choice. You could always tell when the National Assembly in Islamabad adjourned because of the flood of Pajeros on Jinnah Avenue. Another metric of international aid in Pakistan was how many Pajeros a given sum would buy.

The meal wasn't ready when we arrived and we passed nearly an hour without refreshment while the cooks completed their preparations. We were seated, four on a side, on couches in a kind of reception area. In the West, we might have described the time as having been passed in embarrassed silence. But here, there was no embarrassment. There were occasional interludes of conversation:

> You are from Kandahar?

Yes.

> How are things in Kandahar? I hear there is still fighting there.

Kandahar is finished.

> Is it better in the north?

Dostom is strong in Mazar and Ismail Khan in Herat and Qara Baba in Ghazni. But the rest of the country is finished. Afghanistan is finished.

One of our constabulary guards, Mohammed Qasim, passed the time by taking apart his Kalashnikov. He removed the breech cover, extracted the long spring, and then pulled out the clip. We watched as he examined the pieces and then put them back together again, ending by snapping the clip into place. He didn't move a round into the chamber, but pulled the trigger several times and laid the weapon on the couch next to him. He was the younger of the two guards. The older man, Mohammed Sadiq, had the full white beard and considerable paunch of the adult Afghan male. But Mohammed Qasim was thin and fair and had only a light-brown mustache. When he grinned, he revealed one front tooth that had been crowded out and lay in front of the others. It was in a different plane altogether.

Finally, the meal was ready and it was the usual excess. There was enough to feed double or triple our number, but better there be too much rather than too little so the guests would feel no reluctance to eat their fill. There were plates of tomatoes, cucumbers, onions, and sliced lemons. The main course consisted of bowls of mutton curry and roast goat, platters of pilav, and Afghan *nan*, the large flat bread. We ate in silence, each according to his national habit. The Americans ate with a knife and fork, and the Pakistani driver with a soupspoon. Like an Egyptian, he knew that you could move more food with that implement than any other. The Afghans ate with their hands, forming balls of rice and meat with the aid of the bread and projecting the mass into their mouths.

As each man finished he moved away from the table, washed his hands at the basin, and dried them on a common towel, before returning to his place on the couch. But still the food came: plates of diced melon, white plums, tangerines, and mangos. Then there were soft drinks, Cokes, Sprites, and mango sodas. Finally, we finished and left. It was like a Pakistani *valima*, or wedding reception. There, everyone sat for an hour watching the unsmiling bride and her attendants, before the meal was served. Then they fell on the food like a plague of locusts and as soon as it was gone, everyone left. As we drove away we saw the cooks tucking in to the leftovers.

Afterwards, we paid a short visit to the Chaman railway station. The stone blockhouse looked like something on the Hejaz Railway, remnants of which still existed in Saudi Arabia. But this was larger, with ten tracks in a switching area in front of the station. A sign on the wall showed the schedule and the fares: Shelabagh, Gulistan, Kucklak, Quetta. A first-class ticket to Quetta cost thirty-two rupees, or about $1.25. I had planned to take the train to Islamabad from Quetta. It would take thirty-two hours, the first eight through the Bolan Pass. But I couldn't spare the time on this visit and would have to wait for another opportunity.

The drive back to Quetta was the same scenery in reverse, and we were sleepy after the meal. But I still had time to visit our chief logistician, Ghulam Ahmed Khan. He, as usual, had an interesting perspective on our trip

> In 1929 my elder brother and several chaps were on a holiday. They were in a Model T Ford and when they reached the top of the Khojak Pass—you know, where the rest house is now—they met three cars coming in the other direction.

Ghulam Ahmad Khan, Quetta

Like most Pakistanis, he still used many British words.

> You know, they were just students. But the other cars were two Rolls-Royces and another English car, I think a Bentley, and they were carrying the Afghan King, Amanullah Khan, and his women. They were also carrying several large chests of gold. This was in the winter and, you know, they had no tire chains, and these young chaps helped the King down this side of the pass.

> It was after the revolution?

Yes, you see, Amanullah Khan had been to Europe and was, you might say, modern in his attitudes. But when he tried to introduce reforms, the mullahs rose up and forced him out.

> This was at the time of Bacha Saqao?

Yes, Bacha Saqao, "the son of the water carrier."

It was a famous episode in Afghan history. Bacha Saqao had been a Tajik freebooter who seized power in the aftermath of the revolt. He was killed shortly afterward.

And there was no problem with the gold?

No, none whatsoever. This was not like our times, with our modern communications. No one knew that the king had left such-and-such a place, and would be at the border a few hours later. He traveled with only his personal bodyguard. The gold was kept in large wooden boxes made of thin wood, like plywood. Then they wrapped them with the skin of animals, you know, like parchment. The boxes were sheathed in this leather.

I always liked talking with Mr. Khan. He was a retired squadron commander in the Pakistani air force and had served in Burma, at Cox's Bazaar and Imphal, during the Second World War. We talked about the American Dakotas that had been the difference in the campaign, and about Field Marshal Slim, the theater commander.

They say that Slim's is the best general's book ever written. He called the Japanese "the best fighting insects in the history of warfare."

We used to have a saying that the only good Jap was a dead Jap. You know, they had Subhas Bose and the Indian National Army, but no one paid any attention to them.

The son of a Kashmiri contractor who had come to Baluchistan to work on the railroad, Khan was born in Quetta and was the only survivor in the family after the terrible earthquake of 1935. It had killed 40,000 people.

I had three brothers and six sisters and they were all killed. They found me—I was only a little chap and had just started school—a day afterward in what was left of our house. The British troops found me. Our own people, the Pathans, found women alive in the rubble and killed them, you know, for their jewelry. But God spared me, I don't know why.

Khan had the reputation of being a bit of a mullah himself and he looked the part, with a fine, full beard and a very noticeable *zabiba*, or encrusted prayer mark, in the middle of his forehead. But I always thought of him as the best of a certain kind of Muslim, honest, hardworking, and utterly incorruptible. Life was full of ethical choices and he always knew where he stood. We may not have found his attitude about Salman Rushdie to our liking. But then, we never discussed religion. He had had a full life. He ran away from home as a teenager, lied about his age, and joined the air force. After the war, he spent a year at school in the United States and he and several other officers bought an old car and traveled around the southwest. He smiled when he recalled Tucson and Phoenix. Then he worked as an ordinance officer in Riyadh before retiring. He still flew gliders in Quetta.

Khan was just the kind of man we needed to run our warehouses. I think he saw me with my Arabic as a potential Muslim. Like many others I met, he was ready to welcome me at any time into the saving faith.

7

The Prison

> Yeaaah Lord. Help us to be the instruments of your grace . . .
> on this feast of renewal . . . help us to think of the men and the
> women in the prison . . . yeaaaah.

JOHN WAS COMPLETING HIS contribution to the prayers being offered before we set out for the prison. He was the pastor of the Anglican church in Islamabad, an Australian with the flat accent and matter-of-fact manner that seemed to characterize the type. We were going to the main prison in Rawalpindi to bring the Christian prisoners a little Easter cheer. There were supposed to be fifty-five men, almost all of them Nigerians, and almost all in for drug trafficking. The newspapers in Pakistan were full of reports of the arrest of "Afro-Caribbeans" in the Northwest Frontier Province, how they were later made to "lay the eggs" they were carrying, heroin in condoms they had swallowed. It was difficult to understand why drug barons would use people who looked so obviously different. But Nigerian mules had become common the world over, and they were active in the networks in Asia, the Americas, and Europe. It was said that drug abuse was even beginning to appear in Nigeria itself.

We had heard that conditions in the prison were appalling, and we hoped to bring a little cheer on this, the most important feast in the Christian calendar. The weekend before we had segregated donated clothing into fifty-five individual packages, putting maybe two shirts and a pair of pants into each plastic bag. To them we added a couple of bars of soap, a package of crackers, and a few staples like sugar, salt, rice, and *dal chana*, or lentils. It was a fairly complicated logistical exercise, when added to the three large pots of rice and curry that we hoped would give the men at least one decent meal that year. We drove to the prison in caravan and, when we arrived, we attracted the attention that seemed to follow expatriates in Pakistan. Expats were often giving something away and it was certainly the case this time. There were maybe a hundred people—men, women, and children—milling around the doors of the prison when we arrived. Friday seemed to be visiting day.

In the prison itself, men and women inmates were, of course, segregated, and the women in our party entered first. Inside the main gate there was an intermediate area before the prison proper, and the men in the party were kept in a kind of holding cell. It was large enough for about fifty people, and was on the second floor overlooking the prison grounds. We were an international group: John, the Australian pastor; a Brit who worked for United Nations; the Australian Deputy High Commissioner; three Africans—one each from Kenya, Uganda, and Nigeria; Farhat, an Iranian who, with his fluency in Urdu and willingness to get into it with the guards really earned his keep that day; Nigel, an English missionary from London; and me. We thought that the Africans would be especially useful, given the population we expected, and hoped that they would be able to speak to them in one of the several tribal languages with which every African came equipped. Like so much else about the day, we had been misinformed.

A first concern was our own safety. We had been warned to leave anything of value outside, and I had only a plastic comb in my pocket. Everything else—wallet, keys, money and glasses—were left behind. So, it was difficult reading one of the little Christian tracts we had been given when we arrived:

> A man was walking one day in his village in Lesotho, when the
> devil appeared to him in the person of a medicine man . . .

I had even put on a pair of old desert boots. But no one else seemed to be too concerned and there were several Rolexes and spit-shined loafers in the group.

The search on the way in was cursory. We had several large canvas mail-sacks with the clothes, and many more of food: dyed Easter eggs, oranges, and apples, not to mention the pots of rice and curry. None of it was inspected very carefully. The only evidence of a security check was the name "Ali," the officer responsible for out visit, written in ballpoint pen on the fatty part of each of our hands, just beneath the thumb. I think we could have brought in anything. They didn't seem to be expecting us and we spent about forty-five minutes in this upstairs room before we were admitted through a second set of gates into the prison itself. While we waited, we had time to watch the traffic in the yard below.

The prisoners didn't look particularly abused, but the guards looked like guards everywhere. They walked with the swagger of men who were used to the exercise of authority. The *shalwar khamis* was the loose-fitting trousers and shirt that constituted the Pakistani national garb, and most of the prisoners were in light brown *shalwars*. But the guards wore tight pants and gray shirts with epaulettes. I was reminded of Burton's comment that tight pants were a symbol of authority in India, however uncomfortable they may have been for their wearers. Almost all of these guards had big bellies and their pants were hiked up high, outlining the cleft of their buttocks in the back and the knot of their genitals in front. Most carried a swagger stick, a long bamboo baton and, we later learned, they used it liberally.

Once inside, the next question seemed to be why we were there. Ali didn't know, and he and Farhat had a long discussion before anything was decided. They were bellowing at one another in Urdu—one of the world's most incomprehensible languages—and the only words I caught were "Christians," "foreigners," and "professor." It seemed that there was a Christian Pakistani, a professor, in the prison and he was sent for. When he arrived, he appeared to be anything but the abused inmate we had been led to expect. He was about forty, clean-shaven, wearing a spotless white *shalwar*, and aviator sunglasses. He introduced himself in excellent English and told us matter-of-factly that he was in for murder. Then he, Ali, and Farhat resumed the discussion and the bellowing became three-way. Finally, they reached a conclusion and the professor explained it to us: there were no Nigerians in the prison, only a few foreign Christians and a handful of Christian Pakistanis. But Ali, whose patience was beginning to wear thin, had sent for the foreigners. If we wanted foreigners he would give us foreigners.

So, they trooped out and we watched them as they came down the long axis of the prison yard. They were in ragged formation and there must have been about 200 of them. When they arrived near the gate they were ordered to squat and they did so mechanically, looking at us bemusedly or expectantly or just uncomprehendingly. By the look of their color and dress most were Bengalis and, therefore, Muslims. Clearly, this wouldn't do. So, after more bellowing, they were ordered to march back where they had come from. It was probably not the most incomprehensible thing they had done that day. I managed to speak to one of them, an Iraqi, in Arabic. He had been there for a year and was incensed about everything: he showed me the wound on his leg, he worked for the United Nations, he didn't belong in prison, he was not a Christian and, he seemed to be saying, we could take our Easter eggs and stick them where the sun didn't shine.

We were getting nowhere fast and Ali's shift ended at one o'clock. That seemed to be the determining factor. So, we decided to take whatever Christians we could find and get on with the program. Here, the professor was helpful and gradually our little flock grew as the Christians were sent for.

Most had the dark, Dravidian look of Pakistani Christians. But there was one little Afghan who stayed even though he was a Muslim. No one seemed too concerned even though it was a crime to proselytize in Pakistan. Later, when we prayed, he looked utterly befuddled. But he could jump through hoops if he had to. He showed me several wounds, one where a round had entered and then exited just under his left elbow, a second on his right calf, and a third that had left a scar behind one of his ears. He made a gesture like he was pulling a trigger and grinned. He looked a little like Robert De Niro, with a smile always ready at the corners of his mouth.

The prison yard was spotlessly clean. The facility had been built in 1986, according to the date over the main gate, and the rooms we had seen so far were no worse than some of the offices we occupied. But it was outside that we noticed the cleanliness and order. It was maybe a hundred by two hundred yards on a side and there was nothing out of place, or a piece of trash to be seen in all of this expanse. It looked like they employed an army of sweepers to keep the place clean. The sun was now high but it still cast shadows of the bricks in the long walkways, set like cobblestones in a herringbone pattern. The central square was full of flowers, the pansies, petunias, chrysanthemums, marigolds, roses, and sweet peas that carpeted Pakistan in the spring. They used to say that anything would grow in India and the British brought out all their favorites.

It didn't look like an American prison and, from the look of the prisoners, there didn't seem to be that suppressed violence ready to erupt at any moment. There were the usual problems of confined men anywhere, of the interaction between the strong and the weak, intimidation and, probably, homosexuality. But, like the society they came from, these men were not naturally violent. They may have been casually brutal with animals, with their wives, and with each other, but that was different from the barely-controlled violence of American prisons. Part of the reason may have been the population here. There was a notice board just inside the main entrance where the daily count was kept. Of the 3,176 inmates that day, 1,129 were there under "rigorous confinement," and another couple of hundred were scattered among several other categories. But 1,743, or over half, were awaiting trial and had not been convicted of a crime. Many had not even been charged. Judicial backlog, and the need to pay bribes at every step in the process, was the bane of the system. We later saw three kids who were accused of "car lifting" in Murree. None of them had even begun to shave.

Then we picked up the mail sacks and pots and marched off to the classroom where we would hold our service. We turned right about fifty yards from the main entrance, down an alleyway to a sign on the wall that announced a school. It was an English word, but written in Urdu characters:

seen kaf, wow, lam, or *skool*. It was like one of the first signs I had seen in Pakistan: "Notice," but spelled using a *noon, wow, tay, seen*. It was an odd, eclectic language and the borrowed words made it seem odder. After another long discussion between Ali, the professor, John, and Farhat, we moved to a larger classroom where we settled down to the program.

It started with a few prayers and then the group broke into song. It was like the English Salvation Army centers where men had to sing for their supper. They seemed to know the words and the tune, because they all sang in full-throated voices. It was a typical song from this part of the world, with hardly a familiar progression. They went on and on, and up and down, in an odd syncopated rhythm. One of the inmates was wearing chains and they rattled as he tapped out the complicated beat on the surface of the little school desk. Then, just as suddenly as it had begun, they all stopped. It was amazing. There was another song and then John invited Amos, the Kenyan, to lead us in prayer. He had already strutted his stuff before we left for the prison, and he had a power of extemporaneous prayer of prodigious proportions.

    Lawd, we thank you for bringing us heah today . . .

Farhat was simultaneously interpreting, sentence-by-sentence, into Urdu and it flowed easily. He was a Muslim originally from Shiraz and had come to Pakistan about five years before. I spoke with him as we waited to enter the prison and he said that after the revolution there were no religious problems in Iran. In Shiraz the Christian, Baha'i, and Jewish communities were all free to practice as they pleased.

    . . . to make us the instruments of your grace . . .

The Pakistanis were listening but others were not. There were three Sri Lankans in the back of the room and they probably understood only a little of the English. The Afghan just kept his head down. I was sure he found the performance baffling.

    We thank you, Lawd, for you are great . . .

There was even a Frenchman, who was four years into an eight-year sentence for drug trafficking. Nigel, the missionary from London, had moved into the back of the room and was earnestly explaining to him the contents of one of the little tracts we had brought. His words clashed with those of Amos.

    Lawd, you are King . . .

And so, on it went, Amos dipping into an apparently inexhaustible fund of sentiment, Farhat with his simulcast, and the low murmur of Nigel from the back of the room. Periodically, Ali looked into the room, and then at his watch. We had a one o'clock deadline and, he seemed to be saying, time was awasting.

We thank you, Lawd, for these men . . .

By now, everyone was shifting uneasily in his seat. We were about five minutes into the prayer and Farhat was faltering. But still Amos went on.

We thank you, Lawd, for the jailers . . .

It was Islam that came to the rescue. Because now, from the little mosque two doors down the hallway, came the lilting wail of the call to prayer:

Allahu akbar, Allahu akbar, la ilaha il Ullah . . .

The three orisons, those of Amos, Nigel, and the muezzin, joined together in a kind of spontaneous ecumenical apotheosis. It was a fitting end to the session.

John made a few remarks of a commonsense Christian kind, and then we adjourned to lunch. The curry and rice, in pots maybe two feet in diameter and a foot deep, were still hot. The curry was good and a few men burned their fingers sampling a piece of meat or potato. But they had just dined and ate sparingly. So, we emptied several plastic bags and filled them with the leftover rice. They had their own pots for the curry. Ali sat watching in the corner. Unsmilingly, he declined a plate of food. Like everything else about the prison, this building appeared to be well maintained. We were now outside the classroom in a long, cloistered arcade that had the look of one of the missions in California. Bougainvillea climbed over the wall that separated it from the walkway. A patchy lawn was mustering its strength against what would soon be fearful heat. A gecko scuttled down the wall.

With the professor's help, we now lined up the men to distribute the clothes and soap. We tried to move them down the arcade and out the exit, in a kind of assembly line. That way, there would be no double dippers. But several turned around and came back again, including the Afghan who wanted a football. I thought there might be fights over the bags because, in spite of our efforts, some were better than others. The surplus clothes contained things like odd socks, psychedelic swimming trunks, and a Chicago Bears ball cap. But there were also brand-new Levi's and shirts, and there was no way to eliminate the luck of the draw. But everything went smoothly. This was not a violent bunch. Actually, the men looked neat in their *shalwars*, and I couldn't imagine them wearing some of the stuff we brought.

On the way out, we finally saw our first Nigerian. He was a trim little man of about twenty-five in a red shirt and Levi's. He had closely cropped hair and the receding hairline and high cheekbones of some Africans. He was with a group of new prisoners and we chatted as they loosened the fetters that bound him to a sullen Pakistani. He told us he had been in prison for a year and was being transferred here from Quetta. He was in for drugs.

Yeaaaah.

8

The Ambassador

IN THE AUTUMN OF 1993 we were in Delhi for a few days for a volleyball tournament. It was a welcome break from Pakistan. These tournaments were regular events at the International School of Islamabad, or ISI. It was more cost-effective for schools from Karachi, Lahore, Colombo, Katmandu, Islamabad, and Delhi to gather in one place once a year rather than play each other individually. The previous year the basketball and volleyball tournaments had been held in Islamabad and we were host to a pair of Nepali girls from Katmandu. Even though Islamabad and Delhi were only an hour and a-half away by air, there were still the formalities of international travel, with exit permits, visas, customs, and the international departure gate. There were no direct flights between the two cities and the first leg took us only as far as Lahore. We had a long layover and enough time to make it downtown and see the Lahore Museum, which we had missed on our last visit. The first curator had been John Lockyard Kipling, Rudyard's father, and the museum was noted for its wealth of

Martha, Shish Mahal, Lahore

poorly-catalogued exhibits. But we couldn't do it justice in the time available.

On arrival in Delhi, our first impression was of a different world from the one we had just left. India had problems, probably as serious as those of Pakistan, but that particularly Muslim persecution complex was not one of them. We took a tubercular taxi into the city from the airport. It coughed and wheezed its way through traffic, racked by great shuddering convulsions that occasionally brought it to a halt. We were used to cars that had the look and smell of an electronics showroom, all hard plastic, vinyl, and digital precision. Not this thing. A simple conveyance, it made no attempt to disguise its humble role. It was an Ambassador, a replica of the 1954 Morris Oxford, and the Indians still manufactured them. They came in two models, the Mark 4 and the Nova Deluxe, although from the outside it was difficult to tell them apart. It was probably one of the latter in which the world saw the Indian Prime Minister, the ineffectual P. V. Narasimha Rao, arrive at the Parliament building during the Ayodhya crisis the previous year. There was something very Indian about using one of these little domestic things when there were Mercedes and BMWs available. The Bofors scandal—where kickbacks were paid to members of the ruling Congress party for the supply of Swedish artillery pieces—showed that the Indians knew about the alternatives.

Our cab was an older model but, like even the newest ones, it was a simple platform on wheels. Innocent alike of electronics, avionics, and ergonomics, it was equipped to shield the driver and passengers from the most extreme effects of the elements. The steering wheel was attached to a shaft that disappeared through a hole in the floor and, through the floorboard, you could almost see the mechanical means by which the circular was translated into lateral motion. The wheel itself was a kind of lethal weapon, and was among the first things that changed in the West when considerations of safety began to influence automobile design. The Indian driver was intimate with his steering wheel, lovingly stroking and patting it as he maneuvered through traffic. But in a head-on collision the shaft would be driven straight at him and the hub would hit him about chin-high. It was a deadly kind of intimacy.

Actually, it didn't seem that traffic moved fast enough that a collision could do much damage. But Delhi was a huge city and a sign at one of the major intersections announced that, since the first of the year 251 people had been killed on Delhi roads and streets and another 887 injured. The sheer numbers of vehicles and animals—bicycles, auto-rickshaws, motorcycles, motor scooters, cars, trucks, cattle, and smaller animals—made accidents unavoidable. People drove with the same sense of improvisation as the Egyptians and Pakistanis, but with a peculiarly Indian twist. The shortest distance between two points was a straight line, and if that meant driving on the wrong side of the road or encroaching on the space of someone who was already there, that was all right too. Everyone just moved over and made room, which was what you had to do in a country of a billion people and counting. Americans took a violation of traffic safety or common sense *personally*, but here you would go crazy with that attitude. You might just as well move over with everyone else.

That said, the Indians were law-abiding in an odd sort of way. Almost all the motor scooter drivers, except the Sikhs, wore helmets, most of them olive-green and looking like they were army-issue. Passengers typically did not, and it was not unusual to see a family on a motor scooter—not the six, two adults and four children we sometimes saw on a Pakistani motorcycle—but just three or four. The father, intrepidly piloting the vehicle, wore a helmet but his wife and children did not. That also seemed typically Indian.

The Movies, Delhi

The streets were lined with billboards exhorting the citizens of Delhi to do one thing or abstain from another. Family planning was in vogue, and there were slogans encouraging the limitation of family size, ads for contraceptive pills, and catchy little ditties for condoms. The Indian film industry was the largest in the world and handbills for movies were plastered everywhere. This was unfamiliar to one coming from Pakistan, where a columnist in the Islamabad *News* had recently observed that Pakistani morality consisted, particularly and solely, in how they treated their women in public. The blue movies seized in Islamabad or Rawalpindi or Lahore all seemed to come from India. Here, there were several salacious ads, including one of a blond spilling out of her bra and panties advertising *The Girl from Latvia*. There were Russians everywhere and the Sheraton, in particular, seemed to be full of those thick unpleasant people.

Back in the cab, the shift lever was a long shaft that communicated with the gearbox through another hole in the floor. It took considerable effort to manipulate, and the driver changed the gears as if the purpose of the exercise was to move as quickly as possible from first to fourth. It was independent of the speed of the vehicle, although we couldn't imagine this thing actually speeding. If there had been a tachometer it would have shown that the driver was badly lugging the machine. But the instrument panel had only four gauges, displaying the speed, electrical charge, fuel level, and oil pressure. In this cab only one worked and it showed, reassuringly, that we were well into the green area when it came to amperage.

All of the cabs were metered and the meters, mounted on the outside of the cabs, actually worked. However, this ride from the airport was in a pre-paid cab and it was the one time in India that we felt we got value for money. Everything else always cost more, and the convention was that you paid the cabbie 30 percent over the amount that showed on the meter. But still, they asked for more. After a while it became a game and, as you studied the back of each driver's head and neck, you tried to imagine the outrageous sum he would demand. There were thick necks and thin necks, mounted on fat bodies and tiny, birdlike frames. Some had attached earlobes, and others pendulous lobes like the Buddha. The Sikhs seemed to be particularly enterprising and the *taxiwallah* was often a Sikh. Their outfit was generally impressive but the hair varied on the back of their necks. Several days in Delhi taxis made you an expert on the Sikh's method of tucking the hair into their turbans. But fat or thin, Hindu, Moslem, or Sikh, they always wanted more. It was common for driver to brazenly demand a hundred rupees for a fifty-rupee ride, since "we must have 30 percent over." But they accepted the sixty-five rupees with good grace.

It was not only in taxis. The hotel rates were quoted exclusive of the heavy hotel tax. Restaurant prices did not include the 27 percent tax that was added to the bill at the end. That led, at first, to unpleasant surprises. It really wasn't cost that was the issue. When all the levies were added, the prices were about the same as in Pakistan. It was the sense that there was something underhanded, even dishonest, about the system. It was an unusual man who was a lavish tipper in India after all the official gratuities had been paid. I began to think of them as a nation of cab drivers and extortionists. The judgment was probably too harsh. They were friendly and the feeling in Delhi, after Islamabad, was decidedly one of relief. The Pakistanis were not a happy people. Everyone coming from Pakistan to India noticed the difference. But the Indians wore you down with their demands.

The interior of the car was strictly functional, consisting of two long, upholstered seats. No airbag, fuzzy logic controls, travel pilot, heated windshield, interactive steering, power steering, 4-wheel drive, hands-free telephone, computerized seat adjustment, heads-up system, cassette player, or antitheft alarm. And not even the hint of a seat belt. The occupants would be roughly thrown around, bouncing off many unprotected surfaces, when two of these things came together in a collision. The car in the West had become a leisure experience, an extension of our den. Here, it was still just a conveyance on wheels. The Ambassador was manufactured by the Tata Engineering and Locomotive Company, and statistics showed that it was the thirty-fifth largest manufacturer of automobiles and automobile accessories in Asia.

Several days in Delhi gave us an opportunity to sample other kinds of transportation. My favorite was the motorized auto-rickshaw. In Pakistan, they were all Suzuki engines mounted on locally manufactured frames. It was not unusual to see one rolled over on its side or back like a turtle, while the driver-cum-mechanic dealt with a problem underneath. They were called "tuk-tuks," the name supposedly originating in Thailand, because that it what they sounded like: "tuk tuk tuk tuk tuk tuk . . . " Or maybe it was because they "tuk" people places. They were responsible for half the air pollution in places like Peshawar and Quetta, but in the autumn in Delhi the air quality was surprisingly good. The rickshaw was inexpensive and allowed you to become familiar with India at little sacrifice of safety. The driver, often sitting with his legs crossed as if he were just having a chat, was given a wide berth by the larger and more dangerous vehicles. And he could maneuver into places the larger ones could not. The ride was not uncomfortable, aside from the sound and smell of your own—and everyone else's—exhaust. However, the convention was for the engine to be turned off at red lights to conserve fuel. When the light turned yellow, all the drivers stood and activated the starter, a lever mounted on the floor. That made traffic lights in Delhi sound like the start of the Indianapolis 500. A day in a tuk-tuk left you wind-blown and your hair a tangled mat. But it made getting there almost as interesting as the destination itself.

Tourist, Red Fort, Delhi

For real intimacy, there was the pedicab. When I arrived at the Red Fort in Delhi a Nepali with a pedicab was one of many who offered to show me around. When I emerged an hour later, he was still there and something about his ready grin and persistence paid off. So, we agreed that for fifty rupees he would show me the *Jama Masjid*, or Friday Mosque, in the old city, and assorted Jain and Sikh temples along the way. As I watched the little man work, I recalled the Navy and a pedicab ride years before in Kaohsiung, Formosa. There, three of us, each weighing about 200 pounds, were wedged into one little cab. When the driver delivered us to the *wrong* destination, he just mopped his brow and groaned. My family had never forgotten, or forgiven me for that particular bit of western callousness. But actually, it was good aerobic exercise, what millions of westerners worked up to daily on the Stairmaster.

Qutb Minar, Delhi

This time I was alone and a shadow of my former self. The streets of Old Delhi were narrow, very much like the Anarkali Bazaar in Lahore. They had not forgotten the violent sectarian clashes of the past several months, and armed soldiers were everywhere, the weapon attached by a chain to each man. It was the weapon, not the man, that mattered. The *Jama Masjid* was closed for prayer when we arrived—it was a Friday—and when I told the Nepali he must have known that we started out, he just grinned his ready grin. The Jain temple, three stories of lurid, hyperthyroid statues, was tucked away in an alley with other Jain establishments. The Sikhs, as usual, were better organized than everyone else. The guide gave me a tour of the temple and even extracted a small contribution. But I couldn't persuade him to show me how he wrapped his turban. He said it took about five minutes to get himself ready in the morning.

On the third day, we took a tuk-tuk to the *Qutb Minar*, the twelfth-century mosque complex in south Delhi. I thought I had seen everything that the subcontinent had to offer, and that my store of superlatives was exhausted. But this thing was incredible, a thick and powerful structure that, at the same time, was delicately worked with bands of Kufic and Indian *naskhi* calligraphy. I had seen pictures, but photographs didn't begin to do it justice. Even the government buildings, with their odd amalgamation of Indian and Western architecture, seemed impressive.

Qutb Minar detail, Delhi

The Sheraton in Delhi was comfortable and the Indian food was excellent. The curries in Bombay had been a disappointment and I still remembered the buffet at the Oberoi Hotel in Dammam, in Saudi Arabia of all places, as the best Indian food I had ever tasted. But the food in Delhi was better. The clientele in the hotel coffee shop was decidedly Indian, but the conversations carried just a hint of the influence of the hated British. To an Indian (or a Pakistani) the King's English was revered and they prided themselves on speaking it as well or better than the originals. The *Times of India* was even printed on orange paper, just like the *Financial Times*.

Also, the gemstones were cheap and the atmosphere was free. As an added bonus, the girls' volleyball team went through the opposition like Sherman through Georgia. By the time the taxi deposited us at the Delhi international airport, we had sampled an interesting hors d'oeuvre of India.

The taxi was, of course, an Ambassador.

9

Mohammed

THERE WERE MANY KINDS of hardship suffered by Punjabis in the floods of 1993 that killed thousands. Not all of them came from the inundation of houses and farmland in the plains bordering the Indus. The Punjab was actually the *panj ab*, or "five waters" in Farsi. In addition to the Indus, there were the Jhelum, the Chenab, the Ravi, and the Sutlej, and they all contributed their bit to the devastation. But the residents of the mountains also suffered, in a way that illustrated the capriciousness of nature and the susceptibility of the rural poor in Pakistan to natural disasters. Mohammed, our cook-bearer, was concerned about his family in Murree during the monsoon, the heavy rains that came in the autumn in Pakistan and often produced deadly slides in the mountains. The rain at this time of the year was sometimes so heavy that we had to stop the car and wait for a downpour to pass. The windshield wipers were useless against the volume of water.

Mohammed, Islamabad

Mohammed was one of a stable of household help in Islamabad, their duties separated by the caste system although religion was probably no longer a part of the equation. It was a living remnant of the *raj*. The cook-bearer was at the head of a list that included the *mali*, or gardener, the *dhobi*, or washerman, and the *chowkidar*, or night watchman. Mohammed was the only one who stayed with us on a full-time basis and he lived in his own separate quarters attached to the house. These domestic jobs paid well and were a lifeline for many poor Pakistani families. Some people also had a *bhangi*, or sweeper, a woman who cleaned the house. But female sweepers had notoriously light fingers and when we hired him we told Mohammed that if he wanted the job he would act as the sweeper as well. He objected, but not too strenuously since he needed the work.

Murree meant "high place" in Urdu, and was not the name of some nineteenth-century Irishman commanding a detachment of Jacob's Horse. It had been a summer capital like Simla, but many poor families also lived in the hills surrounding Islamabad. When word of slides in the area filtered down to our neighborhood the news was especially unsettling for Mohammed and he left at once for the village. He made his way home, as he did at the end of every month, by bus and then Suzuki cab, to find his house gone. The family, his wife and two young children, had narrowly escaped but the house had been swept away. The accumulated work and savings of seventeen years were gone in an afternoon. The loss, he told me, amounted to two and a-half lakhs of rupees. Mohammed's stories were often difficult to follow, and we could spend the better part of an afternoon listening to a convoluted tale of why he hadn't returned on time. But this was different and a visit later in the week revealed the extent of the devastation.

The Murree road was badly damaged, including several areas where the roadway had been almost carried away entirely and traffic reduced to a one-lane trickle. We had driven to Naran in the lower Himalayas the year before on roads that made the Karakoram Highway seem like a superhighway, but the roads in Murree were reasonably good. Even with the delays, the trip took only an hour and a-half to the place where we parked the car and began the descent on foot to the village. The walk took about twenty minutes. We arrived at a brother-in-law's house where Mohammed's family were now staying. I could tell it was family because one of the partitions was made of the plywood packing-crate that our sea shipment had arrived in, and the stenciled address was still visible on the wall.

There had been some damage to this house as well, a solid-looking structure made of mortared stone blocks on a concrete slab. The roof consisted of corrugated tin from Australia, the local product not being strong enough for the purpose. But there was no structural steel in the walls and, being built on a hillside, the combined pressures of water and earth had produced serious cracks in one wall. A heavy beam propped up the wall. Luckily, it was in an outbuilding and could fall without damaging the rest of the house. Mohammed's house, or what was left of it, had been a mile away across the valley. We walked through heavy grass along a steep ledge for a better view and reached a point from which the site of the slide was visible. The steep, almost deforested hillside was dotted with tin roofs, the metal prominent in the noonday sun. A few pines were still standing, but most had been cut down. A half-mile or so from the top of the ridge the slide had carved the beginning of a long, thousand-yard scar, maybe fifty yards wide, in the hillside. Mohammed's house had been half way down the scar. I looked through the telephoto lens of the camera and saw a light-blue shutter, all that remained visible of the house.

The rains had clearly not visited everyone equally that year. This was not a village where everyone's house had been inundated and their belongings swept away by floodwaters. But slides had brought a different kind of devastation. They were widespread, especially where population pressures had led to deforestation, but most people had been lucky. Mohammed was not. There was no question of recovering anything from the mud and debris. But Mohammed had one reason to be thankful. His wife had heard stones peppering the tin roof as the slide began, and she had been able to get herself and the children out of the house before the full force struck. Others had not been so fortunate, and there were areas that had simply been declared cemeteries where the slides came to rest. He was also fortunate in that he had a place to go. His brother-in-law was a merchant in Rawalpindi and used the house in Murree only a few months out of the year, so the family had a place to stay. But this was not a long-term solution. The harvest had already been poor that year, and none of the apple, peach, apricot, or walnut trees in the yard had borne much fruit.

We were not in a position to rebuild his house, but we could help with extra cash. There were other contributions as well. The American Women's Club in Islamabad took up a collection for victims of the rains, and Mohammed's case was considered worthy of assistance. It wasn't the two and a-half lakhs he needed, but it was a start.

It wasn't only Pakistanis and it wasn't only the poor who were at risk in Pakistan. Two members of the American community had recently died, both relatively young men, one in his early fifties and the other in his late forties. The first was a medical doctor who died of a heart attack. He had chosen to practice here and his wife elected to have him buried in Rawalpindi. His body was washed in the Muslim fashion by an ecumenical group—a Muslim, a Christian, and a Jew—before it was wrapped in a shroud and buried the next day in the tumble-down Christian cemetery that once served the cantonment. It was the middle of July and we all perspired heavily in our wool suits as we lowered the casket into the grave. It was sheer hard work.

Like other expatriates, this man had probably chosen this life because of the better pay and opportunity offered abroad. Or maybe it was just the adventure of it all. There had been a recent article in *Newsweek* about expatriate labor from Asia—Filipinos in Korea, Hong Kong and Japan, Pakistanis and Burmese in Thailand, Vietnamese in Bangkok, almost everyone in the Emirates, Saudi Arabia, or Singapore. With the exception of our passports and better pay, American expatriates were really no different from other migrant workers. More or less isolated from the local communities, we moved from job to job. And like the Pakistani families in Sindh or Punjabi villages that couldn't adjust when the expatriate returned—so used were they to the cassette players or cameras he brought back on his occasional visits—we could no longer adjust to life in the United States. We were like Europeans in the country trade in the Orient in the last century, although they knew they would be lucky if they survived for five years. But they still preferred life on the deck of a ship in the eastern seas to what awaited them in their own countries, ashore or afloat. We often felt the same way.

After a while it became a way of life. By the time the glamor, such as it was, had worn off it was too late to change. We had become international vagabonds, condemned to a lifetime of wandering from developing country to developing country. Without regular medical care our bodies sometimes broke down. Even with the sterilization routines that we religiously observed we were exposed for years to parasites and microbes that had long since been eliminated in our own country.

Fresh in my mind was the other man we had buried in the little Christian cemetery in Peshawar the year before. He had an alcohol problem. Maybe it was an occupational hazard for single men who spent most of their lives in out-of-the-way places like central Africa, the Northwest Frontier, Mali, or Kurdistan. They were always ministering to people in need and duty-free alcohol may have been their only solace. They were often hard to manage because they had no sympathy for the bureaucrats and the rules that were put in place to control them. But they liked, and were liked in return, by those they helped. In the case of the man in Peshawar, the Afghans even covered for him when he was under the weather and never mentioned what everyone knew was his problem. He was warned by the embassy doctor that the combination of the alcohol and a heavy cigarette habit would eventually kill him, and it did. He was only forty-eight years old.

He died in his home over the *eid* and they didn't find the body for three days. In the summer heat of Peshawar that meant rapid decomposition and we had to burn some of the furniture to get rid of the stench. I put Vaseline-soaked wads of cotton in my nostrils and went through his personal effects, to make sure that there was nothing embarrassing or compromising before officialdom found it. They didn't perform autopsies in Pakistan and the body became a kind of football. There had even been a shouting match in the hospital parking lot between the retired Pakistani brigadier who worked for us and the chief pathologist at the hospital. The awful, decomposing corpse was lying on a gurney and they were arguing over who should take custody of it. The hospital eventually did. The brigadier earned his salary that day.

We buried him in Peshawar, where he probably would have been happiest anyway. The monsoon would soon level the mound of his grave. The American consulate in the city were very helpful, notifying the family, making an inventory of his possessions, securing a death certificate, and doing the many things necessary when an American died overseas. But they didn't know what to do with his life's companion, an African grey parrot bought on an assignment in Ghana. It was on the endangered species list and couldn't be admitted to the United States. The parrot was, in its own way, an expatriate. It would also die a lonely death someday, far from the familiar surroundings of its upbringing.

10

Norman Sicily

"Norman Palermo" may sound like a character in a New York City sit-com. But, in fact, it was the setting for one of the most extraordinary cultural and political phenomena in medieval Europe. In the late eleventh century a pair of brothers, Robert and Roger, left the family holdings in Hauteville-la-Guichard in Normandy, fired with, among other things, crusading zeal. A son of Robert, Bohemond, would eventually reach the Holy Land and become prince of Antioch, a vassal state of the Crusader kingdom of Jerusalem. It was a lineage that a descendant of Roger was later to assert in his claim to the empty throne of that kingdom. But the brothers themselves never made it to the Holy Land. During a stop on the coast of Apulia their eyes fell on southern Italy, at the time a plaything contested by Byzantines, Lombards, the Western Empire, and the Papacy. So, they stayed, finding in Italy scope for their abundance of restless energy. By the time the Pope crowned Roger's son, Roger II, King of Sicily in 1129, the Normans had added a fifth ingredient, and not the least of them, to the stew south of Rome.

By this time, the interlopers had pacified and subjugated all of Italy south of a line drawn between Monte S. Angelo and a point of latitude midway between Rome and Naples. In the process, they had ejected the Arabs from Sicily and chased them into North Africa; shaken the Byzantine Empire to its foundations with an invasion directed at nothing less than the Imperial throne in Constantinople; provided a refuge and an ally for the Papacy in its endless feuds with the two empires; and so discomfited a series of western emperors that removal of the Sicilian menace became the most pressing object of imperial foreign policy.

The Western Empire eventually succeeded in taming the Sicilians, not militarily, although imperial armies made repeated attempts, but by subtler means. When in 1184 Roger's aging daughter, Constance, was betrothed to the future Emperor Henry VI, the most prescient in the kingdom knew that the game was up. The throne that had been so jealously guarded thereby passed into the imperial household. Its occupants would become Angevins and Spaniards until the revolt of the Sicilian Vespers in 1282 brought these latest foreigners low. Others, of course, would follow.

But while it lasted, the eclectic little "Kingdom of the Two Sicilies" was the most brilliant in Europe. As might be expected, the original Normans had been men of the sword. Roger II, however, had the benefit of a Lombard mother and an education in Palermo, where the cultural influences of the Byzantine, Arab, and Latin communities mixed and, all too briefly, coexisted in an easy equilibrium. Greek, Arabic, and Latin were official languages of the court and tolerance seemed to have been officially encouraged. It may seem strange to use the word "traditional" to describe a phenomenon as ephemeral as Norman Sicily, but Arabs were traditionally heads of the royal exchequer, Greeks were the traditional admirals of the navy, and all the communities had important parts to play in the administration of the kingdom.

Roger II attracted not only adventurers and ambitious churchmen to his court, but also some of the best minds of the day. They included the Ceutan Abu Abdullah bin Abdullah bin Idris al Hammudi al Hassani, or Sharif Idrisi, whose compilation was the most important work of medieval geography. Issued in 1154, the book has come down to us *Kitab Rudjar*, or *The Book of Roger*, so-called after its royal patron. It was imperfectly translated into Latin in the seventeenth century and, as *Geographia Nubiensis*, became a staple reference work of early Orientalists.

There is probably no more striking example of the cultural mix that Norman Sicily represented than the cathedral in the little town of Monreale. It sits in the mountains overlooking the broad sweep of the *Conca d'Oro* and Palermo. Nestled among Baroque churches and monuments to the *Risorgimento*, the cathedral dominates the town square with its stark Norman facade, looking like it belongs in some chillier northern clime. Its lavish Byzantine interior contains as fine a collection of mosaics as any in existence, and there is more than a hint of *al-Andalus* in its slender-columned çloisters, enclosing a compound of citrus trees and date palms. But I'm getting ahead of myself.

We had discussed a Christmas vacation and wanted something either cold and white, or very much the opposite. In Islamabad, we had seen enough gray for a while. But our first thought, Copenhagen, sometimes went without snow for an entire winter. And an earlier white Christmas, in Vienna in 1987, had been a bit of a disaster, coming as we were from Saudi Arabia and not dressed for the cold. So, we settled on Sicily, and hoped to see plenty of sun while we pursued the Norman monuments. We went armed only with John Julius Norwich's *The Kingdom in the Sun*. I say "only" not because it was inadequate, but because there seemed to be nothing else available on the Norman period. As it turned out there was nothing available in Sicily either, aside from a few coffee-table books. The Norwich book was our constant companion and we were very glad we had it.

There were few direct international flights, into or out of Islamabad, and the first leg took us only as far as Karachi. After an early-evening flight, we spent the night at the Avari Hotel in the downtown part of the city. It would be our last exposure to the developing world for a week and we left it, as usual, with mixed feelings. The facilities were excellent, the equal of any moderately priced hotel anywhere in the world. The staff were unfailingly polite and helpful, not with the perfunctory politeness we sometimes saw in the West. In the United States, courtesy seemed to be good business. Here, at least in the big hotels, it was simply good manners.

But we were anxious to be among our own kind. And for all of the deference, the domestic help, and the freedom of the developing world, it was anonymity that expatriates missed the most. It wasn't the inefficiency, the discomfort, the dirt, or the occasional danger that was most exhausting, but rather the continuously being on display. Women particularly noticed it, especially in the Muslim World. They were stared at wherever they went—quizzically, stupidly, sullenly, sometimes contemptuously. Whatever the reason the attention was relentless. It was a relief for a western woman to walk in an airport, a store or a street without a hundred pairs of eyes following her every move.

The new Qaid-i-Azam international airport in Karachi had just been opened and it was impressive, well laid out and clean. We were scheduled to leave for Rome, via Athens, just after noon and the PIA flight left on time. The equipment was a brand-new Airbus, so new that remnants of the plastic covers from the factory still adhered to the seats. The leg to Athens took five and a half hours, and just about covered the extent of the old Achaemenid, or first Persian, Empire. Over Baluchistan and then southern Iran the terrain was brown and featureless, but about two hours into the flight the first snow appeared below and for the next three hours we saw little else. The flight path was over the Zagros, running the length of western Iran from south of Shiraz to the vicinity of Tabriz, after which we made a noticeable left turn. The snow continued, not only on the mountains, but now as a blanket that covered everything in sight. Then, to the right of the aircraft, appeared a single, very noticeable peak, like a great white boil rising out of the landscape. It must have been Ararat, and I thought of the freezing Armenians below, isolated in their truncated and landlocked country, cut off from supplies of building materials and heating oil. They were still waiting to rebuild, five years after the devastating earthquake of 1988.

We continued over central Anatolia, with only an occasional body of water to break the monotony of the whiteness. At six-thirty a solitary man who looked like an Afghan stood to pray, and I heard a few snickers from the mostly-Pakistani passengers as he arranged himself. We were flying due west and he chose the area near the wing exit on the right side of the plane for his prostrations and so, was facing Rome. The other side would have better oriented him towards Mecca.

After another hour, the snow began at last to grow patchy, and then it gradually disappeared as we approached the cost in the vicinity of Izmir. We left the peninsula and as we entered the Aegean, a few of the islands of the archipelago appeared below. As the plane descended, the familiar terrain of the approach to the Athens airport came into view. The local time was five o'clock and we would have a wait of about forty-five minutes before resuming our journey. No one appeared to get off—or on, for that matter—in Athens, and we all bundled up against the cold as the doors remained open while the ground crew serviced the plane.

After takeoff, the flight path over central Greece and Albania was also notable for the mountains, although these were not the white monoliths of Western Asia, but delicate serrations dusted with snow like confections dipped in sugar. As the sun set, the Afghan prayed again, this time with a companion, but again in the direction of Rome. The Adriatic quickly came and went as we reached the coast of Apulia, where the brothers Guiscard had first seen Italy. Then, the lights went out. The short remainder of the flight on the in-flight monitor showed our track towards Rome, the air speed, altitude, local time, and time to landing with monotonous regularity, in both the English and metric systems.

We landed in Rome at six-fifteen, after a flight of about an hour and a-half and taxied for what seemed as long before deplaning. Passport control was a welcome return to the developed world. Only a passport was required for entry to Italy: no visa, no stamps, no bother. That is, if you were *from* the developed world. We were in a long line that, at first, moved very slowly, not nearly as fast as the line next to us in which most of the passengers on our flight were waiting. But when the first Pakistani arrived at the booth, that line abruptly stopped. Drugs and counterfeit documents had become the bane of flights originating in Pakistan, and the holders of those green passports were suspect everywhere. When we left, ten minutes later, not a single Pakistani had been admitted to Italy.

The flight to Palermo left at eight-thirty the same evening and feeling a little forlorn, but splendidly anonymous, we had just enough time to recover our bags, find a trolley—there were never enough in a western airport—and push it the two-hundred yards to the domestic terminal. The carrier was a subsidiary of Alitalia and the aircraft was a McDonnell Douglas MD-80, a long sausage with the engines mounted on the fuselage in the back. We were stuffed into it as into a sausage. The announcements were in Italian and execrable English and the flight attendants were indifferent. It wasn't the indifference of PIA where they passed out the food and disappeared as quickly as they could, but a truly European sense of world-weariness.

By the time we had recovered our bags in Palermo, made our way into the city, found the Grand Hotel et Des Palmes and haggled with a taxi driver who left the meter running while we argued, it had been a long day. Travel is war, and we had spent the last ten hours suffering little ignominious defeats. But the hotel was expecting us and by the time the bellboy brought our luggage to the room, we were ready to relax. The room was huge: fourteen-foot ceilings, with three very commodious mirrored armoires and a bathroom that, alone, was larger than the room at the Avari. The beds were made to a similar scale and the hot water was plentiful. There were a few drawbacks. The mini bar was empty on our arrival and remained empty throughout our stay, the elevators were small and painfully slow, and there appeared to be no emergency exit until I discovered the magnificent grand staircase between floors, some distance down the hall. Also, the room didn't lock—from the inside or out—without the key, so the only way to leave someone asleep was to lock him or her *in* the room.

But, for the moment, space was all we wanted and the room provided that. The hotel was also centrally located, as advertised, and there was hardly a sight we wanted to see in Palermo that wasn't within walking distance.

Palermo

The morning arrived early with the time change, and I set out on the dark and nearly empty streets for the Palazzo Royale, the former seat of the Norman governors. At five thirty only a few denizens of the night were still around: a stray cat, an occasional dark silhouette asleep in an alleyway, a huddled figure walking rapidly toward me and then as rapidly away. The sidewalks were covered with rubbish, and I reflected that the garbage collectors in Palermo were Sicilian just as, very profitably, they were in San Francisco. After a brisk half-hour walk I turned up the narrow Corso Vittorio Emanuele and passed several blackened facades that looked interesting. As it turned out, they were black with soot even in the daylight, and most of them were much later than the Norman era. But in a little piazza I saw a statue and, in the dim light of the street lamp, could just make out the Latin words "Rogerius" and "Normanus," so I resolved to revisit it in the daylight.

I had a rough map of the city and knew I was going in the right direction, but stopped to ask a Carabinieri patrol about the Palazzo Royale. They were three policemen, two carrying submachine guns and a third man sitting in a jeep. Neither of the two in the street recognized the words, and they consulted the NCO in the jeep. He shrugged and vaguely waved me in the direction I was already walking. This was shades of Cairo, where the typical policeman was a *sa'idi* from a village in Upper Egypt who didn't know the name of the street he was standing on. But then, I thought, here was this crazy foreigner asking directions in the middle of the night to a Norman royal palace, when all they had to know was that I was looking for the Sicilian Regional Assembly which, I later learned, the building now was.

I walked on, through the Porta Nuova, and turned left along a long, slanting wall with arrow slits and crenellations of obvious medieval provenance. I had clearly found part of what I was looking for and the time and the elements conspired together to make it a memorable introduction to Norman Palermo. The sky was clear and the waning moon—it was the twenty-sixth of the lunar month—hung like a partly illuminated ball in the early morning sky. There were times when all three dimensions in the relationship between the earth, the sun, and the moon clearly stood out, and made obvious the Muslim fascination with this changing celestial phenomenon. It was that kind of morning.

It was too early to see much of anything else so, content with the reconnaissance, I returned to the hotel. On the way, I stopped for a stand-up cappuccino at the one open cafe. It was opposite the Palermo cathedral, a jumble of buildings of several architectural styles where Roger II was buried. By the time I had finished the coffee the city was coming to life. Throaty *buongiornos* were being exchanged, the garbage was being collected, the sidewalks swept, and a few cars hurtled up and down the narrow streets at what seemed like break-neck speed. Later in the day, the volume of traffic would nearly bring the city to a halt. But, even then, the habit of alertness that came from living in a country where they drove on the wrong side of the road would refuse to relax its watch. Back at the hotel, breakfast was the typical European plan: black coffee, rolls, cold cuts, and thin juice. Sicily may have been covered with citrus groves, but we saw no fresh orange juice in the week we were on the island.

The hotel was built in the art nouveau style. Naked statuary filled the lobby, which was otherwise dominated by a huge mirror centered on a bronze bust of, for some reason, Richard Wagner. The lighting was soft and combined with the yellow walls and the off-white androgynes who writhed about the ceiling, this gave it a moldy look. The common rooms, including a bar that looked more like a drawing room and a large sitting room with a fireplace, looked like they had once been elegant. In three days, we didn't see either one occupied. An exhibit of modern paintings pointed the way to the dining room, which was also yellow and featured two massive paintings of rural scenes. It was nearly deserted, with only us and a few other guests. The maître'd had very little to do in the buffet-style arrangement but greet each patron, which he did in a voice of astonishing force and timbre. He uttered not just one *buongiorno*, but a whole series, interspersed with other mellifluous sounds whose sense we caught even if we didn't understand the words.

When the Normans came to Palermo, they converted the old Phoenician and Arab fort to their stronghold in the city. It was about a mile from the port. The building was not particularly striking, aside from the restored battlements I had seen that morning. In fact, it now served as offices for the city administration and a sign on the official-looking glass doors in the front announced in three languages that the tourist entrance was in the back. There was a funeral taking place that morning, and we followed the sleek black cars filled with men in dark suits, past the Carabinieri check point and up the little hill to the gate that permitted access to the interior of the complex. The sixteenth-century Maqueda Courtyard carried our eyes up to the second story where an arched vestibule covered with mosaics announced the presence of something much older. It was the *Cappella Palatina*, or Palatine Chapel, Roger II's private chapel, called by Maupassant "the most amazing religious jewel of which the human mind may dream."

Completed by Greek and Arab artisans and consecrated in 1140, it *was* a jewel, tiny and multifaceted. Inside, after our eyes had adjusted to the light, a thousand objects competed for our attention, from Egyptian red granite columns to inlaid marble floors and a marble pulpit. Mosaics telling the story of the creation, fall, and redemption covered every inch of surface area, crowned by the standard Norman feature of the Pantocrator, the All-powerful Christ, gazing benignly from his perch in the apse. But still there was more: little geometric inlaid patterns in the walls, abstract mosaics covering the floor, medallions of saints above the columns on every arch, a sixteen-foot carved marble candelabrum, Latin and Greek inscriptions, and a stalactite ceiling with Kufic inscriptions on the raised octagonal encrustations. And everywhere there was gold, the background of the mosaics conspiring with the soft interior lighting to give the scene a look of richness and warmth.

But, in spite of its extravagant billing, the Palatine Chapel left a mixed taste on our palates. There was much that was beautiful, but it was *too* much, packed into too small a space. The mosaics were undoubtedly fine as mosaics went, but as an art form they were incapable of rendering anything but cartoon-like figures. When compared with, say, the interior of the equally lush Ulugh Beg madrasa in Samarkand, the *Cappella Palatina* failed to convey the same quiet serenity. There was probably the same weight of gold leaf per square inch in both places, the same attempt to lavish on the surfaces everything decorative art was capable of. But where one had an aesthetic unity, this was too crowded and busy.

Carabinieri, Palermo

I had the feeling that I had seen something like it before, and realized that it reminded me of the chapel in St. Catherine's Monastery in Sinai. There, its littleness, even tawdriness, could be explained by its being a lonely outpost, cut off from the mainstream of Christian art and existing entirely on sufferance in the Muslim world. There was the same feeling in the monasteries in the eastern desert of Egypt or the Coptic churches in Cairo. The Muslim stricture against the portrayal of living things spared Islam some of the crudities of Christian liturgical art. I wasn't sure what this said, if anything, about the Palatine Chapel or the kingdom that produced it. Except, perhaps, that the kingdom was short-lived and fought continuously for its brief existence. Created out of an early Western aggressiveness, and with the inferiority complex that was the source of its vigor, Norman Sicily had wedged itself into the space between a dying Byzantine Empire that still had the energy to despise it, and a still-formidable Islam that was undergoing one of its periodic house cleanings, passing the torch from one dominant group to another. When the Palatine Chapel was consecrated in the middle of the twelfth century, 400 years of almost unbroken Muslim successes lay ahead. They would be years of Christian grief.

The Arabs never returned to Sicily but the Mediterranean was still a Muslim lake and would remain so for centuries to come. The eclecticism and tolerance fostered in the Kingdom of the Two Sicilies was not the wave of the future, but only a brief interlude in the play of communal and confessional enmities that were the rule, not only in Sicily but in the wider region as well. The Palatine Chapel may have represented the art not of a mature kingdom, but of a doomed and defiant interloper, conscious of its own transience and determined to compress as much as possible into the short span allotted to it. However, this was only one little church and it was too early to make much of a judgment.

As we left the chapel, we wandered into the courtyard on the first floor, only to be told by a guard in a black overcoat that it was off limits. So was the area behind the observatory on the Pisana Tower and, apparently, everything else on the palace grounds. The same guard watched us warily until we left by the same way as we had come, down the hill and past the Carabinieri post on the street at the back. These federal police were very smart in their red, white, and black uniforms. They would be formidable if they were half as good as they looked. We headed for the Palermo cathedral, retracing our steps for what seemed like the tenth time, although it was only the early morning of our first day in Palermo. The Porta Nuova dated from 1583 and had been extensively rebuilt after an earthquake in 1823. New stuff indeed. How quickly everything after the twelfth century had become fresh and vulgar.

The cathedral produced none of the aesthetic difficulties of the Palatine Chapel. Begun in 1185 by Walter of the Mill, the English Archbishop of Palermo, it was a huge pile of odd turrets, pilasters, and crenels, part of which projected over the street into the adjoining block, the whole thing surmounted by an eighteenth-century dome. The south porch through which we entered, a Catalan Gothic work of the fifteenth century, was graceful, and from a distance the building was not unimposing. Up close, individual features were good. But from an intermediate vantage point the cathedral failed to inspire. The interior was even less inspiring, with little of the original remaining. It was full of rococo statuary, busts of twentieth-century cardinals, stations-of-the-cross, many side chapels, and a huge crèche in

Palermo Cathedral, Sicily

this, the holiday season. One chapel had several relics on display, including a pair of skulls and one of Mary Magdalene's feet. In short, it was a living episcopal church and not a museum. Each of the eight centuries since its founding had added their contributions to the original.

Stuck away in the back, almost as an afterthought, were four red granite catafalques, arranged in a square. They contained the bodies of Roger II, Constance, Henry VI, and Frederick II. Here lay encapsulated the history of Norman Sicily: the first king, his daughter, her husband, and her son. The first had founded the kingdom, and the last had brought it to a close. Henry and Constance were in the front, Roger and Frederick in the back. It seemed somehow fitting that the area was screened off and the individual catafalques could not be inspected. It was not even possible to get much more than a glimpse, through the bars, of the inscription on the tomb of the first king of Norman Sicily.

It had been a busy morning, but there was another building in the area that we wanted to see. It required another trip through the Porta Nuova. It was the little church and monastery of San Giovanni degli Eremiti, or St. John of the Hermits, built in 1132 by Arab craftsmen for Roger, and it left the most lasting impression. We wandered up and down an area east of the palace, past the Baroque parish church of Saints Peter and Paul, before seeing the little orange domes under which the church lay. Norwich compared them to pomegranates, but it didn't seem necessary to look beyond the nearby orange groves for a suitable image.

The entrance to the church grounds was through a gate and guardhouse and there were a dozen people celebrating a birthday as we passed through the grounds to the other side. The sounds of the party quickly fell away and we found ourselves in an immaculate little botanical garden, full of miniature palms, lemons, ferns, philodendron, and frangipani. A stairway led past an excavated Norman archway, through which a subterranean room was visible, and then up a steep rise to the monastery itself. It was a ruin, consisting of unadorned walls on which only a trace of the original decoration remained. If there was anywhere in this most Mediterranean of

Orange domes, Palermo

islands that a bit of the north remained, it seemed to be here. Without the southern flora, it was possible to imagine oneself on the grounds of the abbey in Torquey. Outside the chapel, a path led through manicured grounds to the cloister that was a hint, in miniature, of Monreale. The slender arches were no longer roofed, but that hardly mattered. This was still a refuge, as it once had been from the city on the other side of the walls. There was little to look for here, no special mosaic to see, no famous tomb to remark, no dazzling decorative feature to appreciate. We lingered, without really understanding why, until it was time to plunge back into the stream of people and cars outside the gate below.

The hotel was on *Via Roma*, three or four blocks north of the port and a main east-west artery of the city. The port, dredged so that ferries tied up virtually on the street, looked busy and departures for Naples, Genoa, Livorno, and Tunis were announced daily. Half a mile to the east, the *Via Roma* was intersected by the *Corso Vittorio Emanuele* which ran past the Norman monuments, through the Porta Nuova and up into the hills and Monreale. For those whose ideas of Sicily were shaped by Fellini movies—images of Marcello Mastroianni pursued by outraged husbands avenging rural infidelities, of dusty cactus-lined roads, and black-clad women with facial hair—Palermo was another world. The Mafia was alive and well, and everyone had read of the recent bombing deaths of Falcone and Borsellino. There were plenty of police in evidence, and we later met army roadblocks in the countryside. There was even the occasional mention of how one heard that such and such a teacher or civil servant had not greased the right palms, and therefore had no work. And we had been warned by friends who had lived in the city to avoid wearing valuable jewelry in the street and to take other precautions that were, frankly, standard in any big city.

But, in the week we were in Sicily, we saw no evidence of crime. To outsiders, Palermo appeared to be just another European city, full of expensive food, clothes, and shoes. Food was our immediate concern, and we eventually settled on one large meal a day after breakfast. The late afternoon was a good time for a break from our peregrinations, and the evening a time to rest and read in the room. We found a little restaurant that advertised Sicilian cuisine and, with black and white photos of the turn-of-the-century port on the walls, it felt like North Beach in San Francisco. Although it was a long time in coming, the food was good and relatively inexpensive.

A single dish for the three of us, something like a *calamari fritti* or *spaghetti bolognese*, with plenty of bread, a liter of the house wine, cappuccino and maybe a dessert, generally ran about thirty dollars. The menus always listed the dishes by course, and we never could manage more than one. But others did, and we would watch dumbfounded as a group of working-class men—not the aristocrats in suede shoes we saw in the hotel dining room—would each consume a large plate of pasta topped with seafood, a good-sized broiled steak, mounds of fresh vegetables, loaves of bread, and wash it all down with relays of carafes of wine. They literally stuffed themselves. It was the quantity more than the expense that was surprising.

Clothes and shoes were the main shopping attractions. There was a wide selection, from very expensive stores to moderately priced boutiques, to street vendors selling blue jeans, socks, underwear, and cheap jewelry. I was looking for gloves. I had bought a couple of pair in Rome in the 1960s and thought that, if there was anywhere in the world where good pigskin gloves were available, it would be Italy. But no one could show me gloves other than cheap, fur-lined things. There were plenty of bookstores, but almost nothing in English, aside from small collections of classics like *Moby Dick* or *A Tale of Two Cities*.

No one spoke much English and over the week we had to acquire a little rudimentary Italian. The people were generally well dressed, and everyone seemed to be in a hurry. They looked homogeneous although we saw an occasional African in the street, looking like he came from Somalia or Ethiopia, and groups of what looked like Bengalis washing windshields at the major intersections. The odd Arab sold couscous or *Um Kulthum* cassettes at a street stand. Still, the homogeneity was noticeable and I was reminded of a line from another Mastroianni movie. When asked if he was a Catholic, he had shrugged and said: "Isn't everybody?"

Gridlock came to streets in the afternoon. The cars were typically small. This wasn't New York, and three or four *Via Romas* would fit into one of the avenues on the Upper East Side of Manhattan. After a while we came to think of Palermo as a city of sirens, because they were everywhere, *Carabinieri*, traffic police, ambulances, and fire trucks. The persistent "hee-haw, hee-haw" accompanied them as they hurtled off on their urgent business. In the afternoon, they sat in the traffic with everyone else, but still made just as much noise.

More Palermo

The Norwich book had an appendix listing the major Norman monuments of Sicily. They were starred for importance and cross-indexed to the text, which included descriptions of the more important, like the three-star Royal Palace and the Palatine Chapel. We couldn't see everything in a week, particularly if we wanted to see the rest of the island, but we managed to find most of the major monuments. On the last day in Palermo we had an extra hour, and we drove through a kind of southern suburb to look for the one-star *Cubula*, a twelfth-century pleasure dome of one of the later kings. We found it, a cubicle of *ojival* arches topped with the characteristic orange dome. It sat in a garden of date palms, looking out of place in a neighborhood of drab high-rise apartment buildings. The neglected gardens were fenced off and all we could do was peer through the iron railings at this odd little remnant of Norman Sicily.

Others required more time. One of the more intriguing was the church of S. Maria dell'Ammiraglio, founded by George of Antioch, the Levantine Greek who was commander of the Sicilian navy. Norwich gave it three stars, and it was worth a visit for many reasons, among them the mosaic of Roger II being crowned by Christ. It was the only contemporary portrait of the king in existence. But it also brought to mind another of the influences on the kingdom, that of Byzantine Greece. If the measure were the legacy left in the plastic arts, it might have been the most important.

There didn't seem to be any question that the Byzantine contribution to the preservation of European culture is overlooked in accounts of history written from a Western perspective. We were all familiar with the story of the passage of the Greek classics to medieval Europe through the medium of Latin translations of Arabic translations of the originals. But surely the Byzantines preserved the Greek classics on their own, without the need for Arabic intermediaries. The fact that the West got its Plato, Aristotle, and Ptolemy through the Arabs is testament only to the fact that it was more ignorant of Greek than it was of Arabic.

The prejudice probably had something to do with what we learned from Gibbon, no friend of Byzantium. In addition, there was enough of the tincture of the East about these particular Greeks that we were able simultaneously to embrace the ancient Greeks and still dismiss everything we found objectionable about the Byzantines as "Oriental." Imperial splendor, the bowstring, eunuchs, statecraft—long before Machiavelli—were all things we assumed to be "Oriental" about the Byzantines, as if they sprang naturally from the soil of Anatolia. But the Ottomans probably learned them from these Slavo-Greeks whose empire they assumed and after whom they patterned themselves.

In actuality many things about the Byzantines—including the active political parties, the "Blues" and the "Greens"; the force of public opinion; the small landholding soldier/farmer who was the economic and military backbone of the Empire before the rot set in; the stability of the currency; the importance of trade—made them far more like ourselves than contemporary feudal Europe. The Westerners who overran Byzantium from the First Crusade onward were a primitive horde, and the sack of Constantinople during the Fourth Crusade was among the greatest acts of barbarism in history. It was ameliorated, if at all, only by the fact that the Venetians carried off much of the city rather than putting it to the torch.

For a thousand years, embodying the legacy of Greek thought, Roman law, and Orthodox Christianity, the Byzantines stood as a bulwark of the Christian world against waves of Turks and Mongols. The sack by crusaders in 1204 was their thanks. When Constantinople fell to the Turks in 1453, the Byzantines disappeared like the dinosaurs from the face of the earth. There were still fossil remains in places like Palermo, Monreale, and Cefalu, but they were remembered today primarily as a byword for deviousness and convoluted behavior. When Europeans conceived their nineteenth-century fascination with the democratic Greeks against the unspeakable Turk, it was of a Greece that only briefly existed. It ignored the proud, complex, and profoundly modern state that stood like a colossus astride the Near East for centuries while Europe slumbered.

Meanwhile, George of Antioch's church left an odd impression. We found it after several abortive attempts, wandering through the grotesque statuary of the Piazza Pretoria and asking for it by what we thought was its popular name, the *Martorana*. A block from the church a girl couldn't tell us where it was. But when we saw those characteristic rectangular towers and orange domes, we wondered how we could have missed it. A combination of the Palatine Chapel and the cathedral, it had the elaborate mosaics of the former and the eclectic accretions of the latter. A wedding was scheduled for that morning, photographers were setting up, and flowers were being arranged, so we were hustled in and out with unseemly haste. The visit was made even less satisfactory by the attentions of a *cicerone* who fastened himself onto me like a limpet as we entered the vestibule. He was an older man wearing a heavy black overcoat, and looked like Lucca Brazzi meeting the Tattaglias in that memorable scene in *The Godfather*.

When he learned that we were from America, he said that he had been to Boston where it was obvious he hadn't learned much English. He followed me around, pointing out the mosaics of particular interest, conspiratorially hissing their names into my captive ear. I admired his accent, but one *Christu Pantocratore* was enough and by the time we got rid of him our time was almost up. The mosaic of Roger was the standard two-dimensional thing, and I wondered how Norwich could have seen "a dark, swarthy man on the brink of middle age" with a face that "has a faintly Semitic cast about it."

As we came down the steps the wedding party arrived. They were the usual beautifully dressed Italians, looking vaguely bemused about the proceedings. Although she was in off-white the bride looked like anything but a virgin, and appeared to be in her thirties. I reflected that we hadn't seen a pregnant woman since we arrived in Palermo. But maybe I was becoming too cynical myself, with exposure to too many Greek-Levantines, or Levanto-Byzantines, or Semito-Normans, or just plain Sicilians. It was time for a break.

We agreed to do some shopping. But no one had my gloves and I was still anxious to see as much as I could before we left Palermo. So, I left for Monreale with the agreement that we would all see it together later on. I flagged down a cab on Vittorio Emanuele—actually it was sitting in the afternoon traffic and going nowhere—and we reversed and headed for the mountains behind the city. The cab was metered and the cabbie was a young kid who, in spite of his glasses and bookish demeanor, had that offhand European manner: everything about his job—the traffic, other drivers, the weather, indeed, life itself—seemed to fill him with the greatest angst.

Actually, there was little room for communication as he spoke almost no English and I no Italian. But I repeated over and over again the words *cathedrale* and *Monreale*, and he, just as insistently, tried to explain something about the fare. Finally, as the cab left the flat and began the steep climb up the escarpment behind the city, he called the dispatcher and she succeeded in making me understand that Monreale was outside the Palermo area, a Palermo cab could not pick up a return fare, and I would have to pay double what showed on the meter. After that, we settled into a kind of give and take. It turned out that the cabbie's parents lived in Arizona and by the time he had dropped me in front of the cathedral in the little town, we were more or less friends. It was an expensive cab ride, but at least I was in Monreale.

The cathedral was closed for the afternoon so I had a couple of hours to look around. I cashed a traveler's check and was glad I had the time. There were several tellers in the *Banco di Sicilia* around the corner from the cathedral, but only one seemed to be working. Everyone with business to conduct placed his check and identification documents on the bottom of a pile on the counter in front of his window, from which they were taken in order. We all stood in a cluster around this single teller, enforcing the line—one old woman tried to slip her check into the middle of the pile—and inspecting the contents of each account as it was called up on the computer screen. The teller officiously typed, wrote, invoked, and canceled before each transaction was completed. It took about forty minutes before my stock of lira was replenished.

The town was tiny, which made the huge cathedral seem even more impressive. The streets were narrow and the displays of seafood and fresh vegetables on what passed for sidewalks made them narrower still, so narrow that the side mirror on a passing truck knocked the lens cover off my camera. Christmas decorations were everywhere and, in spite of the fact that it was the siesta hour, the streets were packed with shoppers. The butcher shops were particularly interesting, with whole animals—kids, lambs, and hares—hanging in the windows. They had been eviscerated and the empty cavities propped open, but they were otherwise just as they had been in life. There were also whole hams, cuts of beef, pheasants, wild boar, and loops of sausages artistically arranged on the shelves. One particularly interesting cut was a whole leg of fresh pork still attached to a long slender loin, on which there must have been twenty chops. The vegetables were beautifully presented and the fish looked fresh. Everywhere sat pyramids of holiday cakes in cardboard carrying cases.

I walked up a steep little street behind the city and thought that the tiny apartments were probably more scenic than comfortable. They were whitewashed, which set off the stunning monochromes of the shutters, doors, and clothes hung out to dry, all reds, blues, oranges, and yellows. After four or five blocks, although it was difficult to say what was a block in these little alleyways, the town came to an end and the road continued its serpentine climb into the barren mountains that ring Palermo. It was then that the poor calcareous skeleton of Sicily revealed itself, which the soft tissues in the town below had concealed. No wonder so many Sicilians had left for America.

By the time I made my way back to the town square, there was still an hour before the cathedral opened, so I had lunch. A half a pound of cheese, a couple of hard rolls, and a bottle of wine cost 4,500 lire, or about $3.25, and I sat to eat it on bench opposite the *Scuola Media Statale* of *Guglielmo II*. Although Roger's daughter Constance had married the future Emperor Henry VI, she had been born shortly after Roger's death, and his son and grandson (her own brother and nephew) sat on the throne before her husband succeeded them. William I—"the Bad"—and William II—"the Good"—neither of whom was as bad or as good as advertised, had gone before. This school was named after the second of the two Williams.

The *Duomo*, or Cathedral, was built by William II and, while this was not the spectacular setting we would later see in Cefalu, it still dominated the little town. Superficial changes detracted little from the overall impression. To the spare lines of the original entrance portal, consisting of a pair of rectangular towers separated by a series of delicate intersecting arches, had been added an eighteenth-century marble "porch." An iron grating prevented entrance by way of the magnificent bronze doors, dating from 1186. Peering through the bars of the grating, I could just make out a few of the details of biblical scenes on each of the thirty or so individual panels.

Entrance to the cathedral was now by a side door, also of bronze and also dating from the twelfth century, set in Norwich's north colonnade, itself a sixteenth-century addition.

Divided longitudinally into three parts by massive columns, the interior of the basilica was huge, approximately a hundred by thirty yards, or about the size of a football field. It was all gold above the columns, with elaborate mosaic scenes from the Old and New Testaments laid into the solid gold background. Christ the Pantocrator gazed from the ceiling of the apse, as was his wont in all these Norman churches. Only the sixteenth-century Chapel of the Crucifix broke the spell, and that only if you looked for it. There were no abstract patterns, no extraneous marble inlays, no fussy details, only what seemed to be acres and acres of mosaics. Criticism of individual details, or of the art form itself, seemed out of place amid the richness. There was little to do but sit silently in the presence of something that seemed beyond reproach.

The complex had been built as a Benedictine abbey to escape the long arm of the Pope, and the grounds were equally renowned. For 1,000 lire, a stairway in the back of the basilica led to a gallery on the roof that overlooked the cloisters, and 2,000 lira bought entry to the cloisters themselves. They were a much larger, more elaborate and better-preserved version of those at San Giovanni degli Eremiti, with each pair of the scores of individual columns differently designed and inlaid by Arab workmen. The long colonnades roofed with Spanish tiles and the enclosed gardens of cactus, palm, and pine were a reminder of the Spanish missions in California. Better yet, they resembled *al-Andalus* itself. From the more elaborate gardens on the other side of the cloisters, which contained two massive banyan trees, it was possible to overlook orange groves in the foreground and the curve of the Conca d'Oro and Palermo, a thousand feet below in the distance.

The return to the city took longer but was less expensive. A bus stopped not far from the Cathedral and for 1,000 Lira it was possible to ride all the way to the Porta Nuova. Although I had already done it many times over the two days, the walk seemed long to the hotel where I arrived, tired and footsore, well after dark.

Cefalu

It had been a busy two days in Palermo and it was time to see some of the rest of the island. We needed a rental car and hotel brochure advertised that they would make all such arrangements. The clerks at the main desk had not been unhelpful when we needed a map of the city or directions to a particular place, so we decided to try them first. But the man on duty that morning was unfamiliar. With his morning coat, aquiline profile, and reddish pompadour he looked a little like King Juan Carlos of Spain. Our conversation was a model of miscommunication:

> Good morning.
>> Prego.
>
> I would like to rent a car and I understand...
>> Espeak...eslowly...please.

This was less a request than a demand.

> I...would...like...to...rent...a car...and...

I completed my explanation and he consulted a little dog-eared book of telephone numbers before dialing the one he wanted on an ancient instrument. After a few perfunctory formalities, he got down to business and I understood a few words like "Fiat" and "kilometer."

He broke off to ask how long we wanted the car and when I told him two or three days he resumed the conversation. I understood a little more this time, including something like "quattrocento mille lire" and then he hung up. The car would be a medium-sized Fiat, it would cost 411,000 lire for three days, there would be unlimited mileage, and where would I like to meet it? This was clearly unsatisfactory and I rapidly explained to him that we Americans didn't do business this way. I thanked him for his trouble and left him with the problem working behind his eyes.

There were several car-rental agencies in the few blocks between the Via Roma and the port, and the man in Europe-Car was the most helpful, understood a little English, and had the best price. It would be for three days, we could turn it in at the airport, there would be unlimited mileage, and the car would be at the hotel at noon. It was a medium sized Fiat and easily accommodated the three of us with our luggage.

It was a clear day as we moved into traffic on the coast road to Cefalu. The drive was only about fifty miles, but it took longer than we expected as we went through two little seaside towns, first Bagheria then Termini Imerese. We were looking for a prominent landmark, described either as a "head"—from the Greek *kephale*, hence Cephalonia in the Archipelago and Cefalu here—or a "pair of great, broad shoulders." Almost as soon as we left Palermo a large formation appeared in the distance, but after half an hour we passed to the seaward side. An hour later we rounded a long sweeping curve in the coastline and the dramatic setting of Cefalu came into view. We were still about five miles up the coast, but this first view was so striking that we turned back for a couple of hundred yards so we could experience it again.

Set at the base of a great limestone head lay the yellow mass of the town, set against the intense blue of the Mediterranean. From its midst rose, very prominently, the twin spires of Roger's cathedral. He had been shipwrecked here in 1127, and vowed to build a church if he was spared. He was and he did, and it was said to be the most magnificent of all the Norman churches in Sicily. We drove into a kind of commercial outskirts, and then up the hill into the densely-packed center of town. After one unsuccessful attempt, where we wound up back where we had started, we finally succeeded in reaching the core. Threading our way through the tiny streets, hardly wide enough for the car to pass, we suddenly emerged in the town square at the head of which lay the cathedral itself.

Cefalu Cathedral, Sicily

It looked like Monreale with the massive, unfinished stone exterior, and the square towers with lancet windows on either side of the facade. They were separated by interlaced Arab-inspired arches and date-palms were strategically placed in front on either side of the little piazza. But where the entrance to Monreale had been closed and the clean lines interrupted by the eighteenth-century marble porch, here the three arches were unobstructed and they were still in use. Moreover, the entrance was on the main axis of the square and we had a clear view of the facade. So confined was the church by the streets and the hill behind it, that there was hardly any *other* view.

As at Monreale, it was the early afternoon and the cathedral was closed. So, we parked the car and looked for a place for our main meal of the day. We found a little restaurant, the *calamari* and *tagliatelle* were excellent, the wine was good, and the bread plentiful. Our corporal selves fed, we walked back up the hill to nourish our spirits. Inside, the impression was of mass and repose. It was earlier by fifty years than the cathedral in Monreale, and simplicity was its most obvious feature. We had seen the three most notable monuments of Norman Sicily in reverse order of their complexity: first, the too lavish Palatine Chapel; then the sustained mosaic *tour de force* of the cathedral in Monreale; and now, Cefalu.

But where the lines of the two cathedrals were the same—the same basilica plan with the nave divided into three longitudinal sections by powerful columns with Roman and Corinthian capitals, the same *ojival* arches supporting the walls of the nave and the ceiling—here, the surfaces were almost bare. The strong simple statement of the nave carried the eye to the transept, where the familiar gold of the mosaics took over and pointed the way to the crowning achievement of the building, the great Christ Pantocrator in the apse. In Monreale, he had competed with the biblical history of mankind. Here, there were no Adam and Eve attempting to cover their nakedness, no Noah in his ark, no camel-ride into Egypt. There was just the all-seeing eye of the most magnificent of these Pantocrators, gazing the length of the basilica.

Cefalu was also a living church, not a museum, and there were many concessions to everyday spiritual needs, including confessionals, statuary, stained-glass windows, and side chapels. But unlike the cathedral in Palermo they seemed insignificant, too small to detract from the magnificence of the place. In a way, it was both austere and spiritually nourishing. It had been Roger's choice for his own crypt, and it was easy to see why. We wandered, looking for details of interest. There was a pair of small marble catafalques in the rear but they didn't seem to be of the royal family. The marble mosaics of the floor were impressive and the presbytery was magnificent, but this church seemed to defeat piecemeal appreciation.

The next order of business was a place to stay. So, dropping down from the central plateau of the town we found the Hotel Riva del Sole. Located on the beach it was set up to do a booming summer business. But in the winter, it was dead, and we saw no other guests during our stay. When, later that day, the man at the front desk asked us at what time we wanted breakfast, it was probably because he wanted to tell the cook what time to come to work. In the evening, we walked the half-mile back to the center of town and by now it had come to life. It was the twenty-third of December, the shops were open, and the streets were packed with people doing their last-minute Christmas shopping. There were clothes, confections, compact disks, ice cream, books, shoes, more clothes, leather goods, and more shoes. But it seemed to be as much a social as a shopping occasion, and families walked, arm-in-arm, and greeted other families, also out for the evening. The occasional little car crawled through the crowds, but this was definitely a walking town.

In the square in front of the cathedral, a band was playing a kind of dirge. They were all in uniform, both men and women, and produced that mournful

Sicilian music heard on festive occasions, as if even their celebrations were tinged with melancholy. After a while we had a *gelato* and wandered with the crowd towards the other end of the little town. This was going to be a musical evening. Posters on the walls advertised a *Concerto di Natale* at nine o'clock in the *Duomo* and after a short nap in the hotel I returned for the performance. It began late and the audience was small and tended to drift in piecemeal. But it was no amateur show and the *Academia Cantori Nuovi* was thoroughly accomplished. They were four sopranos, four mezzo-sopranos, four tenors, and four basses, accompanied by a piano and organ. The individual notes of a toccata were sometimes difficult to distinguish, but the unamplified voices of the choir filled the cathedral like liquid filling a jar.

The program, with pieces by Palestrina, Schubert, Brahms, and Benjamin Britten, lasted just over an hour. The performance ended with the choir coming down to the entrance of the transept and singing familiar carols, and we were invited to join in. Afterwards the audience mingled with the performers, greeting them like rock stars. We left by the front doors of the cathedral, thrown open for the occasion. Down the hill there was another performance, just as enjoyable in its own way as the one above. They were a band—an accordion, a trumpet, several guitars, a couple of saxophones, a flute, and a triangle—playing in a darkened little street. They were just kids and they sang as they played, the same mournful tunes we had heard earlier in the evening. Even late at night and late in December, people were out on their balconies listening to the concert. After a while I drifted away and fell asleep to the sound of the soft slapping of the waves on the shore outside the hotel window.

To Taormina

The next morning, breakfast was in the dining room that must have served hundreds during the summer. We were the only ones there. It was a travel day, and after finishing our coffee and breakfast bun we set out by the coast road towards Capo d'Orlando. Our eventual destination was Taormina on the east coast, a little over a hundred miles away. Names on the signs were interesting. Some were people we knew, other names we had just heard in passing. We saw Nicolai, Nicolini, Torretta, Prizzi, Mendolia, Caminiti, Casale, Paterno, Cefalo, and Corleone. My favorite was Taormina, and I thought of Sal Taormina, a journeyman outfielder for the San Francisco Seals in the early fifties. He was a solid left-handed hitter who briefly made it to the big club after the Red Sox bought the organization. The ace on the staff had been Jerry Casale, who later pitched for the Red Sox.

After an hour, we had seen enough of the coast and turned off toward Mistretta, Nicosia, and Leonforte in the heart of the island. It was a bad decision. The coast was clear, but as we climbed into the hills it became increasingly overcast. By the time we reached Nicosia we were *in* the clouds, and for the next several hours it was wet and dreary. In Leonforte we headed east after first missing the turn, and then dropped into a valley with a large lake, *Lago di Pozzilo*. There were many good-sized farms and the freshly plowed fields looked dark and rich. This was definitely not calcareous, and I remembered reading somewhere that Sicily had once been the granary of Rome. We passed several flocks of sheep, some of them on the road and looming up unexpectedly out of the mist.

We stopped in Regalbuto to buy cookies, delicate little Sicilian things covered with confectioner's sugar. It was nearly an hour by the time we had parked the car, found the shop, and then crawled through the narrow and packed streets to the other end of town. This was Christmas Eve and everyone was in the streets. It would be very different the next day, when not even the gas stations were open. When we reached Paterno, we'd had enough of this half-blind groping through the highlands. So, we headed for the autostrade outside Catania that would take us straight on to Taormina. The scenery changed as we descended, the ground becoming yellow and rocky again. Large groves of citrus and olive trees began to appear, and the roads were lined with the flowering cactus whose reddish fruit appeared in the markets at this time of the year.

We quickly covered the twenty-five miles to the turnoff to Taormina. The overcast had broken a little, but not enough to reveal Etna, sitting up there somewhere to the southwest, at nearly 11,000 feet the tallest active volcano in Europe. We paid the toll and wound back and around, down and then up to the little city, half sitting on and half carved into the rocky cliffs, a thousand feet above the water. It was about as picturesque a setting as could be imagined, and Taormina knew it. We found a place to park, a quarter of a mile from the center of town, and walked back. At two o'clock nearly everything was closed, but we found a restaurant and settled down to a meal of linguine with pesto and Taormina ravioli.

After lunch saw a little of the city, walking the length of the *Corso Umberto* and back again. The *Duomo*, or cathedral, had been founded in the thirteenth century by St. Nicolas of Bari, a great friend of the Normans. But it was small and had been extensively renovated, and so had little historical interest. We made a note of the location, intending to return for midnight mass. As the afternoon lengthened, a few shops opened. But bigger things were obviously planned for the evening, and two huge piles of limbs and trunks, including whole stumps with much of the root structure still attached, were being prepared for the fire. One was in the square near the Duomo, the other in front of the *Chiesa S. Catarina*. They were about ten feet high and maybe fifteen feet in diameter, and would burn through the night and into the next day.

We then looked for a hotel, and by the time we had settled into the Diodoro, near where we parked the car, we had made another complete circuit of the *Corso Umberto* and the *Via Roma*. Our first thought had been the San Domenico Palace, a sister to the Grand Hotel et Des Palmes in Palermo. It was a converted fifteenth-century convent, and the place to stay in Taormina for artists and crowned heads of state. Thomas Mann and John Steinbeck, among others, had worked in its rooms. At 800,000 Lira, it was more than we wanted to pay. But the staff in the Jolly Hotel Diodoro were just that, and everyone made an attempt to be pleasant. This hotel, like the one in Cefalu, was set up to do a booming summer business, and it was virtually deserted in December. The dining room was cavernous and the complex, overlooking the Ionian Sea below, was in a spectacular location. The room was large and, since it would be our home for Christmas Eve and part of Christmas day, we spread out of our suitcases into some semblance of comfort.

We spent the early evening resting and reading, before going out about ten o'clock. After the long walk to the center of the city, we turned left into the *Corso Umberto* and found it packed. The fire in front of S. Catarina, a noble little church of Baroque simplicity, was roaring and spitting and kids were throwing firecrackers into the inferno. It sounded like war, and with each report Martha winced as if she had been shot. We sat over an Irish coffee in the little cafe opposite the church until the din became too great. Farther up the street we met the familiar sight of families walking arm-in-arm, and exchanging prolonged *buon natales*. If Cefalu had been a walking city, Taormina was even more so. We saw a few cars on the *Corso Umberto*, Fiats or odd little three-wheeled vehicles, but it was laid out like a promenade and meant for pedestrians. The overhead was festooned with Christmas decorations, shooting stars, and wise men in lights, and holiday cheer filled the shops. Mounds of confections beckoned from bakery windows, along with heaps of dried fruits and candies, Brazil nuts, chestnuts, walnuts and hazelnuts, sugarplums, apricots, apples, and pears.

Mufflers and scarves and whole bolts of woolens reminded us that it was cold, and displays in the antique shops conjured up *The Night Before Christmas*. Outside the Duomo a huge fir tree was decorated only with oranges, a nice touch. Inside, through the crowds, we could just see the priest, already in the middle of his sermon. The people looked warm in their pews, and in spite of the fire on the other side of the square, we were not. It was a reminder of a Christmas Eve in Salzburg several years before. I had gone to have a prescription filled, and several of us stood, or rather hopped and danced in subzero temperatures and falling snow, while we watched the pharmacist through the tiny aperture in the locked, steel door. Warm as toast, he pushed the medicines through the opening to each of us in turn.

Mass was out of the question and so, after a brief grilling at the fire, we returned to the hotel. On the way, we met a group of Sicilian bagpipers in traditional dress, and it was the sound of the pipes, punctuated by the bursts of firecrackers, that lingered as a reminder of an odd Christmas Eve in Taormina. Early on Christmas morning I took the familiar walk along the cliff road, past San Domenico and up to the center of town. There were a pair of cops in the cafe where I had a cappuccino, and the garbage men were out sweeping up the litter from the night before. It was otherwise deserted. The fires were still smoldering, and by the look of the embers, they would probably continue to burn for several days.

We had an elaborate breakfast buffet at the hotel before visiting the nearby Greco-Roman amphitheater. The theater, a fifteen-minute walk up the hill from the hotel, was the crowning glory of Taormina. It dated from the second century BC, having been built on an earlier Greek structure. On a clear day, the coast of Calabria and the cone of Etna were visible from the site. But for us the overcast had still not lifted, and we never saw the mountain. However, we wandered over the graduated seats of the theater and peered through the few standing columns to the Ionian shore, a thousand feet below, and it was picturesque enough.

Palermo and Home

We left Taormina about noon and took the coast-road north towards Messina, about an hour's drive away. After Taormina Messina looked muscular. The road continued through a drab suburb, and then a light industrial area before it reached the waterfront, where we suddenly entered a changed scene. Cranes and piers were everywhere, and ships were tied up at the street's edge. Beyond them, other ships were riding at anchor. And beyond them lay the narrow straits and then the coast of Calabria. It looked close enough to touch.

We followed the waterfront for half a mile or so, before leaving the city. After another five miles, we rounded the tip of the island and turned to the south and west as the road climbed back into the hills. By now, the gas gauge was nearly on empty. But on this Christmas day most of the gas stations were closed, with chains across the entrances. A few were open but unattended, with an automatic dispenser that took 10,000 lira notes. Fortunately, we had a few of those, but the next trick was to find a station that was open and had unleaded gas. We eventually found one and a kid on a motorcycle to show me how to use the pump, but not before we had a few anxious moments.

What was true of gas stations was doubly true of restaurants. Nothing was open and the streets in the little towns—Sparta, Spadofora, and then Barcelona Pozzo di Gotto—were deserted. There was nothing attractive about the scenery, a winding road through scrub with an occasional view of the sea. So, we decided to take the autostrade again and press on to Cefalu for the night. It was a different world. The speed limit may have been a hundred kilometers an hour, but no one seemed to pay attention and the miles flew by. The divided highway was excellent, with an elaborate network of tunnels cut through the coastal mountains. The broad plains in between were covered with citrus groves, and every few miles a *wadi* drained the interior northward into the Tyrrhenian Sea. It was the kind of landscape that lost nothing at speed.

The head of Cefalu looked different from the back, and we left the autostrade several miles inland of the city. As we made our way down the coast and then up into the square in front of the cathedral, we realized that Cefalu, too, was dead. Everything was closed, including the restaurant where we had eaten the first day. It looked like this was going to be a hungry Christmas. However, by the time we checked into the hotel and returned to the square at the more reasonable hour of seven o'clock the restaurant was open for business. We fell ravenously on a Christmas dinner of several courses of pasta, fried gambari, calamari, and dessert. Just as we started a man and his wife we had met in Palermo arrived, along with another couple. He was a retired television producer and now a journalist, a New Zealander although they now lived in Melbourne, and they were traveling around Europe. He was filing an occasional story with the *Melbourne Post*. The other couple were a professor of Spanish at UCLA and his wife. Both couples had rented apartments in Cefalu. So, we pulled the tables together and shared the meal.

A light rain was falling the next morning as we set out for Palermo. The drive seemed shorter than we remembered it, and when we arrived we still had a couple of hours before the flight to Rome. So, we made a return visit to Monreale and had a last view of the mosaics. Afterwards we looked around the northern suburbs for remnants of Norman pleasure gardens, and found the *Cubala*, looking intact but a little forlorn in the middle of the residential neighborhood. We looked for catacombs in the same area, but didn't find any. It was probably just as well, since they contained thousands of mummified bodies, including some from the early part of the twentieth century, and were said to be grisly. Afterwards, the airport was packed, and so was the plane. The flight for Rome left at two thirty, and the weather had cleared at Leonardo da Vinci by the time we landed, an hour and a half later.

We had an early morning flight to Germany the next day, and so wanted a hotel close to the airport. We found the Sheraton to be about midway between the airport and the city, and it was a relief to be in an American atmosphere again, with everyone efficient and courteous, although a bit plastic. After dinner, we saw a little of Rome, including the area around the Coliseum, the Roman Forum, and the monument to Vittorio Emanuele. During the war, American soldiers had dubbed it "the wedding cake," but it looked like baked Alaska that night. It was bitterly cold and we weren't dressed for the weather. Everywhere there were hints of what else the city had to offer, looming up out of the chill and dark, and we resolved to return when we had more time.

The next morning the Alitalia flight to Frankfurt, where we would catch Lufthansa to Karachi, was a last exposure to the south. The stewards and stewardesses were their usual laid-back selves:

>Signori, avanti, grazi . . . Signori, avanti, grazi . . .

They seemed hardly to care whether we moved or not. The passengers were in a voluble mood, the women beautifully-dressed and the men affecting designer stubble and looking like Versace. A bottle of wine came on every dinner tray as if it were in the natural order of things.

After banking over the Adriatic, we left Abruzzi and then Lombardy behind and I was reminded of why we had come to Italy. The Alps were a solid mass of white, with jagged peaks showing through the cloud cover. It was not hospitable terrain. Campaigning in the south was a seasonal affair, just as it was for sailors in the Mediterranean. For the Emperor to cross the passes in the spring, deal with "the Sicilian," and return before they closed again in the fall, required luck and coordination with the Pisans, or whoever his allies were at the time. It almost never worked out that way, and invasion after invasion ran out of steam before it reached Campagnia. The empire eventually brought the Sicilians to bay, not by conquering them but by marrying one of them.

Frankfurt was cold but dry. As we taxied to the arrival bay, the ugly profiles of several C141s and C5s were visible on the military airfield nearby, sprawled like giant cormorants at rest. Once a month for the past seven years, planes like these had brought surplus medical equipment and clothes to Islamabad, in return taking away Afghan-war wounded. It was the longest sustained airlift in US military history. The flight to Karachi left in the afternoon, and by the time the efficient and attentive aircrew had seated us and passed out the venison or duck that Lufthansa always seemed to serve, it was dark. The long flight was broken only by a short stopover in Bahrain. There were Bibles for sale next to the Qur'ans in the duty-free shop, and the clerk was a Bahraini *girl*, a reminder of what a different phenomenon that little island was on the Arabian Peninsula, to which it was now attached by the causeway.

We had a three-hour wait in Karachi before the flight to Islamabad. We sat among wild-looking Pathans and Baluchis with mounds of luggage, cheap suitcases, gunnysacks, and cardboard boxes tied up with string. They watched us intently and when boarding didn't know what a line was.

Then we knew we were at home.

11

The Mosque

THE FAISAL MOSQUE LAY in the western suburbs of Islamabad nestled against the Margallas, the range of hills that separated the Punjab from the Northwest Frontier Province. Architecturally, it was one of the largest freestanding structures in the world. Completed in 1986 it had been financed by the late king of Saudi Arabia—hence the name—and built by a Turkish architect and contractor. It was a landmark in the city and tours were organized for non-Muslims on weekends. Along with the expanse of glittering white marble, inside and out, there were also displays of calligraphy in massive Qur'ans dotted around main prayer hall. The structure was not particularly graceful or beautiful. But the size made it impressive.

Close by the mosque sat the Islamic University. It was probably attached to the mosque in the same way that al-Azhar University was attached to the mosque of the same name in Cairo. Or, closer to home, the way *madrasas* in Central Asia, in places like Bokhara and Samarkand, had often been attached to mosques there. *Madrasas* were traditional Muslim educational establishments, and those in Central Asia had sent some notable graduates into the world. Jamal ad-Din al-Afghani and Mohammed Baha ad-Din al-Bukhari were probably the best known. But there were many others. Al-Azhar, founded by the Fatimids in 970 was the first and probably the most famous Islamic university in the world, and the students lived in *riwaqs*, or quarters, organized by nationality, or what passed for nationality in those earlier days. Students from Java were in one *riwaq*, those from the Maghreb or North Africa, were in another, those from Afghanistan in a third, and so on. Each was supported by a separate *waqf*, or pious foundation. When Richard Burton made his pilgrimage to Mecca and Medina, he used as his local address the Afghan *riwaq* at al-Azhar, whose nationality he had temporarily assumed.

By the look of the student body the same general plan was probably true of the university in Islamabad. The dormitories were located three hundred or so yards from the mosque complex itself. A walk along the road to the dormitories was a study in the faces of a resurgent Islam. Indian Muslims could be light or dark, the lighter coming from the areas of the subcontinent to the north and west, present-day Pakistan. But the darkest Indians were not Muslims at all, and some were Christians. Christian missionaries had little success in India, and many of the few converts were untouchables who had nothing to lose and everything to gain by abandoning the faith of their fathers. Many domestics in Islamabad were Christians, dark people with names like Grace, Robinson, Johnson, and Edward. They lived in their own ghetto in the city and in periods of unrest were subject to persecution by the majority Muslims.

However, it was the other ethnicities that stood out in Islamabad: Africans, Asians, Europeans, and occasional Arabs, and it was a reminder of the catholicity of Islam. The quiet flow of students up and down the street seemed, somehow, timeless and appropriate. Secular universities in Pakistan were wracked by dissent and periodic violence, the student bodies often controlled by Islamists. As in the West, these oases of intellectual freedom and higher learning were often hotbeds of intolerance. But there was something about a Friday morning walk behind the Faisal mosque that recalled an earlier, less contentious time, and the manifestations of typical student behavior seemed very remote.

The most striking here were the Africans, probably because they seemed so foreign. The East Africans had a different look from those from the center or the west. They typically had the high forehead, small lips, more delicate features and *cafe au lait* coloring characteristic of the Arab-African mix. That made them attractive to the Arabs, and Abyssinian woman, legendary for their charms, had always been favored concubines. East Africans were products of a triple heritage, that fusion of Islam, Africa, and Europe that Ali Mazrui had chronicled in his series on public television. The Central Africans were different, much darker, with broader noses and lips. They often had tiny ears, high cheekbones and deep-set eyes. Where a Somali might have a shaggy beard, a Central African's beard was often made up of tight little curls that lay flat on his face, clinging to the skin like a creeper. Farther west they seemed to become lighter in color again.

A good example of the type had been a systems-engineer in Saudi Arabia. His people had originally been from Chad or Niger and his surname, Takrouni, came, some said, from the trilateral Arabic root *ka-ra-ra*, "to do repeatedly," since they poured into the peninsula in a steady stream. Like other African Muslims they crossed the Red Sea to Arabia to make the pilgrimage and had stayed on in the area around Mecca, supporting themselves as hewers of wood or drawers of water. But Eissa was no hewer or drawer, and the best of a young group of computer specialists in Petroserve, the services branch of Petromin. He looked like an American black. But here in the subcontinent there were few Africans who looked like American blacks, large and thickly muscled. Most blacks in the Americas came from the west coast of Africa, from what are now Senegal, Sierra Leone, Ghana, and Nigeria. East coast slavery fed the markets of Jidda, Istanbul, and the Persian Gulf. In the nineteenth century, there were reportedly 50,000 Hadhramis, natives of the Hadhramaut, in Jidda alone, engaged in the slave trade. Most of the Africans here wore a white gown and skullcap, and the contrast with their darker complexions was particularly stark. Islam had proselytized heavily in sub-Saharan Africa and won many converts.

The Asians were also unfamiliar to someone not from the area. With the breakup of historic India, the Indonesians were now the largest nationality in Islam, as measured by population. The Javans, called after the island that produced the most migrants, had the sparse beards characteristic of the region. But they lacked the epicanthic fold and were darker than the East Asians, bordering, as they did, on Melanesia and Polynesia. The Central Asians did look "oriental," and were typically light in coloring. They were the most interesting to me, probably because I hadn't really seen them before. They also had sparse beards, and the hirsute Arabs and Persians who carried Islam into Asia at first thought they were eunuchs, a phenomenon with which they were quite familiar. Here, they were more or less white and, although we couldn't tell the difference, an expert eye immediately knew the difference between a Turkman, an Uzbek, and a Hazara. In addition to these students, there were Central Asians all over the Northwest Frontier Province. They sold carpets in Islamabad and Peshawar and for some reason all the fried-potato vendors in Islamabad seemed to be Uzbeks.

There were even a few students who looked to be European. Bosnian families had settled in Mansehra and it seemed that a few of their sons had matriculated. The Bosnians were ethnically Slavs and, with their light, often blond hair and European features, they looked the most foreign of all. They could be mistaken for Afghans, some of whom were as light as Germans or Englishmen. There were only a few Arabs unless, by stretching the point, the Sudanese could be called Arabs. But the Arabs had their own institutions of Islamic learning and there was no need to send their sons abroad.

Behind the mosque lay the jungle and there it was easy to lose oneself in the world of Indian flora and fauna. This area, bordering on the Margallas, was different from the hills themselves. The Margallas were covered with dense scrub and stands of what looked like Ponderosa pine, distributed over limestone outcroppings. The scrub and limestone gave them a rugged appearance, and the evergreens meant that they looked much the same the year round. But just below the hills there was an entirely different ecosystem, lush without being tropical, particularly during the monsoon. The southwest monsoon visited northern Pakistan in July and August, the Indian months of Sawan and Bhadun, solar months that had existed in the subcontinent for hundreds of years. Babar, an early conqueror from Central Asia, had mentioned them in his *Memoirs*, dating from the sixteenth century. They were the first two months of the rainy season:

> The natives of Hindustan, who have divided their seasons into terms of four months each, have confined the appellation of the violence of the season to two months of each term . . . the first two months of the rainy season, Sawan and Bhadun, they regard as the period of the rains.

Any driver in Islamabad today knew these same names, which clearly had existed in the popular culture since Babar's time. Most drivers were not, otherwise, experts on Babar.

The rains during the monsoon were torrential and they fed the green of the jungle. *Jangl* was originally a Sanskrit word, passed through the Urdu or Hindi, and it referred to a forest or wooded area. It had none of the English connotation of rain forest, creepers, or tropical damp. Here, the jungle behind the mosque—the *jangl shetout*—had the leafy green look of New England in the summer. There were thick stands of deciduous trees with large green leaves, and stands of wild mint and marijuana. In the winter, the trees lost their leaves and what was once green and dense became a sea of gray sticks. The animals moved with the change in seasons into the foothills, still covered with their evergreen scrub. Troops of monkeys moved up toward the ridges. Just as in the jungle below, they were easier to hear than to see. It was surprising, the amount of noise a twenty-to thirty-pound animal made in the trees. When disturbed, a troop would crash through the tamarisks, bending over the small branches, sounding like an army on the move, shrieking and chattering in protest at the intrusion. They were Himalayan Rhesus monkeys, medium sized, brown to gray-green in color, with a long furry tail and tufts of white whiskers. But if they were like an army in the trees, they made surprisingly little noise on the ground. There were monkey-and bear-tamers in Islamabad and the monkeys looked like those in the jungle.

There were other animals here as well. Before the capital was built the ground laid out in the geometric grid of Islamabad was covered with the same green jungle. Even today, no one liked to be in the area after dark: too many animals and too many unpleasant surprises. We saw wild boar, barking deer, fox, and jackals, and an early-morning walk in the jungle behind the mosque was exposure to its teeming wildlife. Sometimes, the animals could only be heard, or evidence of them seen. There would be the sound of a primate dropping to the ground from a tree around the bend, or the grunts of the wild boars as they rose unseen, but only ten yards away in the underbrush. More often there were only their tracks, visible in every path or clearing in the area.

The boars were not so visible now that the garbage dump behind the Islamic University had been closed. When it was in use groups of pigs could be seen rooting through the leavings, finding much to their taste. They were small, the largest weighing maybe seventy-five pounds, the males heavily tusked. Pig sticking had been a favorite sport of the British and, like many things British, it had survived in Pakistan in modified form. But it was mainly foreigners who shot wild boars these days and the meat was occasionally served at dinner parties in Islamabad. The flavor was not at all gamey and in fact was rather bland.

There were small animals as well—rabbits and mongoose—as well as the carnivores—foxes and jackals—that preyed on them. I once saw a small dog-like animal move away into the underbrush and moved quickly to where it had been, certain it would stop to look back. It did, and we stared fixedly at one another for a few seconds before it bolted into the green. It was gray-brown in color and had sharp pointed ears. At first I thought it was a jackal, but it was probably a fox.

But the most common wildlife were the birds. In the subcontinent they were spectacular, with pheasants, partridges, quail, great pied hornbills, parakeets, and families of songbirds. Even the city was full of birds and the Common Myna, the House Crow, and the green Alexandrine Parakeet were common in every neighborhood in Islamabad. The jungle was home to the more exotic species. It wasn't like bird watching in North America, where people stayed up for days to catch a glimpse of a tiny, two-legged, egg-laying vertebrate with feathers and wings. These were *real* birds, and their names were as exotic as their plumage. I wasn't a serious birdwatcher, but I bought a copy of *Collins Handguide to the Birds of the Indian Subcontinent* and it was a constant companion on my walks.

The calls of the birds accompanied an intruder as he made his way, he thought noiselessly, along a jungle path. They became a cacophony in the presence of the Laughing Thrush or the Brain Fever Bird, the latter looking like a small hawk with a plaid tail. They were hard to see but the racket they made was earsplitting. Some of the birds spent most of their time on the ground. It was not uncommon to put up a covey of quail, exploding into flight out of the low grass in a clearing, disappearing as quickly as they appeared. Sometimes they could be heard running though the heavy underbrush, their feet making nearly as much noise as the whirring of their wings. The Khalij Pheasant, the most common of the Himalayan pheasants, still occupied pockets in the Margallas, and one would occasionally be surprised in a clearing or a path below. The male was about the size of a barnyard rooster, iridescent blue in color with a long drooping tail.

The streams were full to overflowing during the monsoon, and nearly dry in the winter. But what little water remained collected in a few stagnant pools, and a varied bird population cautiously gathered to drink. An hour with a pair of binoculars near a pool would be rewarded with views of birds that spent hardly enough time drinking to make identification possible. There were White-cheeked Bulbuls, spectacular Paradise Flycatchers, Shamas, Babblers, and Long-tailed Tree Pies. They would land at the edge of the water and, after a careful examination of the scene, dip cautiously. The slightest movement disturbed them and, with an explosion of wings, they disappeared into the surrounding trees. After a minute they were back, to repeat the process.

Doves were common, as were the Hoopoe and the Indian Tree Pie with its rust-colored back and gray foot-long tail. The male and female Paradise Flycatcher were both black with tufted heads, but the male had a white body and a long white tail while the female had a shorter tail that was rust colored, like her wings and back. And there were Blue Drongos, Blue Rock Thrushes, Starlings, Yellow-cheeked Tits, Red-whiskered Bulbuls, and Common Wood Shrikes.

The students from the Islamic University occasionally wandered in the jungle. There was probably as much chance of encountering a cluster of grave, bearded men in gowns as a barking deer or a jackal. Their coloring and dress could be as different as those of the animals or birds. But Islam seemed to be a religion of the city, and the students had other preoccupations. It would probably be some time before religion and environmentalism were combined in the jungles of Islamabad.

12

The Roof of the World

ONE OF THE ATTRACTIONS of Pakistan was its proximity to the "Roof of the World." Taken together, the Himalayas and the Karakorams were the highest places on earth and we had planned more than once to see them. But there always seemed to be a problem in the north. With heavy rains, there could be slides and the road would be closed for weeks at a time. Even without the rains, the Karakoram Highway (KKH) passed through many places where a slide could stop traffic for days. And the people in the northern areas often used the highway to advertise their grievances, and they always seemed to have a grievance. The Kohistanis had recently closed the road for several days in protest over some government policy to which they had taken exception. There was also the religious divide. Many of the inhabitants in the northern areas were Shia and recent converts to Islam, and this led to conflicts with the older Sunni population. There would be armed clashes, leading to reprisals and the inevitable counter-reprisals. In one incident in 1992, three entire Shia villages had been destroyed and access to the north had been restricted for several weeks because of the unrest.

Air traffic was subject to the same uncertainty as that on the roads. There was an airport in Gilgit in the middle of the territories and, at about forty dollars for a round-trip ticket from Islamabad, the flight was inexpensive and spectacular. Mount Everest may have been the highest mountain in the world, but peak-for-peak the Karakorams took the palm. There were more mountains over 25,000 feet in the Karakorams than in any other range. The flight passed between many of them, skirting the western Himalayas, on its way to Gilgit. But flight control was visual and dependent on the weather. Once you were there was no guarantee you would return on schedule since the flight that would take you back to Islamabad first had to reach Gilgit. In fact, the same was true of the KKH. Any of the above problems could occur while you were *there*, and people would often be stranded until a slide was cleared or the heavy weather had broken. In addition, fuel was often a problem. Diesel and gasoline were trucked from Islamabad, and the truckers were subject to the same, and other, uncertainties as everyone else. It was not unusual to be stranded for days at a time because there was no gas or diesel available.

We decided to take advantage of the *eid* holidays in June of 1993 to try the north once again. This time we were lucky. There were a few slides over the six days we were on the road, but none was serious enough to interrupt traffic. Diesel was unavailable briefly in Gilgit, but it was on a day when we weren't traveling. So, the trip went almost exactly according to schedule. It would be from Islamabad to Chilas on the first day, Chilas through Hunza to Karimabad on the second, the Kunjerab Pass on the third, and back to Islamabad in the reverse order on days four, five, and six. We rented a company car—right-hand drive, 4-wheel drive, and diesel powered. The right-hand drive was probably the most important part. The left-hand drive Blazer worked in Islamabad, but in the mountains seeing around a corner or a bend was critical, and with left-hand drive you were always half blind. The handicap could be fatal.

The drive to Besham and the Indus was familiar since we had done it the year before on an abortive first attempt at the north. We had gotten as far as Naran in the lower Himalayas, and then over the Shangla Pass into the Upper Swat Valley. This time, we pressed on. The leg took about five hours from Islamabad. These lower levels of the mountains were typical of Pakistan, green, terraced, and deforested. The upper slopes, once covered by pines, were now mostly barren. In the fields wheat was being harvested by hand, and large bundles lay by the side of the road. Other fields were planted in rice, and water in the irregularly shaped paddies gave the area the look of Southeast Asia.

Rice paddies, Karakoram Highway

The bridge at Batgram signaled our arrival in the Indus Valley and we picked up the KKH at Mansehra before winding another hundred kilometers to Besham. By then we had become used to the sight of the river below. There was nothing pretty about the Indus. Lower down at Attock where it joined the Kabul, the water was light blue with whitecaps, and there was a brief mingling of the blue of the Indus and the muddy brown of the Kabul, before the Indus swallowed up the smaller river. Farther up, we would see many glacier-fed streams, clear and blue-green, that would tumble into the larger river. There would be a brief swirl of colors before the gray took over and flowed relentlessly onward. The Indus did that, absorbing and dominating other rivers.

Here, the gray of the water was the predominant color. In fact, it was the *only* color and Besham was a preparation for the next several hundred kilometers. The river was maybe a hundred meters wide and it flowed rapidly. The banks on either side were gray, and large deposits of gray alluvium had collected in the flat areas. The silt was finer than sand, and it was as much a part of the scene as the river itself. The Indus was a powerful, malevolent body. We never saw anyone swimming in it. The water was too cold, too rapid, and too rough. Laura said it looked like a giant stream of Maalox, a sharp observation.

Above Besham, the valley began to narrow and we left the terraced hills behind. The green remained but now the slopes were too steep to cultivate. An occasional hut might cling to the hillside, and a few tracks wound into subsidiary valleys, but there was little evidence of habitation and the drive settled into a long, barren marathon. The KKH was visible for miles ahead, first disappearing then reappearing beyond a bend in the river, snaking its way along the slope, thousands of feet above the valley floor. There were only a few settlements on this stretch—Paten, Dassau, Sazin—made up of miserable little mud-brick and rock buildings and dilapidated store fronts. There were occasional slides and a few rough spots. But the great cliffs and alluvial fans lay ahead. Surprisingly, the road improved the farther north we went from Islamabad.

Just before Sazin, the road and the river turned to the east-by-south, along the primary axis of the river as it flowed between the two mountain ranges. Oddly, the Indus rose nearly a thousand miles away to the *southeast*, not far from the source of the Ganges. It then flowed in a northwesterly arc, between the Himalayas and the Karakorams, confined by the two until it found an escape just short of Gilgit. But this was only an illusion of freedom, and it went south for only fifty kilometers or so before resuming its northwesterly flow. After another 120 kilometers at Sazin, where we now were, it finally broke free and began its thirteen-hundred-kilometer race to the south and the Arabian Sea.

The valley began to widen after Sazin and the friendly greens of the lower valley disappeared. The elevations had not been particularly great until now, and we had seen only few peaks with patchy snow at about 16,000 feet. Maybe that was because we were only now approaching the western extremity of the Himalayas and had not yet entered the Karakorams. But as we followed the river down to Chilas, the great mass of Nanga Parbat gradually came into view. It was not a single promontory, but a series of peaks. At 26,650 feet, the tallest of them made it the ninth-highest mountain in the world.

At Chilas we stopped for the night. It had been 478 kilometers and nearly eleven hours since we had left Islamabad. Our average speed, about forty-three kilometers or twenty-six miles per hour, was a measure of the difficulty of the road. We bought diesel three times—twelve, fifteen, and twenty-two liters—only because it was available, and keeping a full tank was insurance against a shortage farther north. Chilas lay in the wide part of the valley. The river lay just below the hotel and we walked down to the water after dinner, where we skipped rocks over the surface. It was just as fast and gray as at Besham. We had climbed to only about 4,000 feet at Chilas. This was surprising since we were about to enter the valley between the two highest mountain ranges in the world. But that was what made the heights so spectacular. The rise to over 26,000 feet was from a base not much higher than that at Chilas.

The Shangri-La Hotel was adequate, although it was already hot and the air-conditioner blew warm air into the room for most of the night. We were up early and on the road just after dawn. Nanga Parbat again revealed itself, the rugged white mass appearing very suddenly out of the cloud cover. It was stunning. At Gunar we began the climb to Gilgit and the mountain gradually fell away behind us. It was in this stretch that the geological forces that had shaped the valley seemed most obvious. We had long since left the green behind, and now everything was gray or brown. Around Chilas, the rocks had a dark brown crust and looked like they had been baked in the sun. Farther up, the landscape resembled the high desert in southern Sinai. The plutonic rocks were of many colors, often intermingled. One formation looked like a well-marbled steak, with regular veins of white in a reddish-brown field. In many areas, the road had been blasted out of the cliff face and the jagged overhang looked like it might fall at any moment. Cracks were visible in the surface and the debris on either side of the road showed that pieces were constantly breaking off. It looked like they might do so at any time.

Across the valley, the alluvium was laid down in different patterns. Great fans spread from fissures in the cliff face. The long slopes were sometimes covered with a fragrant blue-green plant that smelled a little like anise. Other material looked like it had been laid down horizontally and over several millennia the river had carried most of it away, leaving remnants on the walls of the valley looking like bits of ice cream sticking to the wall of a container. Some of the deposits were swirled like pralines and cream, or marble fudge. The deposited material probably came from the mountains themselves, and they must have been even more massive in remote geological time.

In early June it was hot, but tolerable. In July and August, the reflected heat off the bare rock faces would be particularly intense and this stretch would feel like an oven. There was something magnificent about the landscape, like the river itself. It didn't have the variety of southern Sinai, and you wouldn't call it beautiful. But it made the lush greens and 16,000 feet of the lower slopes we had earlier passed through seem like child's play. We crept like ants along these rock faces for what seemed like hours at a time, the landscape varying only in degree of difficulty.

Maintenance of the road was a constant problem. The areas where the highway had been carved out of the cliff face were relatively stable, but in the gorges material was constantly flaking off and it occasionally blocked the road. Each attempt at repair seemed only like a Band-Aid. Masonry buttresses, consisting of local stone mortared into walls, were undermined or overwhelmed everywhere. With each slide the road moved sideways, progressively up the gorge, and a part of the original roadbed would be left—when it was left—thirty feet away from a temporary passage bulldozed over the slide area. The paths were generally only wide enough for a single vehicle at a time. But, still, this was only rock and loose scree, not producing the heart-stopping sensation on the road above Hunza, where the water and soil conspired together to make the passage very unstable. A thousand feet below was our constant companion, the swift, gray river.

We gradually left this lunar landscape behind and the green began to appear again. But where, below, the green had been everywhere, here it only carpeted the masses of the alluvium. They were hundreds of feet thick, and portions of them had been carried away by the river. The green sometimes began very dramatically, half-way up the cliff face, where a fissure allowed the exit of subterranean water. Everything was green below. We passed Gilgit, sitting on one of those alluvial monoliths, and looking downright tropical in comparison with what we had just seen. We would save the town for the return leg. Just above Bunji we finally left the Indus behind and picked up the Hunza. It was the same color, but without the volume of the Indus. It would be our companion for the rest of the day. Actually, the day was a short one. We arrived in Karimabad in the Hunza Valley, just before noon, after a drive of about six hours from Chilas.

Karakorum Highway, northern territories

Hunza was supposed to be the setting for James Hilton's *Lost Horizon* and *Shangri-La*, and it *looked* the part. It would be hard to imagine a more picturesque setting: the little towns of Aliabad and Karimabad set in groves of apricots, mulberries, and plane trees in the center of an alluvial fan that poured down from the Ultar glacier. The elevation in the little towns was only about 8,000 feet, but directly behind them, rising nearly sheer to 25,545 feet, was Ultar itself. Across the valley, equally dramatically, rose Rakaposhi at over 24,000 feet. And in every direction, there were peaks equally stark in appearance. Even in June they were still covered with snow, as they would be throughout the year. The white was dazzling.

But it was more than just the setting. The people had the look of what we imagined to be medieval Europeans, and we saw many pink complexions and blue eyes. They seemed to be stunted, the staple diet of dried apricots apparently leading to longevity but not to stature. It was not unusual to see what appeared to be a child, maybe four feet tall, before we realized that it was an adult woman. They were not unfriendly, and always responded when we greeted them, but they didn't seem particularly outgoing. The children were also unusually small but they seemed well educated. One sober little being waited on us at a store and his English was textbook perfect:

What's your name?

My name is Ali.

Where did you learn English?

I learned it in my school.

And how old are you?

I am twelve years old.

He looked about nine. The words were chosen only after suitable reflection and uttered with considerable gravity. I gave him a 500-rupee note and he bolted down the hill to get change. We had the run of his store while he was gone but, as usual in this part of the world, there was no concern about theft.

In Karimabad we had reached a halfway point of the marathon and it was time for some sightseeing. Two little picture-book forts, Baltit and Altit, dominated the scene and we climbed to Baltit first. But it was undergoing restoration and was closed. The Agha Khan Foundation was financing the work, as it was with many other works—schools, community centers, and health clinics—in this Shia area. Earlier we had seen graffiti spray-painted on the cliff walls welcoming his eminence to Hunza with the clarion Shia call: "Live like Ali, die like Hussein." The Agha Khan had recently seen a sharp drop in the value of his hotel portfolio, stemming from overextension on a project in Sardinia. So, construction of the Serena Hotel, which should have opened in Karimabad the year before, had not even been started.

Altit was supposed to be more impressive than Baltit, but it was hard to imagine that it could have been less so. The location was dramatic enough, and peering out one of the windows we were greeted with a sheer drop of about 1,500 feet to the river below. This was another setting out of *Grimm's Fairy Tales*, tiny, dank, and cramped with doors maybe five feet high. The interior was begrimed with the smoke of thousands of fires, and the floor was covered with straw. It looked and smelled like a stable. The place reeked of treachery and violence, of pretenders to the throne butchered like sheep in its little rooms, or pitched from the windows into the abyss below. We imagined that a single sharp earthquake would shake the individual stones from their mud settings, or collapse the ridiculous beams and headers that lay crookedly everywhere.

Outside, there was some nice carved woodwork on the exterior jams, and we sat in the shade of the little tower and surveyed the village below. A sign at the entrance to the fort, placed there by "The Youth of the Village," announced that the women did not want their pictures taken, although the women themselves didn't seem to have been consulted. On the way into the grounds of the fort, we had passed an orchard full of dwarf sheep and apricot and mulberry trees. The mulberries were a revelation. These were not the bushes of Central Asia, cut every year to feed the silkworms. Here they were large trees, hundreds of years old, and the branches were heavy with fruit. I could reach a few that were riper than others, and they were sweet and delicious. The apricots also looked old, but they didn't appear to be pruned and the fruit was smaller than we were used to in the United States.

Verdure was everywhere in this little oasis, a product of snowmelt from the glacier behind the town. A system of community waterworks carried the flow into every garden and orchard in the town. From some forgotten recess of my memory a little ditty came to mind:

> In der vintertime
> In der valley green
> Ven der vomenfolk
> Of der vatervorks
> Ride velocipedes
> Down der vaterfalls.

Here the gray water tumbled down the hill in a constant stream. But it looked unappetizing, with precipitate matter making little eddies and swirls in suspension like egg-flower soup. It was probably the same gray silt we had seen hundreds of miles to the south.

We walked back to the hotel, followed by groups of children all wanting "one pen." It had become a refrain until one independent little creature demanded "one balloon." The PTDC (Pakistan Tourist Development Corporation) hotel was adequate and inexpensive at about $22 a night for a double. The standard dinner of curry, chickpeas, vegetables, and *nan* was good and filling. The BBC news was dubbed only in Chinese, and we could make little sense of it. So, we read and turned in early. We were tired and it was probably no wonder. We had hiked about five miles at a steady pace that afternoon at an elevation of over 8,000 feet. And we wanted to get an early start for the Kunjerab Pass the next day.

We were up before dawn and on the road with first light. The man at the front desk told us that the trip to Kunjerab and back would take about ten hours. He was spot-on. From the map, it looked to be about 400 kilometers, or 240 miles. It actually took nine-and-a-half hours, with half-an-hour at the top of the pass. He also said that the climb was very gradual, with a hardly perceptible rise to the summit. At 4,733 meters, or 15,528 feet, it was the highest metaled surface in the world.

In Islamabad, we had heard that the road might be closed past Karimabad. There was evidence of several slides after we crossed the Chinese bridge below Altit, but nothing serious enough to block the road. Then we negotiated a very loose and wet stretch where a slide could easily have blocked passage for several days. About fifty kilometers above Karimabad we came to Khaiber, a little village of the same name, in both Urdu and Arabic, as the Khyber Pass and the ancient, low-lying village north of Medina in Saudi Arabia. The names were occasionally cited as evidence that these northerners were one of the lost tribes of Israel. The village in Arabia had originally been inhabited by Jews and it was said that one of the events portending the end of the world would be the return of the Jews to Khyber. Doughty had looked for them in 1881 but found the place inhabited by blacks, the descendants of slaves. We had seen the Saudi Khyber in 1987 on a trip to the Nabataean monuments of Meda'in Saleh.

At the Pakistani border post at Sost we were stopped, eighty kilometers from Karimabad at an elevation of about 10,000 feet. We had become used to these checkpoints and our northward progress had already been registered in half a dozen logbooks. But here, we waited at the roadblock until a civil servant in a Pajero came to check our passports. He asked if we were going on to China and, when we said no, he told us to be careful anyway, as the Chinese were "crazy people." Beyond Sost we picked up the Kunjerab River and it was clear and pretty, like a stream in the high Sierra. The road was surrounded by snowcapped peaks, all of them over 22,000 feet. But after the extravagance of Hunza everything now seemed small and insignificant. Two hours later we reached another checkpoint and gained a passenger, Mohammed Rihan, a policeman who would accompany the final three miles to the summit. We were at about 14,000 feet and the road began a steep climb to the pass itself.

Now, the landscape changed. A light snow began to fall, and the ground was covered with white patches. Underneath, it looked oddly different, and we later found that it was tundra, soft and yielding to the step, or crunchy where a thin crust of ice covered the surface. Then, a brilliant little orange animal loped across the white expanse, then another, and another. We stopped, and soon they were everywhere. Mohammed said they were *torshin*, or marmots, about two feet long and covered with thick fur the color of the rusty drums that littered the landscape. The remains of a yak, the head, horns, and a long string of vertebrae, lay by the side of the road.

At the summit, we entered a different world from that only 2,000 feet and five kilometers below. The grade gave way to a flat plateau surrounded on every side by mountains. Everywhere, it was white except for occasional patches where the tundra lay exposed. A pair of pillars marked the border, in red letters and Chinese on one side and green and Urdu on the other. The Chinese border post was at Pirali, ten miles on the other side of the pass. A herd of yaks grazed on the Chinese side, pawing through the snow for the edible stuff underneath. We drove through the pillars and stopped for a look. The first sensation, at over 15,000 feet, was one of slight dizziness. I had been at 19,000 feet on Kilimanjaro, but there the ascent had been gradual. Here, we had driven the last 5,000 feet in an hour and the last 1,500 in a matter of minutes. We walked around, sampling the soft footing and examining the lichen on the surface. It was very still, almost eerie, with not a sound to be heard. We felt that we really were on the roof of the world.

After a decent interval, we left. As we drove away, the scene looked particularly bleak, with only the pillars, the yaks, and Mohammed, waiting for another car and looking a little forlorn with nothing to keep him warm but a pack of cigarettes. The drive back to Karimabad and Hunza was anticlimactic.

Hunza was a staging point for day trips in the area and we spent the next morning hiking part way to the Ultar glacier. There was a track behind the little town and the climb at 9,000 feet through the boulder-strewn gorge next to the little stream, was strenuous. Even at this elevation the water was gray, the same color as the stuff that came out of the tap in the hotel. We left for Gilgit early in the afternoon. There was no diesel at the station five kilometers outside of Aliabad, but we had three-quarters of a tank and twenty liters in the jerry-can on the back of the car, so we were not concerned. There were a couple of slides on the way down, one that had been recently cleared and one that was just then happening. We watched the falling gravel in a little caravan, each driver gauging a favorable time to dash across the slide area.

Gilgit spread over an alluvial fan that occupied the south side of the river. In any other circumstance, it would have been impressive. Sitting at 5,000 feet, it was cool and the white mass of Rakaposhi stood up starkly across the river. We crossed the Chinese bridge and entered from the east. The KKH had been a joint Pakistani-Chinese project, with the Pakistanis building the road and the Chinese the bridges. Like the others this one was a delicate little arched span with temple dogs supporting the railings.

The town was the hub for serious treks in Pakistan, the ten-and twenty-day trips to Masherbrum or the K2 base camp. The dusty little streets were lined with fruit sellers, bookstores, mountaineering shops, butchers, and hardware stores. There were also tourist cabins, huts, villas, and hideaways. We settled on the Hunza Tourist Inn where we found another group of Americans, waiting to buy diesel. There wasn't any in the town and they said you needed a permit from the governor. There was also a Serena in Gilgit, a five-star facility, but we didn't have reservations and were, anyway, not in a five-star frame of mind.

Gilgit too was a military town, like many others in Pakistan, and the cantonment dominated the eastern part of the city. Military police in crisply pressed uniforms and ascots directed traffic at the little intersections with parade-ground precision. There were also Frontier Constabulary everywhere, armed men in pairs on the streets and even on the little roads outside the town. They were there to keep the lid on in the event of sectarian violence, and we should probably have been reassured by their presence. But we found it oddly disconcerting. In the afternoon, while the Americans went trout fishing, we looked for L.M. Baig's bookstore and George Hayward's grave. We saw them in reverse order. It took us several attempts to find the Christian cemetery in the western part of the town, and the same policeman must have waved us through the same intersection three or four times before we finally found it. That was odd since it *looked* like a cemetery: green, overgrown, and surrounded by a wall. A cobbler across the street had the key, and he let us in to the little Christian oasis in this Muslim town.

Hayward was an intrepid explorer and he had paid the price. His grave was marked with a plaque on the ground, and I perched on the granite wall above to get a clear view of the inscription:

> To the memory of G.W. Hayward, Gold Medalist of the Royal Geographical Society of London, who was cruelly murdered at Darkot, July 18, 1870, on his journey to explore the Pamir steppe. This monument is erected to a gallant officer and accomplished traveler at the instance of the Royal Geographic Society.

There was also the grave of an English schoolteacher who had died here in 1988. The cemetery didn't have the neglected look of the Christian cemeteries in Peshawar and Rawalpindi, with the headstones falling down and the graves falling in, collapsing like the bodies they contained.

Back in town we found L.M. Baig. The shop was supposed to carry hard-to-get titles and it did. I found Rawlinson's *England and Russia in the East*, a late nineteenth-century Great Game classic, an appreciation by the Commander in Chief, India of Russian designs on the subcontinent. I had seen it elsewhere, advertised for hundreds of sterling pounds. This was only an Indus reprint, but it was offset from the original and looked like the real thing. And the price was right. Early the next morning we drove to the east of the town to see the Buddha carved in a cliff face. A little boy pointed it out to us, and then ran alongside the car for a hundred yards, looking for a pen. But we had run out.

It was the first day of the feast and the children were in their *eid* finery, the little girls particularly festive with new dresses and hennaed hands. But the Frontier Constabulary were everywhere and as we drove back through the now-shuttered streets to the tourist inn, something about the atmosphere told us it was time to leave. As we left the town a crowd of men blocked the road, but we persuaded them to let us through. At the checkpoint on the KKH, we breathed a sigh of relief. We were glad to be free of the army, of the children and their elders. Religious passions ran especially high during the feasts, but they were often the only times we could travel. A shipment of diesel had arrived the previous afternoon, and the full tank and jerry can on the back meant that we had enough fuel to take us back to Islamabad. We had seen Gilgit and now set out for the south and home.

The dramatic scenery behind us, the drive to Besham became a long, boring slog. We stopped in Chilas to see the petroglyphs, rock carvings left by generations of travelers, the earliest dating from the Sakas, or Scythians, in the first century BC. We found only a few stick figures, crudely scratched in the rocks, and didn't have time to look for the leopards and other animals that were advertised. But we encountered, again, a phenomenon as puzzling as it had been on the journey north. Periodically, thousands of logs would be stacked by the side of the road, before being sent by overhead wire to the other side of the Indus. They were about ten feet long and looked like they had been dressed with an adz to maybe a foot-and-a-half square. We always rolled down the windows as we passed because they were deodars or Indian Cedar, "timber of the gods," and their fragrance perfumed the air. We thought they must be used in road building, but we never saw them anywhere except in these redolent piles.

We stopped for the night at the PTDC hotel in Besham. After the usual curry we watched the BBC, this time in English. It was our first news in nearly a week, but it seemed that we hadn't missed much. Afterwards we walked down to the river and the play of the nearly full moon on the water was spectacular. We were on the road early the next morning. At Batgram we watched a chairlift make its precarious way across the gorge. Almost the first news that greeted us in Islamabad was that a cable on the lift at Batgram had failed and thirteen people, including ten women from the same family, were killed in the fall.

It had, literally, been all downhill from Kunjerab and as we descended into the heat and thronging humanity of the Punjab the roads were packed. We crawled through crowds and traffic in the little towns on our way to Abbottabad. Higher up, we sometimes hadn't seen another vehicle for hours at a time. After Abbottabad, later made famous or notorious as the last refuge of Osama bin-Laden, it was the scenic route through Taxila. Among its several incarnations was a period as a Greek settlement, dating from the time of Alexander the Great. We missed the familiar ruins, but saw the Bhallar Stupa rising dramatically out of the valley. The drive was very pretty.

At Wah we picked up the Grand Trunk and after nearly a week in the north it seemed like a miracle of modern road building, not the bad old GT we all knew and hated. In Islamabad, they sold T-shirts with the logo "I survived the Grand Trunk," but we hurtled up this novelty of a divided highway at 120 kilometers an hour. When we pulled into the driveway at home the odometer said that we had gone 1,806 kilometers over the past six days. That was only a little over 1,000 miles. We were used to driving nearly that far in a day in the United States.

But there we hadn't gone to the roof of the world.

13

The Sale

As projects wound down and Americans prepared to leave Pakistan, RONCO was tasked with selling the excess government property that had previously been stored. The American withdrawal was based on the Pressler amendment that, since its passage by Congress in 1985, had attempted to deal with an alleged Pakistani nuclear program. The law required a yearly finding that Pakistan was not in the business of acquiring a nuclear weapon and presidents Reagan and George H. W. Bush, with larger fish to fry in the subcontinent, had provided the necessary certification. But after the Russian withdrawal from Afghanistan in 1989 the immediate threat seemed to have passed and we were now prepared to lean on the Pakistanis, although it took several years for the full effect to be felt.

In the early 1990s, RONCO had acted as the procurement agent, logistician, and general factotum for the USAID Representative for Afghanistan, or AIDREP. It seemed odd to be using a private company to conduct government business. But Afghanistan was still too dangerous for an embassy or aid mission, even after the end of the war against the Soviets, and Americans were forbidden to cross the border from Pakistan. So, the Afghan program was managed remotely from Islamabad, Peshawar, and Quetta. The American role in the Afghan conflict had been anything but orthodox, and we occasionally had to deal with problems left over from the wild early days. Whatever else could be said about the old cold-warriors they had a collective sense of humor. We inherited a stable of organizations to fund including the NAACP (National Afghan Construction Project) and the ACLU (the Afghan Construction and Logistics Unit).

This sale would be a change from our normal course of business. Instead of warehousemen we would become merchandisers, proprietors of a wholesale furniture and heavy-equipment outlet. But everyone pitched in and we soon became very good at it. Mohammed Aurangzeb and his merry band of men at the warehouse led the effort. Aurangzeb himself was a little like Babu in *Kim*, a native of the subcontinent who made a fetish of the English language. After the first sale he had said, with evident satisfaction, that the success was due to the fact that the items had been "minutely, not to say microscopically, displayed, sir." When I earlier asked him how things were going, he had replied "perfectly, just perfectly, sir." I reminded him that perfection was not of this world, but was an attribute only of God, and his eyes momentarily glazed over. But it was only a short pause before he was off again, intent on bringing his brand of perfection to some other, yet undiscovered, corner of the warehouse.

And perfect it very nearly was. The goods in the first sale were a combination of household furniture—living-room sets, dining-room sets, china-cabinets, and bedroom sets—as well as washing machines, refrigerators, and a few pieces of office equipment. Later sales would dispose of the big-ticket items—forklifts, tractors, and Mitsubishi Pajeros, as well as assorted computers and accessories. It was all used and some of it had been badly used. But like a good merchandiser, Aurangzeb understood that display meant everything. The crew at the warehouse were augmented by day laborers and everyone willingly pitched in. They polished and they polished so carefully that when the doors opened on the first day the goods had never looked better.

The merchandise was organized in lots. A dining-room set might be a lot, consisting of a table, eight chairs, a sideboard, and a china cabinet. Or, several air-conditioners might constitute a lot. They were carefully arranged with a sign attached to each, describing what the lot contained. This was important since everything was sold by auction. On the opening day of the sale, the public viewed the goods and submitted sealed bids, by lot. The bids were then reviewed and the winners announced several days later and it was important that everyone understood exactly what he was bidding for. The knobs were even taken off appliances during the viewing. That was a problem since people sometimes surreptitiously took them.

The buyers were a combination of individual Pakistanis and dealers. Many of the items—American refrigerators, freezers, and washing machines—would otherwise have been subject to customs duty, and so were available at greatly reduced prices. The furniture was local, but it was all hardwood. There was no particleboard with a thin veneer, and so it was all good value. In fact, furniture made of *shisham*, or Indian Rosewood and the state tree of the Punjab, was probably the greatest bargain in Pakistan and there was hardly an expat who didn't take home at least a chest of drawers or a rocking chair. Many took back whole rooms of furniture. It was hard to say how much of the value of the items was realized by the sale. But the proceeds were substantial. It was not unusual for a bedroom set to sell for 30,000 rupees, or $1,000, and an air conditioner to go for half that amount. There were estimates that these auctions brought in about fifty *paisas* on the rupee, or fifty cents on the dollar. But in some cases, it was higher and Aurangzeb's display probably made the difference.

As part of the effort we had to train the cashiers who would be dealing with large amounts of cash. I say "train" but that hardly described the reality. People in this part of the world imbibed a commercial sense with their mother's milk. I think it was Calvin Coolidge who said "the business of America is business." But the same was true of the Muslim world. In this most practical of the world's great religions, every man was a businessman, especially familiar with transactions in cash. My introduction to the cash economy had been in Egypt when I accompanied a landlord while he bought furnishings for three flats. He had the equivalent of about $10,000 in cash in his briefcase and tossed bricks of money, still in their wrappers from the bank, at the girl in the appliance store. She put the money in the drawer of an unlocked desk. In the United States only the underground economy—drug dealers and money launderers—operated this way.

Each country has its own method of counting cash. In Egypt, the bills were clasped between the second and third fingers of one hand and the thumb on the other hand was used as the counter. In Saudi Arabia, it was the same. In Pakistan, a pile of bills was held in the left hand, and the thumb and third finger of the other hand counted them with a very rapid, and very accurate, chopping motion. If the pile were especially thick, they were laid on a table and a moistened finger rapidly scanned them. I had recently counted $9,000 in hundred dollar bills and was struck at how clumsy I was in comparison with Pakistanis. They seemed to share the fine motor movement with the Chinese.

So, the cashiers were already used to handling large amounts of money. They would need to be since all the transactions were in cash. Each bidder was required to deposit 25 percent of the value of the bid as earnest money on the first day. Sometimes, thousands of rupees came through the grating of a cashier's cage in ten-rupee notes. The piles were counted three times, each time by a separate cashier. A receipt was then written and the earnest money was sealed, individually, by bidder in its own envelope. The envelopes were my contribution. Most of the bids were unsuccessful and the earnest money of the losing bidders had to be refunded on the second day. It was much easier to refund them envelope by envelope, rather than rupee by rupee.

Dealing with the successful bidders was even more complicated. The earnest money had to be refunded before they returned the full amount of the winning bid. Sometimes this was more, and sometimes less than the deposit. In fact, we had a computer program that showed the "net" that each successful bidder owed. But it was easier for the cashiers to deal with each transaction on a gross basis rather than struggle with the arithmetic required of the net.

The greatest problem, needless to say, was the press at the cashiers' windows. Many times, there would be several people attempting to thrust their money through the grating at the same time. We were ruthless about the chaos. The cashiers were already under enough pressure without having to be line monitors at the same time. They worked nonstop, counting, writing, and re-counting for five hours at a stretch. So, we hired extra SMS security guards to keep the lines in check. But it took constant attention, so great was the tendency toward the normal state of entropy or disorder.

SMS was the company used by the American Embassy to provide guards at the gates of the compound. They were also hired to supply the night guards, or *chowkidars*, at the homes of expatriates and we grew fond of our own man, Nawab Khan, who always saluted smartly as we came and went. Most of them were ex–military. We heard complaints that they were worked on back-to-back shifts, and that they were underpaid. They certainly slept on the job. In our first house, we had been awakened in the middle of the night by the sound of the chowkidar's snoring outside the bedroom window. A reading of *Plain Tales from the Raj* suggested that not much had changed in India over the years: runners ran, writers wrote, and *chowkidars* slept.

The sales were surprisingly successful. Almost everything sold, from Pajeros to trashcans. Aurangzeb would have listed the latter as something like "cans, trash, plastic, 2 each." On the second day, the crew worked overtime to move the goods to the front of the warehouse where an odd assortment of vehicles was waiting to carry them away. It all worked like clockwork. There were inventory lists, receipts, lot chits, and checklists. The last stop was at the gate where the SMS guard, looking slightly out of place with a spectacular hennaed beard and tight-fitting western uniform, checked the receipt against the cargo. The winners left in caravans made up of everything from large Hino flatbeds to tiny Suzuki trucks hardly more than toys. One bidder departed with his typewriter proudly lashed to the top of an old Morris cab.

Then the cashiers opened the envelopes and counted the money. It was generally spot-on. In an average sale, the take was about 1.5 million rupees in earnest money, and 600,000 in final proceeds. It was always a relief when the SMS armored car arrived to relieve us of the money. We later learned that a bank a quarter-mile away had been robbed on the first day of the second sale. The loss was about 4 lakhs, or 400,000 rupees. They could have quadrupled their take if they had visited us. But we decided not to provide armed guards at the sales. With arms, and hundreds of innocent people milling around, someone would surely be killed in any robbery attempt. It wasn't worth the risk.

Even an operation as serious as this had an inimitable Pakistani flavor. The armored car had three attendants, an officer, an NCO with a pistol on his hip, and a guard with a sawed-off shotgun. As usual, we shook hands all around. The guard had to shift the shotgun to free his hand. Then they put back on their serious faces and packed and sealed the cash bag. Everyone breathed more easily as the car pulled out of the gate. But this was only Islamabad. The next sale would be in Peshawar. We might as well be holding it in Dodge City in 1875.

14

Central Asia Revisited

IT WAS OUR SECOND visit to Central Asia and it would be very different from the first. The photographs told the story. Where the first had been of things, of magnificent edifices, *madrasas*, and mosques, the pictures this time were mostly of people. We had already seen Samarkand and Bokhara, but we wanted to see Khiva, the other city on the old slave route north of Bokhara. And we understood that the Fergana valley was beautiful. We also had an onward flight from Tashkent to Almata in Kazakhstan the first afternoon and had scheduled a drive to Bishkek in Kyrgyzstan for the following day. But it was our interaction with people that dominated the trip. The experience was often frustrating. In situations like this I often thought of Richard Burton's voyage from Suez to Jidda in the *Golden Wire*, a leaky tub commanded by an incompetent but engaging ruffian. Burton traveled as a local, in steerage and, to compare great things with small, his adventure put our little inconveniences into perspective. He had approached the experience with his characteristic gusto and the least we could do was the same. I think we succeeded. We thought we had a nearly inexhaustible fund of good humor and it never ran dry, in spite of the gravest provocations.

We were only three, the rump of the earlier Central Asian group, a kind of hard core who had the time and the inclination to return and refine the impressions of the first trip. John, a political officer in the embassy, did the legwork and made the arrangements in Pakistan. He had spent years studying the Arab and Muslim worlds and this would be his parting shot before a posting back to Washington. Elizabeth, a Fulbright scholar doing research on arranged marriages in Pakistan, came along as the only one of her gender, sensibility, and age group. Needless to say, she brought her own perspective, personal as well as professional, to the party. Actually, the three of us had a great deal in common, including the fact that we all had a connection with the navy. I had served three years in destroyers. John's father was an academy graduate and he had once considered a career in the navy himself. And Elizabeth's father was a naval architect who had sailed on the *USS Manhattan* on its first polar voyage.

Check-in at the PIA desk in Islamabad was the usual mild aggravation. But by the end of the week we would long for the familiar certainties of Pakistan. Departure was on time and the two-hour flight to Tashkent passed quickly. The weather was poor, with a heavy overcast, and we saw little of Afghanistan. By the time we had landed and taxied to a halt in the familiar surroundings of the Tashkent International Airport, we almost felt like we were coming home. Just as on the first trip, an impressive array of aircraft lay on the tarmac, and I stopped counting at fifty. In an American airport, the planes would be moving in and out, taxiing, taking off, and landing. Here, they were all parked. Aviation fuel was a problem since it came from Russia and the Russians demanded hard currency in payment. The array was varied: propeller-driven Antonov An-24s; a few huge Ilyushin Il-86s, the Soviet answer to the Boeing 747; and ugly, droop-winged Ilyushin Il-78s, one of which we later saw in Peshawar. There were also Yakovlev Yak-40s and Yak-50s, small executive jets. And finally, the workhorse of the fleet, the Tupolev Tu-154. The display was, again, a convincing reminder of what could be achieved in a command economy.

Each model was a replica of an aircraft in the west. Most had been around since the 1970s. But there were several new ones as well, including the massive Antonov An-124. It was the answer to our C5, with a hinged nose and wide doors in the rear, and could be loaded from both ends at the same time. All the airports in the former Soviet Union (FSU) seemed to have an aircraft graveyard attached, containing planes in various states of scrap or cannibalization. But these were all gleaming, newly painted in a variety of colors. Some had the old Aeroflot markings, others had those of Uzbekistan Airways or Air Kazakhstan. Some were in Latin, others in Cyrillic characters. The planes weren't going anywhere at the moment, but the republics had already begun the process of sharing out the capital goods of the old union.

There had been two recent accidents with planes leased from the FSU. On a flight to New Delhi several months before we had seen the charred hulk of a Tu-154, on charter to India Airlines, by the side of the runway. It had flipped over on takeoff but, miraculously, no one was killed. Poor maintenance seemed to have been the cause. More recently, an Il-78 leased by the

UN to carry aid to the Tajiks near Termez had damaged its undercarriage on a rough landing in Peshawar. Stories of the crudity of the interiors and the rudeness of Russian aircrews were making the rounds of the subcontinent. But, although there were characteristics of Central Asian air travel that we would later find amusing, the planes seemed sound and the service was better than we expected. We found flying in the Tu-154 to be oddly comforting, and it may have had something to do with its characteristic long, slow ascent. The pilot never took it up abruptly, but prolonged the takeoff in a display of patience and power that was very reassuring.

We were taken to the terminal building in the same truck-drawn transporters of the first trip, and the building was in the same state of disrepair. But they were making progress. The previous October passport control had been a long-drawn-out agony. Now, simple stands had replaced the sealed booths with their angled mirrors and remote bureaucrats, and we stood eyeball to eyeball with the officer. There was the same awkward pause as he compared each passport photo with reality that stood before him. But by comparison with the last trip, this part of the process was easy. However, other hurdles quickly followed. For a people who had spent the past seventy years regimenting their populations, these former Soviets seemed ignorant of anything resembling an efficiency study.

Customs clearance required multiple declarations and they were *for sale* for ten rubles each. There were no signs advertising this and the information was passed by word of mouth. None of us, of course, had any rubles and when a man eventually set up an exchange booth he, of course, had no change. The alternative for those with large bills was to exchange too much money at a rate that would be better the next day, or the next hour. Or we could wait until the man had accumulated enough dollars to make change. But everyone wanted change. I waited for several minutes and returned to the booth, but he had just given away all of his small bills. Eventually, an American from the embassy in Tashkent loaned me fifty rubles. At the rate that day, it was the equivalent of about six cents.

Customs also meant X-ray and manual inspection of the baggage. The caution of the customs people was understandable. We were, after all, a flight from Pakistan, and drug smuggling and forged travel documents had made the bearers of those green passports suspect the world over. Central Asia had already begun to supplant the more familiar European and far-eastern routes for heroin from the Northwest Frontier Province and Afghanistan. Most of our Pakistani fellow travelers seemed to be young gallants in an impressive array of denim trousers and flowered shirts, and they were probably up to nothing more sinister than a little whoring and an inexpensive binge. But the Uzbeks were clearly on their guard.

There were no schoolgirls with gladiolus to greet us this time. Instead, an odd little man appeared outside the terminal building and asked us to follow him. We did and he led us several hundred yards to the Intourist offices in the domestic terminal. It was an introduction to the officialdom that would plague us for the rest of the trip. We were shown into the offices of Mr. Alexander Akharov, the airport office manager for Intourist. He was on the telephone, bellowing a succession of harsh, unintelligible sounds at someone on the other end. There were parts in operas written especially for Russian voices, since only they have the *basso profondos* with the necessary range. He had that kind of voice. He was thickset with a large belly and hairless butcher's arms.

But he was a decent sort and made an effort to help. After he hung up the phone, he introduced himself and explained our predicament. It appeared that our onward flight to Almata that afternoon simply did not exist. Akharov just shrugged when we asked how this was possible, since we had tickets, coupons, and confirmed reservations. There was no flight to Almata that afternoon, and we might as well accept the fact and make alternative plans. There was a schedule on the wall behind his desk and it seemed that the next flight to Almata would be in two days, but he didn't have much faith in that. So, he spent the next fifteen minutes trying to reach one of the contact numbers we had been given by the travel agent in Islamabad.

Like most Russians—actually, he was half Russian and half Uzbek—Akharov chain-smoked. His desk was littered with papers, half-empty cigarette packs, telephones, and stacks of rubles and dollars, the last held together with paper clips and tossed in a box. He tried several of the phones, but either there was no answer or he couldn't get a line, because he finally gave up. The telephone system was as poor as his English, he confessed. We assured him that this was not the case. But we accepted his advice that our best plan was to check into the Hotel Uzbekistan where Mr. Anwar Saeedov could perhaps help us. Incidentally, Intourist provided a bus to the hotel and if we would each pay him the six-dollar fare, he would make the arrangements. The dollars went into the box on his desk.

Now, this was alarming. We had paid hard currency—at hard currency prices—for these internal flights and we had a full, tightly-scheduled itinerary. A delay of two days in Tashkent meant that we would probably miss a more interesting city later in the week. In the end, even though the delay was only for a day, we never made it to Bishkek. But Elizabeth made the sensible suggestion that since everything seemed to revolve around getting back to Tashkent for the flight to Urgench and Khiva, why not move Khiva up on the schedule and do it the next day? With Khiva out of the way, we could go to Almata and drive back through Fergana. It was a straw, and required a wholesale rescheduling of our flights. But since the schedule didn't seem to mean anything anyway, we grasped it. By the time we had checked into the hotel, settled into our rooms on the thirteenth floor and gathered at the hard-currency bar in the lobby, we were ready to do battle.

Anwar Saeedov was in his office and he appeared ready to help. Yes, what we proposed seemed possible. However, we would first have to see Svierta about the flight and Ludmilla about the visas. Svierta, an Uzbek with platinum blond hair, found that there was an afternoon flight to Urgench the next day. She would see about getting us seats. Then Ludmilla examined our passports and dropped the second bombshell of the day. She announced, rather triumphantly, that we didn't have visas for Urgench. The visa was a separate document with each of the cities of our itinerary listed by name. Ludmilla was right: there was no Urgench. The travel agent had planned the itinerary, bought the tickets, and bought the visas, listing Tashkent, Almata, and Bishkek, the capitals of the republics we were visiting. He apparently thought that since Urgench was in Uzbekistan, separate visas were not necessary.

But they were, and we would not be allowed on the flight without them. Helpfully, Anwar suggested that even though the office of the Foreign Ministry at the airport was now closed, tomorrow was another day and maybe we could persuade them to give us visas then. As to the likelihood of this happening, he said there *had* been cases like this before. But we had to be firm with them, even pound the desk a little. No, he couldn't call and tell them we were coming. He was, after all, only from Intourist and we would be dealing with the Foreign Ministry. But Ludmilla winked at me and rubbed a thumb and forefinger together: US dollars could accomplish anything. And, by the way, since we had changed our schedule, there would be a charge of eight dollars each to arrange the new flights. She knew that it wasn't our fault, but those were the rules. Did we want the flights or not? We agreed to the arrangements. Anwar was right, tomorrow was another day.

So, we settled down to our enforced evening in Tashkent. We made reservations at the Asr restaurant, one of our haunts from the first trip. It was better known as the Tijuana and, at first, we were met with blank stares. We agreed on a price of 5,000 rubles—about $6.50–apiece, inclusive of everything. It was three times the price in the fall, but the ruble had gone from 250 to 800 over the same period so it seemed fair. Even so, it was more than the monthly salary of some of our Intourist guides. We walked the few blocks to the restaurant at about eight o'clock. The meal—champagne, vodka, salads, pickled vegetables, smoked fish, ham, smoked turkey, sausage, and a main course of Stroganoff—was good but not great. There was a floorshow with dancing girls like something out of the Arabian Nights. All the waiters were in the familiar tuxedos. We were a little suspicious when our waiter poured over the itemized bill, and used a calculator to come up with the total. It was 18,373 rubles.

The difference was only about four dollars, between the equivalent of nineteen and twenty-three dollars. But we were tired of unpleasant surprises and tired of the people who authored them. We told the waiter that we had agreed on 15,000 rubles and that was all he was getting. We tossed three 5,000-ruble notes on the table and John added his business card to the pile. He said he was a diplomat and if they had a problem they could see him at the Hotel Uzbekistan. Then we walked back past the sculpture of the drill bit and I fell into the hard, little bed about eleven o'clock. But the day wasn't over quite yet. The phone rang and there was a woman's voice on the other end:

> You vant gorls?

> I beg your pardon?

> You vant GORLS?

> I'm sorry. I don't understand.

> SEX??!!!

I must have sounded very naive. But I later thought that Uzbekistan was full of pretty girls, one commodity that lost nothing in translation and didn't suffer from a lack of quality control. Everyone was selling their artwork and carpets and there seemed to be no reason why they shouldn't sell their bodies as well.

To Khiva

Breakfast the next morning was standard Hotel Uzbekistan fare: cheese, bread, yogurt in a glass, and green tea in a saucer. Anwar Saeedov had told us that our voucher for the hotel included breakfast, but the waitress followed us out of the restaurant and into his office, protesting loudly that we hadn't paid the bill. Then Anwar told us that he had been wrong. We didn't begrudge the waitress the 912 rubles and we paid. But it was not an auspicious beginning to the day.

The hotel arrangements on the trip were a source of constant amusement. We had agreed that since Elizabeth was alone, while John and I would share a room, we would put all the room costs into a pot and divide by three. Here, a double room was eighty dollars, and a single sixty. That worked out to about forty-seven dollars per person per night. However, that was only for the first night. Anwar took our vouchers and didn't return them so that on our subsequent stays we paid the full fare. That was a hundred-four for a double and sixty-four for a single. But since John was a diplomat, he paid only 7,500 rubles for his half of the room. That was about nine dollars on our second stay and less on the third. The second time around I was about to protest to Anwar that we wanted the vouchers back when John gave me a look that was the equivalent of a sharp kick in the shins. The new arrangement meant that Elizabeth's sixty-four, my half of a hundred-four, and John's nine added to a total of a hundred twenty-five dollars, or about forty-two per night per person. But that was for the first night of the second stay. On the second night, Elizabeth's room cost more. Elizabeth and I paid with credit cards. We were the beneficiaries of this arrangement, and John must have wondered what use it was being a diplomat if he couldn't realize the perks. But he bore it with his usual good humor. We demanded payment from him in hard currency.

After breakfast, the first order of business was our appointment with the Foreign Ministry at the airport. We paid Anwar six dollars for the van. All the vehicles in Uzbekistan seemed to have cracked windshields and this one was the same model, but a different van and different cracks, from the day before. We found the Foreign Ministry office upstairs in the international terminal and, with some trepidation, knocked on the door. On entering we found a thin Uzbek in suit and tie sitting at a desk, and his female assistant across the room, near a wall radiator on which a teakettle was whistling. They were watching a Russian soap opera. We introduced ourselves and learned that his name was Ghulam ed-Din. He apologized for his faulty English, and would prefer some other language. By the way, did we speak any Arabic?

It was the break we were looking for and the discovery of the trip. Ghulam ed-Din had studied classical Arabic in school and spent a year in Damascus in the 1970s. John and I trotted out our rusty but serviceable dialects, John's Lebanese closer than my Egyptian to Ghulam ed-Din's Syrian, and we almost fell on each other's necks. It was like old home week and in five minutes he had written "Urgench" and "Khiva" on our visas and attached the Foreign Ministry stamp. No money changed hands. We parted with profuse "*Ya salaams*," and "*Ullah ya khaleeqs*" and he gave us his telephone numbers, both office and home, and told us to call him if we had any more problems. We later did and he virtually parted the waters for us.

But our success with Ghulam ed-Din had an unpleasant sequel. We learned that Rahima, Anwar's steely replacement, had afterwards visited him at the airport and the rules had changed. We later met a Dutchman in her office who had made arrangements in Amsterdam for a tour of Tashkent, Bokhara, and Samarkand. But the Russian embassy had neglected to write the names of the last two cities on the visa. Rahima told the Dutchman he could go to Bokhara and Samarkand as long as he came back to Tashkent every evening! Helpfully, we suggested he see Ghulam ed-Din at the airport, and her reply was only "Yes, *you* succeeded. But that was three days ago." In a country that was badly in need of foreign exchange, relations with visitors were still in the hands of people like Rahima. With Intourist the attitude seemed to be "thwart, extort, and abort." We never found out what happened to the Dutchman.

We almost flew back to the hotel. The only obstacle now was the flight. But Svierta had made the reservations and, with visas in hand, Ludmilla pasted the little change stickers on the flight coupons. These people weren't so bad after all. They were almost all ethnic Russians, and we came to know them individually: the unsmiling blond at the bank; the tough brunette at the main desk; the sweet girl with auburn hair at the bar; the massive woman in the purple knit dress. The Intourist offices were in a hall off the main lobby and over the next week we wore a rut in the floor towards that inner sanctum. After a while, they saw us coming and their faces were perfect barometers of their thoughts: "Christ, here come the Americans again."

We spent the rest of the morning visiting museums and art galleries we remembered from the last visit. Then we took the subway to the *Prospekt Kosmonavtov* station. Along with the equipment at the airport, the subway represented another of the anomalies in the FSU. It was clean, well-engineered, and efficient, the opposite of almost everything else in the country. Each station was decorated in a different motif. This one was modernistic, with large medallions of Yuri Gagarin, Valentina Tereshkova, and other heroes of the Soviet space program. Digital clocks in every station announced the time since the last train and there was never more than a few minutes between them. At three rubles for a token they were virtually free.

I bought a nice little oil painting of Khiva for 20,000 rubles. It was signed, the date showing it had been done in 1954. Most things for sale were on consignment, 25 percent going to the gallery. There were bargains to be had, particularly with paintings, but you had to be careful with carpets. Old carpets were a fraction of the price in Islamabad, which were much less than in Karachi. The same carpet in Paris or London was double or triple the Karachi price. Other things like lacquer boxes with Central Asian scenes, for example, were expensive. The galleries knew the exchange rate and the prices ratcheted up with inflation. And they didn't bargain.

Lunch was at the Blue Dome, and the *shashlik*, rice, and *nan* were inexpensive and filling. *Shashlik* were skewers of meat, whole pieces, not minced, and they became our staple diet. Someone said that the only people in the world who knew how to make bread were the French and the Russians. But we found the Russian bread to be bland and preferred *nan*, the thick, round local loaves. Our flight to Urgench was at one twenty, so at noon we arranged for a van to take us to the airport. The driver said it had been taken care of and wouldn't accept any money. But he met us on our return the following day, in the company of the Intourist duty officer, complaining that he hadn't been paid. The institutional memory of Intourist was a constant source of amazement.

Even though this was a domestic flight, foreigners were still kept in the Intourist terminal in their own waiting room. Each of us checked a bag on this outward flight and they arrived intact. We were lulled by this early success into a carelessness that later cost us dearly. Half an-hour before flight time we were taken by a departure attendant to our own truck-drawn airport transporter. It looked like the kind of thing used to transport horses in the United States, and we were the only three on board. We were the first on the plane after the crew and wondered, incredulously, if we were to be the only passengers. We had our choice of seats, but ten minutes later the locals arrived and the plane quickly filled.

The "equipment" was an Antonov An-24, a twin-engine propeller plane with about fifty seats. It was like the Fokkers PIA flew to Peshawar, but more comfortable. The flight attendant was a Tajk and I had spoken to him in Farsi when we came aboard. So, after passing out the small glass of mineral water that constituted the in-flight service, he settled himself next to me for a chat. It was mostly in pidgin English, since my fund of Farsi was soon exhausted. His name was Hassan, but he had never seen it written in either Arabic or Farsi, so I wrote it for him in my best *naskhi*. Then he asked if I wanted to see the cockpit and we went forward, through the baggage hold and onto the flight deck. The pilot and engineer were Russians and the copilot was a Tajik. There was actually very little to see, the area being packed with instrumentation, and the windows were tiny. The glare off the very white cloud cover was blinding, but none of the flight crew wore sunglasses. The instruments showed that we were at 6,100 meters and the airspeed was 340 knots. At that rate, the flight to Urgench would take about two hours. Coming back, with a tailwind, it took only an hour and a-half.

I had a quick look at the radarscope before returning to my seat. After a while the cloud cover disappeared and the barren *Kara Kum* and *Kizil Kum* revealed themselves below. They were the "red sands" and the "black sands" but were no more red or black than the Red Sea or the Black Sea. Caravans had come this way for centuries, and the two *kums* were famous for their barren, inhospitable terrain. There were also tiny specks that looked like wells, with tracks like ant trails radiating out from them. The wells required hundreds of feet of rope, and special animals had to be assigned to carry the weight of the rope. Khiva, where we were going, had preyed on the caravans and literally lived off the slaves captured from passing *qafilas*.

As we approached the end of the desert, patches of green and white began to appear. The green was the sown, but the white was salts and there were deposits everywhere. Irrigation had not created the problem, but only aggravated it. The soil had always been saline and tombs in Khiva were always above ground. Bodies buried beneath the surface were rejected, hydrostatic pressures pushing them back up through the crust. The Uzbeks were now flushing the soil, washing the salts into a secondary system of canals. But a great deal of damage had already been done. And the diversion of the Oxus, or Amu Darya, for irrigation had virtually dried up the Aral Sea, into which it flowed.

The landscape eventually became a dusty brown and green, and we banked sharply and began our descent. The landing was very smooth. The plane taxied to a halt, the pilot shut down the engines, and the most extraordinary scene ensued: no one moved. The minutes ticked by, one, two, three, four, but still everyone sat motionless. Finally, the pilot, followed by the rest of the crew, strode the length of the cabin and, with a perfunctory *dasvidaniya*, deplaned. Only then did we stir. We were used to PIA where the passengers were in the aisles emptying the overheads before the plane touched down, and we found the whole performance astonishing.

We caught a cab to the hotel where our Intourist guide, Saeeda, was waiting for us. Anwar Saeedov had telexed our revised itinerary. Khiva was forty minutes away by car and it was too late to see anything that day. But one day would be enough to see the old city and we walked to the nearby Aeroflot offices to confirm our reservations for the return flight the following afternoon. Then, we settled down for a good read. We were exactly twenty-four hours behind schedule. But our real trip was, we hoped, about to begin. My only regret was the loss of my diary, which I must have left on the plane. Martha had lost *her* diary on a flight to Rostov on Don in 1964 and I thought the bastards could now complete the family album. But then I remembered that it had been in her maiden name.

Khiva

Khiva was the old Khwarizm, and had an even older pedigree as the possible home of the Avesta, the Zoroastrian sacred books. Herodotus mentioned its fertile valley and delta as important Central Asian sites. The Khwarizmians, or Chorasmians, formed a unit in Xerxes's army and, apparently, the capitol of the province had the same name. But by the time of the visitation by Alexander the Great, the old Persian satrapy of Chorasmia was independent and he received a delegation from the Chorasmian king in the spring of 328 BC. The name Urgench was probably Chinese. The names could be confusing, in part because in the literature they were sometimes used for the province and sometimes for the city. But if there was a convention it seemed to be that Khwarizm and Chorasmia were used for the province, and Urgench and Khiva for the city. Between the early period as a Persian satrapy and the Arab conquest in the eighth century AD, little was known about Khwarizm, except that an ancient Iranian and Zoroastrian culture had apparently survived. Qatiba bin Muslim conquered the province for Islam in 712 AD. There was also a Christian, Greek Orthodox, community in the area.

With the Muslim conquest came a period of disintegration, after which the unity of old Khwarizm was reestablished and the ruler became known as the *Khwarizmshah*. The Seljuk Turks moved into the area in the eleventh century and maintained sovereignty until the next century and a reversal of fortune. The *Khwarizmshah* became the successor to the Seljuk sultans in their rule over all of western Asia. Khwarizm became a world power, with territory that stretched from the *Syr Darya* (the Greek Jaxartes) in the east to the Tigris valley in the west and as far south as the Arabian Peninsula. The source of Khwarizm's power was trade and this precipitated conflict with Genghis Khan. No one emerged intact from such a confrontation, and the province fell to the Mongols in 1221, with the city being razed to the ground. The inhabitants of Urgench were either massacred or drowned in the river. The city was rebuilt shortly thereafter on another site, and Ibn Battuta mentions it in 1333. It gradually returned to its earlier prominence as an emporium, and became the most important land link between eastern Europe and east Asia. Islamic learning and the arts flourished, and the cultural importance of the city gradually grew to rival its commercial importance.

However, this was only a brief respite. Tamerlane conquered Urgench in 1379, razed the city again, and sowed barley over the remains. In the year 1391, he permitted a small part of the city to be rebuilt, although it never regained its previous splendor. After short periods under, first, the Timurids and then the Persians, it fell to the Uzbeks in 1511. Another period of cultural eclipse followed. The caravan route lost most of its importance after the Europeans discovered the seaward passage to India. A decline in the arts followed the commercial decline, or vice versa, in an uncertain relationship. The city of Khiva rose on the old site in the seventeenth century, but it was almost completely destroyed by the Turkmans in 1770. It was rebuilt shortly thereafter. In the following years, there began a series of Russian attempts against Khiva, the Tsars viewing it as a staging point on the road to India. The early attempts were bloody and disastrous, no one in Moscow understanding the difficulty of the sixteen-hundred-kilometer march from the eastern shore of the Caspian where the invasions usually began. Pressures from the Bokharans, Turkmen, Persians, and Russians kept the Khans of Khiva busy and particularly sharpened their powers of intrigue.

Whenever the city had declined over its long history, it had become a center of lawlessness and brigandage, at least in the view of the outside world. Such a decline prevailed throughout most of the nineteenth century and, along with Bokhara, Khiva became notorious in Europe for its malevolent khans and slaving propensities. There were pathetic stories of European slaves, and generations of Russian children heard terrifying tales of the khans of Khiva, the way they had once heard of Genghis Khan or Tamerlane. The Russians finally conquered Khiva in 1873 and reduced the Khan to vassalage. Most of the buildings in the city were of no great antiquity, but dated from the period of Khan Muhammad Amin in the mid–nineteenth century. The Soviets had done a great deal of restoration, as they had elsewhere in Central Asia, and the Khiva we were about to see was billed as a kind of open-air museum.

The afternoon had been restful, reading and chatting on the balcony of the hotel. In Urgench the spring weather was beautiful and we watched chickadees, mynah birds, and mourning doves come and go in the plane trees behind the building. Summer had come early to the Punjab, and Islamabad had been unpleasantly hot when we left. The Hotel Khwarizm was huge, and they expected a trainload of American tourists in the next few days. But I think we were the only ones there at the time. We bought a bottle of the local vodka at the bar from an ethnic Russian who was firmly European in this Central Asian exile. He understood only Russian and looked blankly at us when we tried to describe what we wanted. We thought vodka was vodka in any language, but he seemed to recognize the word only if it was uttered by a native Russian speaker, and we had to point to the bottle to make him understand. The English of the desk clerk was adequate, but he preferred German and John handled the formalities. Even though he had spoken to me in English when we arrived he would afterwards speak only German.

Dinner was *shashlik, nan*, and raw vegetables in the lurid hotel dining room. The vegetables were beautiful—firm, brilliantly red tomatoes, fat cucumbers, green and white onions, and various slaws and grated carrots. This menu, which extended from the Northwest Frontier Province of Pakistan through Uzbekistan, was good, inexpensive, and filling. None of us was sick on the trip, although we ate everything on offer and drank the tap water. Breakfast was more of the same vegetables and nan of the night before, but there were also blintzes, fried eggs, cheese, and salami. Tea came in the usual deep saucers. Coffee was not to be had.

We met Saeeda at eight-thirty for the drive to Khiva. The car was a very clean Lada and Saeeda, the car, and the driver came in a package: thirty-five dollars for six hours. Urgench had the look of new Bokhara, dusty and dun-colored, with the usual monumental medium-rises dominating the skyline. But we soon left the city behind and entered the intensively cultivated countryside. It was difficult to tell what they grew, since the fields were just then being prepared for the seed. The salts appeared heavy on the fringes, but the recently plowed fields looked clean and inviting. The flushing seemed to have worked.

Saeeda had visited San Francisco the year before, the guest of a Chinese-American couple who had come through Khiva. She stayed in Chinatown. She had also seen southern California and her already large eyes widened as she recalled the experience. Her English was excellent. After a drive of about forty minutes we arrived at Khiva and entered the

Khalta Minar, Khiva

city by the *Ata Darwaza*, or western gate. There were a few landmarks in the old city, and they appeared as soon as we were inside the walls. The squat *Kalta Minar* was built, it was said, in a bid to outstrip the Kalyan minaret in Bokhara. But where the monolith in Bokhara dated from 1127, this one was begun in 1852. It was never finished and, rising to a height of only 14.2 meters, it was only about twice as high as it was wide. The horizontal bands were blue, green, and yellow, and it made a nice backdrop to photographs taken from elsewhere in the city. But old it was not and couldn't hold a candle to its counterpart in Bokhara.

Just inside the gate was the Ark, or citadel, dating from 1806, and the view from the rebuilt watchtower was probably the best in the city. The monuments seemed to be clustered around Karl Marx Street, which was the main east-west axis. The minaret of the Dzumha mosque (1789) was straight ahead and that of the taller Islam Khoja madrasa (1908) was visible to the right. Afterwards, we climbed the 118 steps to the top of the latter for another panorama, but the view was restricted and the close little keep stank of the pigeon droppings that covered the floor. The descent was tricky, the spiral staircase narrow and the steps uneven, especially since we had to assume an attitude half bent-back at the waist. My thighs ached for days afterwards.

There were fifteen madrasas in our little map of the city, the earliest listed as dating from 1720 and the latest from 1910. We visited the mausoleum of "Pakhlavan Makhmood," part of which dated from the fourteenth century. There was no "H" in Russian, and the Cyrillic "X" was used to render the aspirated "H" of the Arabic. It was then transliterated as a "KH" into the English, as in the above names. Russian shared this lack with Hebrew and the two languages were hopeless with Arabic, especially with a sound as important as the aspirated "H." Families were coming and going in the mausoleum in a regular stream, and dropping ruble notes into the recess where the catafalque lay. It was hard to tell how much they knew about Islam.

Around the corner, the grim little jail had exhibits of manacles and instruments of torture. On the walls were exhibits of the preferred methods of execution, by hanging, impalement, stoning, and burial alive upside down. Some of the columns in the Dzumha mosque were said to date from an earlier, tenth century building on the same site. It was the most striking visual image of the day, with the sunlight playing like spotlights on several delicate leafy trees in the center. The building was constructed of wood in a city otherwise of dun-colored brick. It seemed low ceilinged, undoubtedly because of the expanse, as it covered about half an acre. When our eyes had adjusted to the dark, we saw that it was being used as a storeroom for carved doors, column bases, and other artifacts, including a black lacquer carriage still in beautiful condition. It had been given to the Khan in the nineteenth century by one of the Tsars.

Khiva had none of the antiquity or beauty of Bokhara. But, in its favor, was the fact that none of the supposed shortcomings of this Central Asian tourist trap was particularly noticeable. There were people here, but they all seemed to be Uzbeks and all seemed to be going about their daily business. The "souvenir hawkers" we had read about were selling the usual unappealing collection of stuff, and there wasn't a tourist brochure to be had. The department store in the restored *caravanserai* was the equivalent of the stores we had seen elsewhere in the FSU, selling everyday tools and clothes. I bought a pottery plate for 200 rubles, passing over the plastic hubcaps, books in Russian and Uzbek, electrical cover plates, cheap tools, insecticides, teapots, and women's winter coats.

The bazaar outside the western wall was a replica in miniature of those we had earlier seen in Tashkent and Samarkand. Although this was not the harvest season of the previous October, there were still green onions, tomatoes, a few squashes, and mounds of peanuts. Snuff, dark green and packed in little plastic bags, was everywhere. We visited a few of the museums and there were some nice collections of carpets, carved woodwork and fabrics. One had a grotesque display of photographs of human birth defects and a pickled fetus with two heads.

We met Saeeda for lunch in the lee of the Ak mosque that dated from 1842. The familiar *shashlik* brazier—a metal stand six feet long by about eight inches wide and the same deep—was set up and we had skewers of meat, raw onions, bread, and bottles of the local beer. A group of young Khiva bloods was sitting at the next table, hooting and snorting and looking very pleased with themselves. Groups of giggling schoolgirls passed by, arms linked, and the boys became quiet as the groups checked each other out. Times had changed. In the jail, there had been a painting of the execution of a pair of young lovers from different social groups. He was hanged and she, buried up to her breasts, was being stoned to death.

We returned to the car through the western gate. On the drive back to Urgench, we all agreed that Khiva had been a disappointment. Bokhara was much more impressive and had the added advantage that it was on the railroad. You could see Tashkent, Bokhara, and Samarkand by buying a single train ticket. Khiva required a separate flight and now we felt that, if we had missed it, we wouldn't have missed much. Our flight to Tashkent was scheduled for five thirty and, after saying goodbye to Saeeda and giving her the customary hard-currency tip, we arranged for the driver to take us to the airport. He insisted on carrying our bags upstairs to a kind of VIP lounge, where pots of still-warm tea and cakes were set up at a table. But four places were set and we decided they were not intended for us.

When we checked in, one of the airport staff inspected our tickets and said that they were not acceptable as Aeroflot did not take tickets from other airlines. But he left when Lucy, the Intourist hostess at the airport, arrived and made everything smooth. She was a large bleached blond with heavily applied lipstick. Lucy walked us, separately, to the plane but then we waited with everyone else for fifteen minutes on the tarmac until the crew arrived and plane was cleaned. During the wait, I asked her what she thought of my ceramic plate and she said it was "not so good." The flight was smooth and we touched down in Tashkent just after seven o'clock. The driver dunned us for the cost of this trip and the previous one, before delivering us to our friends at the Hotel Uzbekistan. They didn't seem overjoyed at seeing us again. We had *shashliks* in the hotel dining room, watched the dancing for a while, and then turned in. This time, there were no phone calls.

To Almata

After breakfast the next morning, we had another unwelcome day in Tashkent. We had asked Svierta to make reservations for us on the afternoon flight to Almata in Kazakhstan, and she had done so. Ludmilla pasted the little change stickers on the coupons and we were set for a five o'clock departure. But it meant that we had most of the day to kill in the city. We used it to pay a return visit to the Museum of Applied Arts where we looked more carefully at several of the carpets. There were many fine *Tekke Bokharas*, Turkman rugs from old Russian Turkestan. The *Tekke* part of the name was a tribal confederation that occupied the area between Khiva and Herat, east of the Caspian. The Bokhara part was just the name by which the carpets were commonly known. If you asked a carpet dealer for a "Bokhara" he knew that you were looking for one of these characteristic Turkman designs.

It was forbidden to take the carpets out of Uzbekistan and the airport at Tashkent was a carefully watched terminus. The few dealers in Islamabad with authentic *Tekke Bokharas* used their Afghan nationality or Pathan ethnicity—foreigners being forbidden—to ride the train to Ashkabad on the Iranian border with Turkmenistan. There they bought the carpets and bribed the customs officials on the way out. I saw several beautiful pieces in a few shops in Islamabad, all of them having been used as wall hangings. The prices differed widely from shop to shop. Some were half the prices another shop asked. But even those were twice the prices in Tashkent. I had looked for several months in Pakistan before buying one at a price I thought was a steal. But the prices here were much better.

At the museum, we also met the entrepreneur we recognized from our first visit. He now had a partner, along with his collection of coffee table books on Central Asia. His English seemed to have deteriorated over the six months and we communicated by means of sign language and pidgin English. The only word we seemed to have in common was "bucks" and we haggled over how many bucks the books were worth. He said the ones we wanted were at his home, so we agreed to meet him at three o'clock under the statue of Karl Marx in the park across the street from the hotel. He was not welcome in the hotel itself.

Each of us went separately to our surreptitious rendezvous. By the time I reached the park, John had already completed his transaction. The man and his partner were parked in a Lada at a corner of the park and they motioned to the back seat when I reached the car. It was all very furtive. The illustrated book on Khiva was nice but they had an even nicer one on all three cities Khiva, Bokhara, and Samarkand, beautifully printed in Moscow in 1987. After negotiation, we agreed on a price of fifteen bucks. The text was all in Russian but I could use it as an excuse to learn the Cyrillic alphabet. Elizabeth arrived just as I left and took my place in the back seat of the car. She bought a book on Central Asian handicrafts and we walked back to the hotel feeling a little like parasites or social undesirables.

We had just enough time to check out and pay for the van. We arrived at the airport at about four o'clock and took our familiar places in the Intourist departure terminal. There were several other foreigners there, including a pair of reptilian Indian tea merchants on their way to Almata, and the Reverend Nathaniel Ungam Kiel, the emeritus pastor of the Korean United Presbyterian Church of New Jersey. He was now pastor of the Calvary Presbyterian Church of Almata, but his home was Glen Ridge, New Jersey. Elizabeth's father was from Glen Ridge and they had a bit of a chat on the unlikely chain of events that had brought them together in, of all places, Uzbekistan. Stalin had moved minorities like chess pieces around the Soviet Union during the 1930s and there were 50,000 Koreans in Tashkent alone.

We checked our bags and went upstairs to the lounge. At five-thirty there was an announcement that the flight to Almata had been delayed and would now depart at eight o'clock. We were sitting in the lounge with the two Indians, three Russians with gunnysacks full of purses and backpacks for sale, and two Africans from Sierra Leone. One of the Africans, an agricultural student who was the spitting image of James Baldwin, was returning to school in Almata. The other had been waiting here for two days for a flight to Moscow, and they were both asleep at one end of the lounge. We had dinner in the cafe and returned to the waiting room in time for the announcement that the flight had been further delayed. We discussed the problem among ourselves and the Indians said that the problem was that there probably was no fuel. I wondered aloud if we would even get out of Tashkent, but one of the Africans bestirred himself just long enough to say that everything would be fine if we were patient. And, so it was.

Because, very suddenly at eight-thirty, came the announcement for departure and we were taken in our own transporter to the Tu-154 that had just arrived from Almata. After the usual wait, the locals arrived and the forward part of the plane quickly filled with passengers. They were like passengers everywhere, rushed and burdened, and they sank into their cramped seats with obvious relief. At nine-thirty-five the plane took off, the engines humming very reassuringly as we rose into the inky blackness. The seat belts worked and no-smoking signs in both Russian and English showed on the forward bulkhead. The only difference from an American flight was the service. The cabin soon filled with the aroma of food, but the plates were carried the length of the plane and onto the flight deck. Only the crew were fed. After a very smooth flight, the plane touched down at ten-forty-five, Tashkent time. But there was a difference of two hours, and in Almata it was almost one o'clock in the morning. We waited, as usual, for the crew to deplane and then left.

We were taken to the Intourist arrival lounge where the Rev. Kiel offered us a ride to the hotel in his church van. After about forty-five minutes the baggage arrived, but there were several cases of religious tracts missing and we grew tired of waiting while they tried to locate them. Meanwhile, the little man from Sierra Leone said that he was concerned about traveling late at night by himself. They didn't like blacks in Almata and he was afraid the cab would be stopped and he would be beaten up. So, we agreed to share a cab and he would drop us at our hotel. It wasn't easy because the African had two huge bags and each of us had one, plus carry-ons. After we had put one of his monsters and one of ours in the trunk of the Lada, it was full and we wedged ourselves and the remaining bags into the front of the car. The African had his other bag, which must have weighed seventy-five pounds, between his legs in the front seat, and it was so high he couldn't see over the top. We hurtled off into the night. The African made the arrangements and each of us paid 1,000 rubles. He said he would pay 2,000, but I am sure we financed his trip. It was two-thirty when we arrived at the hotel. The lobby was deserted and so was the rest of the hotel. When we finally fell into bed it was nearly three a.m.

We awakened on Tashkent time. There was plenty of hot water in the bathroom and the heated towel racks actually worked. But the towels were, as usual, small and thin and the soap was the standard quarter-bar. We were to meet at eight o'clock for breakfast and as we left the room we met with an extraordinary sight. There, visible through a window at the end of the hall, were the snow-covered Tian Shen, or Heavenly Mountains, at 15,000 feet, very rugged and framed by the soft greens of the spring foliage in the foreground. It was even more breathtaking for being utterly unexpected. We had read that Almata was not in the steppes like the rest of Kazakhstan, but had its head or its feet—I forgot which—in the mountains. But we were not prepared for this view and we went back to see it, over and over again.

The restaurant was in the shape of a yurt, the felt tent of Central Asia, and the walls were covered with Persian miniatures. Breakfast was the familiar yogurt, cheese, bread, and green tea. Afterwards Miriam, the lady in the Intourist office, outlined our touristic options. This was the thirtieth of April and the following day was a Saturday, and the first of May. There would be a "demonstration"—a happy demonstration, she stressed—on May Day, and everything in the city would be closed. The likelihood of finding a car to take us to Bishkek in Kyrgyzstan was very remote, as all the roads would also be closed. Therefore, we should see as much of Almata as we could today and spend the next day, like everyone else, at the fair. We were already more than a day behind schedule and wanted to see the Fergana Valley before we left. So, we made the decision that had been obvious from the first day: we would skip Bishkek, and return to Tashkent the following afternoon. Miriam said that she would make the arrangements but it would cost five dollars per ticket. We could pick up the tickets the next morning.

She was a funny little lady with short, hennaed hair and a ready wit. When I said that I had been taken for a Turkman the day before, she said that I must have had a "steppe-grandfather," and we all had a good laugh. She looked to be in her fifties and was an ethnic Kazakh. Unlike several others we met in the city, she had actually spoken the language as a child. We talked about the systems of writing that had been used in this part of the world and discussed the Arabic, Latin, and then Cyrillic alphabets that had rapidly succeeded one another in the 1920s. She knew about them but growing up hadn't seen either of the first two:

> I may be old but I'm not *that* old.

She pronounced the name of the city "Almat*uh*," and so did everyone else we met over the next two days, explaining that this was the authentic sound in the Kazakh language. The State Department had recently sent out a cable to all diplomatic and consular posts with the information that

> Department is adopting 'Almaty' as the official spelling of the capital of Kazakhstan and the Embassy Alma Ata will henceforth be known as the Embassy Almaty.

The cable went on to say that this was a correction of the Russified version of the name and that the change had been made at the request of the Kazakh government. But no one we talked to in the city pronounced it "Almaty." I later learned that it meant "a place of apples" in Kazakh. Etymologies were always suspect, and we had no way of knowing whether this made any sense. It sounded plausible enough. But I later looked in Redhouse's *Turkish and English Lexicon* and there was a tantalizing connection:

> Elma. The apple tree and fruit . . .

The name of the "Kazakhs" as a people and a country was apparently of relatively recent origin. They were originally all known as Kyrgyz, a nomadic people from Mongolia. Grousset says that after their separation from the Uzbek Khanate in the fifteenth century, some of these nomads came to be known as "Qazaqs." But I had long since given up trying to make any sense of Qazaqs, or Kazakhs, Kyrgyz, Mongols, Turks, Uzbeks, Tungus, Uigurs, Kipchaks, Turkomans, and Tatars. They were all nomads from the same general area and they had flowed in an epochal surge to the west that took place over centuries. What we knew for certain was that, after the Russian Revolution, "Kazakhstan" became an administrative unit and later a republic in the USSR.

There were a few exceptions to the rule of Turkic peoples in Central Asia, including the remarkable survival of the original Iranian stock in the Tajiks. The Russians constituted 40 percent of the population of Kazakhstan, and that made Almata almost a Russian city. Bokhara, Khiva, and Urgench had been dusty, steppe cities full of Asians. But Almata was thoroughly European and there would be times over the next two days, particularly at the fair, when we thought we might have been in Europe or the United States.

We arranged for a mountain tour and it was expensive by Central-Asian standards, twenty dollars an hour for the guide, car, and driver. Miriam said that if we were clever we could get a little city tour thrown in at the beginning or the end. At ten o'clock we met our guide, Deena, in the lobby. She looked very Japanese, with lacquered hair worn in a kind of 1930s bouffant, stylish and with very white skin. The car was a van with the usual crack in the windshield. Deena also pronounced the city "Almatuh." We were soon in the foothills of the Tian Shen and it was very pretty: little streams of snowmelt, and stands of birch, just coming into leaf. We drove for half an hour before coming to the end of the line in a kind of bowl where a large stadium lay. Deena told us it had been built for the 1988 speed-skating world championships and had artificial ice. She added, with evident pride, that it was a world-class facility. However, the championships had been a disappointment. Americans had won most of the races and "we"— she meant the Soviet Union—had been shut out.

Deena seemed to be a representative of an old-style, unrepentant Marxism. She was Kazakh but had never learned the language. Her parents, now retired, had both been party members and they didn't like Yeltsin. She had traveled widely, particularly to socialist countries like Egypt and Yugoslavia. She maintained another flat in Moscow and considered it her second home. What was happening in Russia was terrible. As a matter of fact, there may have been a little of the Chinese model at work in Kazakhstan: economic change before political change. The local strongman, Nursultan Nazarbayev was a pal of Yeltsin, but he kept the lid on politically. Prices were higher than in the old days, but people seemed well dressed and well fed.

The stadium was impressive, particularly from the vantage point of the earth-fill dam high above at the head of a valley. We walked to the top but, at an altitude of over 5,000 feet, the 800 steps were hard work and we stopped to rest several times. The surrounding slopes were still covered with patchy snow and there were what looked like many ski runs. This was a recreational area in the winter. The dam was designed to prevent flash floods, as too much snowmelt or too great a volume of water could threaten the city below.

On the return to the hotel we passed a convoy of armored personnel carriers, with their headlights on. The hatches were open and several heads, in the rounded Soviet tanker's caps that looked like second-world-war aviator's headgear, made bulges in the otherwise smooth surfaces. The vehicles looked menacing, somehow like prehistoric animals. It was only a few years since we had done everything we could to drive these same people out of Afghanistan. Some of these men had probably served in that disastrous war.

Miriam's advice had been sound, and we managed a short tour of the city before we said goodbye to Deena and the driver. We had lunch at the hotel. The tour may have been expensive by Khiva standards, but the food was not. The lunch, a plate of smoked horsemeat, Kazakh noodles in a heavy broth, *nan*, and a bottle of Georgian wine, cost next to nothing. The meat accounted for most of the cost and Elizabeth declined to taste it on principle. She was a rider and explained a sociological study that related the animals we ate to their distance from the symbolic hearth. Horses were definitely not candidates for the pot. The meat was a little sweeter than beef.

We spent the afternoon walking around the city. The Zenkov Cathedral, supposedly the tallest wooden structure in the FSU, was across the street in Panfilov Park. Later, we went up to the top floor of the hotel and a combination of the spires of the cathedral, the green of the park, and backdrop of the Tian Shen was even more spectacular than our first view. However, the cathedral was being restored and was closed and locked. We strolled up *Ulitsa Furmanova* towards the Central State museum, which we had seen briefly that morning. On the way, we came across an unexpected sight: the American Embassy, newly painted in

Spetsnaz, Almata

pastel blue and white. The flag was lying limp in the afternoon stillness, but the red, white, and blue was still striking against the light-blue background. The embassy guards, members of the *spetsnaz*, or Soviet special forces, were recognizable in their blue and white striped T-shirts. They were the only Soviet troops that had amounted to much in Afghanistan.

The museum was impressive, with displays of everything from primitive man in Central Asia to space travel. We watched a slide presentation in the round, showing the process of evolution from the primordial soup to early man, and the children present were rapt. It would probably be easy as a child to grow up in Almata and believe that you were in the vanguard of everything in the world that was modern and scientific. The distress of some at the disintegration of the Soviet Union became more understandable as I looked at those little faces, so open and eager and interested. But the other side of the coin was the inertia of the system, and what it made people do to one another. It wasn't so much an evil empire as a monstrous system that devoured its own. What the outside world now represented was openness and freedom. We would see plenty of that the next day.

The museum also had carpets for sale, most of them large, dark Kazakh pieces in geometric patterns. They were nice but none of us had room to spare in our bags, even had we been interested. We took a cab back to the hotel. Dinner was more noodles in a side room in the restaurant. There was a wedding in the yurt, and earlier in the evening we had seen the staff making preparations: bottles of scotch, vodka, and champagne set next to the flowers on each table. When we arrived, the place was packed and we shared a table with a couple who were there for dinner. He was Russian and she was Kazakh. There seemed to be many mixed marriages, although I don't think these two were married. With the perfunctory politeness of this part of the world he offered to buy our dinner, but we wound up buying them a bottle of champagne. After dinner, we had a vodka in a nightclub in Panfilov Park, across the street. The place was full of young Russians and Kazakhs dancing to a band playing live western music. Then we turned in. Tomorrow would be the "happy demonstration" and we wanted to get an early start.

More Almata

I was up early the next morning and before breakfast I walked to Gorky Park, fifteen minutes away on *Ulitsa Gogolya*. Gorky and Gogol were storied Russian names and I read somewhere that Leon Trotsky had been exiled in Almata before the revolution. The park was huge and leafy green. After breakfast, we settled our outstanding bills. We paid Miriam the fifteen dollars, collected our tickets and checked out of the Otrar. There was another surprise, but this time a pleasant one. Since we had arrived at two thirty in the morning on the first day it was considered only a partial day and the bill was for a day and a-half. Probably no other hotel in the world would have calculated it this way. After we added the individual bills together, weighted them and divided by three, it worked out to thirty-four dollars a night per person.

We strolled the mile up Furmanova Street at a leisurely pace. When we arrived at the area where had seen yurts being set up the day before, the demonstration was in full swing. The square was dominated by several hot air balloons, painted psychedelic colors and straining at their moorings. The technicians periodically admitted more gas to the flame and they surged briefly, before hissing and falling back to the ground. Everyone's eyes were drawn upward because biplanes were dropping parachutist after parachutist who came in very fast over the square, their legs pumping before landing in a large circle in the middle. Later, another plane came back and ran through its paces, steep climbs followed by what looked like a stall, loop-the-loops, and perpendicular dives at the crowd, before pulling out at the last minute. There was a collective gasp and then a roar with each pass.

May Day, Almata

The aerial acrobatics, especially with the Tian Shen as a backdrop, were spectacular. But it was really the people who stood out. There were tens of thousands of them, of every ethnic background and in every kind of dress. It was difficult to say which ones were Korean and which Kazakhs or which, for that matter, were the mixtures. There were also many Caucasian and Eurasian faces, about the percentage you would expect in a place whose population was 40 percent European and the rest Asian. Most people were happy to have their pictures taken. Armies of little girls in uniforms of red, yellow and blue tutus, with huge bows in their hair, were everywhere.

There were a few old men and women in ethnic Kazakh dress, and girls in what looked like eastern European peasant outfits. We missed the remarks from the reviewing stand, a quarter of a mile away across the square. It looked like it belonged in Red Square, a monolithic red granite wall with hatted, faceless functionaries peering over the top. In the crowd, there were the usual old men in the suit coats that constituted a kind of proletarian uniform. On the lapels were rows of medals, probably from the Great Patriotic War, during which the Red Army had systematically raped its way across Eastern Europe. The thought added a somber note to the festive atmosphere. But the men and their medals looked like anachronisms. This was a young crowd and images from America were everywhere. Jack Lang's cultural imperialism was alive and well.

Baseball caps, not those things with limp bills that everyone else seemed to make, but real American ball caps with high peaks and stiff brims, were on thousands of heads. They were probably made in Taiwan, but that was only another refinement of the phenomenon. I saw one with "USA" and "California" stenciled across the front, and the little boy underneath it gave me the thumbs-up. Someone described the ball cap as the tonsorial equivalent of the T-shirt, and there were plenty of those as well with the usual international signatures: "Chanel, Paris," or "Tanglewood," or "Def Leppard." It was not unusual to see a little boy in Levi's, T-shirt, and ball cap and wearing shoes that were probably endorsed by Diego Maradona or Michael Jordan.

All this must have been incomprehensible to the old men, and there were the usual grumblings about things not being the way they used to be. But times had changed and there seemed to be promise in the changes. It was evidence of a common cultural language that would probably be all to the good. We hoped that things like the yurts and horsemeat and fermented mare's milk would stay, and that these people would be spared some of the excesses of our own popular culture. But we could hope all we wanted. Change had come and there was no holding it back.

At lunch the attempt to buy almost anything brought us down from our international high and sharply back to reality. There were too many people struggling for too few goods, and the lethargic attendants simply turned their backs when the press became too great. They were gratuitously unpleasant, but we bore it patiently, standing with everyone else, rubles held out. Eventually we bought a few pastries filled with cream cheese and green onions. There were other things to see: organized competitions involving the medicine-ball toss, skipping rope, and weightlifting. There were also a few yurts set up and furnished in the traditional fashion. They had a wooden latticework frame, around which the felt was draped. The lattice was held together with hard leather balls.

Our flight to Tashkent was scheduled for five-thirty, and we began the trek back to the hotel early in the afternoon. It had been a leisurely day and a-half in Almata, and we were sorry to leave. There was nothing particularly Central Asian about it. The city may have been an old Silk Road site, but it was heavily Russian and very different from Khiva. We were sorry to have missed Bishkek and the Pamirs, but there was always Fergana where we looked forward to a sylvan retreat. We imagined leafy trees and crystal-clear brooks, and maybe a picnic while we dangled our feet in the stream. The reality would be somewhat different.

At the Otrar they told us that calling a cab would take an hour, so we flagged down a car in the street and the driver agreed for 200 rubles to take us to the airport. His name was Rahman and he was different looking, but I couldn't put my finger on the difference. He might have been Azeri or Armenian, but he turned out to be Daghestani. They were the Muslim people in the eastern Caucasus and had been as difficult to subdue as the Circassians in the west. He parked the car and insisted on carrying our bags into the terminal building. We asked for the departure desk and were directed to the Intourist terminal where we had waited for our bags that first night. It seemed like weeks before. Check-in began promptly at four-ten at the Air Kazakhstan counter, and we were impressed with the efficiency. This was a real airline, with a pretty uniformed attendant, a computerized reservation system, baggage tags, and boarding cards. We went through a security system that actually worked, and took our places in the departure lounge. Then we boarded the ubiquitous Tu-154 and the plane lifted off at five twenty-five, five minutes early.

Shortly after takeoff the stewardess came down the aisle with a tray of snacks for sale, including caviar and Snickers bars. Snickers, at 348 rubles for the small bar, were everywhere in Central Asia. The weather was good and we watched as the Tian Shen gradually disappeared behind us. But then cloud cover appeared and it was overcast when we landed in Tashkent. The time change meant that it was still early in the evening. The van was waiting to take us to the Hotel Uzbekistan where we checked in for the third time in the past six days.

After leaving our bags in the rooms, we went to see Ludmila about arrangements for Fergana. By now we were veterans and we uttered hardly a word of protest when she said that we didn't have visas for Fergana. She was right, again. In our relief and haste at Ghulam ed-Din's we had gotten visas only for Urgench and Khiva. However, we had his telephone number. We called, but he didn't answer at home. Tomorrow was Sunday, added Ludmila with more enthusiasm than necessary, and the office would be closed. But we weren't beaten yet, and we decided to gather in our room, have a drink and review our few options. We had a liter of *Rasputin* vodka we had bought in Almata almost for the name alone, although when we read the label we saw that it was imported from Germany. But vodka was vodka. I had packed it, wrapped in layers of clothes, and it had survived the flight. John had bought a couple of tins of caviar, which he had also packed. At least we could enjoy ourselves while we considered our conundrum.

John was talking over his shoulder as he rummaged through the left side of his suitcase, but he grew silent as he moved to the right, then back to the left, then again to the right. The caviar was gone. And so was his camera. I remembered that I had packed the leather jacket I had just bought in Islamabad on the top, to cushion the vodka. It, too, was gone. Elizabeth was the only one who locked her suitcase and hers was the only one that arrived intact. Now, we weren't so sure that this was funny anymore. Our fund of good humor was dangerously close to exhaustion. But we did have the vodka, and we did what any Russian would have done under the circumstances: we got roaring drunk. Our mood swings were wild. First there was helpless anger, followed by shame as we considered our stupidity. The loss to the two of us was about $500, and it was criminal on our part to have put temptation in the way of people as poor as these. Finally, the whole situation—the missing visas, the wasted time, the lost property, the entire trip—struck us as ridiculous. If there had been someone in the hall outside the door he would have heard an eruption of hysterical laughter, rising to a crescendo before fading away into individual, pitiable whimpers.

The next morning, more soberly, John drafted a letter to the ministries of tourism in both Uzbekistan and Kazakhstan. He informed them of the theft and suggested that if they wanted foreign tourism and the hard currency it brought, they had better do better than this. He used what leverage he had as a senior diplomat. We didn't expect the camera and jacket back again, or even that they would make restitution. But we hoped to make enough noise that those responsible would think twice about doing the same thing again.

Meanwhile, there was Fergana. We had one card left and now we played it. The other Ludmila, our old guide from the first trip, lived in Tashkent and we had her telephone number. John placed the call while Elizabeth and I watched a Russia-Sweden hockey match on television. The old CCCP jerseys were gone, but the Cyrillic "S" in Russia meant that there were almost as many "C's" across the front of the new jerseys, and the squad was as powerful as ever. They were beating the Swedes handily. Ludmila was at home, celebrating the birthday of one of her children. Yes, it sounded like we had a problem. Fergana was about six hours away by car, not the two hours Omar had told us in Pakistan, but it could be managed in a day. There was a family friend at the party and he had a car—it wasn't much of a car, she added—and he might be willing to take us there. There was a pause in the conversation while she discussed the proposition with him.

Yes, the friend was amenable and the sixty dollars John mentioned seemed reasonable. His name was Yuri and we agreed to meet him in the hotel parking lot a six o'clock the next morning. He was about fifty, said Ludmila, and we would know him by his red car. And, she added, he had been a world-class cyclist when he was younger. We weren't sure what this meant on a trip by car. But we were to discover that he drove the way he rode, with a great deal of body English, as it were. The people at Intourist had all pronounced the Fergana trip impossible, as anything out of the ordinary was in their world. We didn't have visas, and two Dutchmen we had seen earlier in the evening had been turned back at the bus station in their attempt to go to Samarkand. They also didn't have visas. But we had tried to go *through* Intourist and, only when that didn't work, were we now going *around* Intourist. We had risen from the ashes once more and would soon be on our way to Fergana.

Fergana

Yuri was there at six a.m., standing by his red car. It was an older Lada and we gave it a rapid, but discreet, once-over as we introduced ourselves. It would be our home for the next thirteen hours. The tread looked adequate, but there were problems with the sidewalls: there was an external patch on one of the rear tires and a noticeable hernia on the right front. But this was no time to be faint at heart, and we got in. To begin with, I rode in the front seat with Yuri. There were no seatbelts and the windshield, like every windshield in Uzbekistan, was cracked, this one in two places. I sat well back in the seat as we pulled out of the parking lot, but after a while I grew tired of leaning backwards. If we hit something it wouldn't make any difference anyway.

Part of our reason for wanting to see Fergana was F. M. Bailey, the British officer sent to Tashkent in 1919 to find out what the Soviets were up to. He spent eighteen months in Central Asia, most of the time in disguise and most of it trying to stay one step ahead of the Cheka, predecessor to the NKVD, and then the KGB. His book, *Mission to Tashkent*, was a masterpiece of understatement. In fact, it was so understated that it was almost boring. We knew all about the banality of evil, and these Central Asian Bolsheviks had been simple thugs and murderers. But his account also seemed to say how commonplace it was to be a spy. It was not the "Great Game" thriller it was supposed to be. As far as I was concerned that counted in its favor.

Bailey had spent several months at a bee farm sixty miles east of Tashkent and I somehow identified this with Fergana. But as we left the environs of the city I read some of the names on Bailey's itinerary to Yuri, he looked puzzled. He wanted to look at the map in the book, but we persuaded him to give his full attention to the road. As the miles went by it became clear that we were not going in the direction of Bailey's bee farm. But another attraction of Fergana was that it was the source of the "heavenly horses" of Chinese fame, and it was supposed to be very fertile. We had bought some extra *nan* and *piroshkis* at the restaurant the night before and we still had a little of the vodka. Yuri had brought along some bottled water and soft drinks, and we were all looking forward to our sylvan picnic.

At about six-thirty we saw mountains ahead of us and thought that they were the Pamirs. But Yuri said that they were the Tian Shen. Our conversation was in monosyllables as he understood very little English and we almost no Russian. He knew a few of the German numbers and they were useful later in the day. He was a trim little man with graying sandy hair and a mouth full of gleaming gold teeth. He *looked* like a cyclist, and managed to make us understand that he had been to Prague, Berlin, and Sofia for competitions. Several of Bailey's acquaintances in Tashkent had been executed because their hands were too smooth. The same could not be said of Yuri. He had the calluses of a mechanic with grease under the nails and on the cuticles that no amount of scrubbing would remove. We asked him what he did and he told us, in sign language, that he was, in fact, an auto mechanic.

The weather was good and we were making excellent time. After half an hour, we turned parallel with the mountains and Yuri began to give the Lada its head. The speedometer climbed to 120 kilometers per hour, or about seventy miles per hour, and the rural scenery flew by. I am sure Ludmila had told him the foreigners wanted to go to the city of Fergana, and he knew how long it would take. He had done the trip by bicycle several times before. The road was good and there was almost no traffic, this being a Sunday. At seven-forty-five we saw the ominous shape of the cooling towers of a power plant ahead. But although they looked like Three Mile Island it was a conventional facility and burned soft coal from an open pit nearby. Yuri told us that the name of the plant was Angren. The pit was huge, and must have been one of the largest open-pit coalmines in the FSU, if not the world. The terraced levels of the immense scar disappeared from view as they wound into the earth, and the tracks and rail cars on the opposite side were barely visible. The name of the pit was also Angren.

We then climbed to the top of an earth-fill dam that kept the water away from the pit below. Yuri said that the name of the dam was Angren, and he must have been as tired of answering the question as we were of asking it. He talked expansively with his hands and we soon learned to ration our questions, asking them only on relatively straight parts of the road. He had a few stock gestures, one a kind of gathering motion with both hands, another that meant "one half," and a third that said he didn't know. I thought of the fine motor-movement of the Chinese as he talked, but Yuri was a Russian and his hands were blunt instruments. Now, we began to climb and the stupendous mountains unfolded on either side of the road. Yuri was getting into it. He grinned his golden grin and gradually became one with the car, leaning with it on the curves and relaxing as we plunged down some particularly precipitous grade. He seemed to know all the tricks of a racer, and if there had been another car to draft on he probably would have done that too.

We stopped to stretch our legs and take a few pictures near a village. It was smooth and green up to where the snow began, then rugged peaks up to their junction with the sky. Clouds like cotton balls went scudding by. Tall poplars, straight as reeds, had just come into leaf and they filled the spaces between the little houses. We would see other poplars farther on that were still barren, the difference in elevation meaning a difference in their biological clocks. Still we climbed, and the scenery began to look like the lower Himalayas, perhaps the Kagan Valley. The green gradually disappeared and then it became all snow and ice. The road was washed away in many places and Yuri slowed just enough to negotiate his way between the slides—wet masses of earth and ice—and the gorge, a thousand feet below. I would have slowed still more, but Yuri knew what he was doing. He had to deliver his charges to Fergana before noon and he was right on schedule. We gradually understood that, for him, Fergana was the city on the far side of the valley of the same name.

Finally, we reached the summit at over 8,000 feet, with mountains another 9,000 feet higher all around us. We slowed just enough to read the numbers on the monument and do the mental arithmetic that changed them into the English system. Then we plunged down the other side. The landscape was the same, in reverse, as what we had seen on the way up. The river was running in spate, and many little bridges were damaged or washed away. Gradually, the poplars became green again and by the time we reached the bottom, we were back in relatively familiar surroundings. But this was different from the Tashkent side. Flocks of sheep and shepherds on horseback dotted the hills, which were all rocks, loose scree, and scrub. However, we quickly left this little nomadic interlude behind and the landscape and the sociology changed again. We were now in the Fergana Valley.

It was not what we imagined. Dusty, dun-colored fields fringed with green stretched away as far as the eye could see, and there wasn't a mountain in sight. Except for the mulberry trees, it looked like the Sacramento Valley.

At nine-fifty we crossed the Syr Darya, the old Jaxartes. It was wide and brown. Ten minutes later Yuri slowed as we entered Kokhand, and we stopped to see what was left of the old city. He didn't fool around in the populated areas and religiously observed the speed limit. We had passed several radar speed traps, but he seemed to know them all. We were stopped at a couple of checkpoints and had rehearsed our story if they asked who we were. I tried to lounge inconspicuously in the front seat and hoped I still looked like a Turkman. But each time Yuri left the car with his documents and handled the formalities himself.

Kokhand had once been second only to Bokhara in Central Asia, with hundreds of mosques and madrasas. Politically, it formed a kind of unholy trinity with Bokhara and Khiva, the three competing for the prize as the most inhuman of these Central Asian khanates. But after its brief fling with independence in 1918, the Bolsheviks razed the city to the ground and massacred thousands of its inhabitants. There had been recent problems as well over the number of mosques the government would permit. Only the Khan's palace remained from the pre-revolutionary period. It was now a museum and we wandered through exhibits of cotton and silk culture, old photographs, maps, and stuffed animals of the Fergana region: wild boar, coyotes, bear, porcupines, badgers, deer, and antelope. Done well, taxidermy could be beautiful. But these were amateur efforts, with the ears falling off and the stuffing coming out, pathetic approximations of the real thing.

We saw what little remained of the palace grounds and took a few photographs. One pretty Uzbek girl in a blue denim dress agreed to pose in front of the gate, and then orchestrated a whole series of portraits. She lined up what looked like brothers or sisters or cousins and monopolized me for several minutes, moving them in and out and rearranging the grouping. But we left before she could give us her name and address, clearly what she intended. Yuri now became lost, and we began to second-guess him since we could see and read the signs ourselves. But he proved to be as resourceful as ever, and at twelve-thirty, six and a-half hours into the trip, we passed through an arch that announced the limits of the city of Fergana. The immediate impression was of green, with huge trees overhanging the wide boulevards so that we couldn't see the sky overhead. We made a little tour of the town before Yuri found the bazaar and we stopped for lunch.

We now saw a side of Yuri that made him even more endearing. He offered to pay for lunch, but we declined and I gave him a 500-ruble note. He returned with the change, 270 rubles, all in ten-ruble notes, and they made a fat bulge in my pocket. But it was his manner that we noticed and by the end of the day we would come to recognize it as vintage Yuri. The table in the little outdoor restaurant was dirty, so he cleaned it. He used the white towel the old babushka was using to wipe the plates, and she was furious. We couldn't understand a word of her Russian, but we didn't need to, to see how angry she was. Yuri didn't pay her the slightest attention. He brought us bowls of broth, big deep things filled with a mixture of what looked like pearl barley and vegetables, and a couple of plates of pilav. It wasn't our babbling brook but we were hungry, so we broke out the *nan* and *piroshkis* from the night before and ate like trenchermen. The crowds in the nearby street were mostly Uzbek, but there was a fair number of young Russians in the mix. This was a garrison town and it was full of soldiers. An unfortunate with Down syndrome appeared, baying and howling and hopping over puddles. Everyone ignored him. The victims of Mongolism looked the same the world over, even here among the Mongols.

After we finished the meal Yuri went back for tea and served us all in deep saucers. It wouldn't have surprised me if he had been in the kitchen, telling the cook that there was too much barley and not enough meat in the soup. Then he gathered the bowls and saucers together in a little pile and then we left. Half a plate of the pilav went to an old woman sitting at the next table. The babushka was still muttering and she delivered a parting shot on the way out, but Yuri ignored her. Elizabeth and I turned and tried, unsuccessfully, to get a photograph of the trees and the avenues as we left town. But we had seen Fergana and Yuri now turned the nose of the little red car towards Tashkent and home.

We made better time on the way back. John took my place in the front seat with Yuri and they talked a little in German. Yuri didn't seem to have much use for the locals, and he gestured contemptuously at a cluster of houses under construction. They were built in the Uzbek style, wood-frame with balls of mud filling the walls, and the whole thing plastered over with mud. He called them *serays*, the Turkish word for palace or mansion, and there was no mistaking the sarcasm in his voice. We stopped for gas and discovered that he had two jerry cans of fuel lashed upright in the trunk. He set up folding picnic chairs for us as he carried out the refueling operation. Afterwards, the miles in the valley flew by and we passed the short steppe interlude, before entering the mountains.

On the way through the mountains, we stopped several times by the side of the road to buy mushrooms, huge things eight inches in diameter in piles tended by men sitting in chairs. Yuri bought mushrooms the way he did everything else, utterly oblivious to everyone and everything around him. He negotiated a price for the pile and bought them all, leaving the two nicely-dressed gentlemen waiting in line behind him empty handed and a little befuddled. The second time we emptied the contents of Elizabeth's backpack and he filled it with mushrooms, some for Ludmila. They pickled them. As we hurtled down the Tashkent side of the pass we began to hear the troubling sound of vibration in the suspension on the right side of the car. Yuri stopped and we all had a look. A plastic bushing that held the shaft of the tie-rod in place had come off, and the whole assembly was vibrating. At the speed we took some of the potholes, it was not surprising. But nothing was broken and we pressed on.

Later, children were selling bunches of bright red poppies, and Elizabeth wanted to buy a bouquet. But we passed too many and by the time we stopped, it must have been the last of them. As they approached the car I stood to take a photo and they bolted like deer, disappearing over the side of the mountain. It was the last we saw of the children or the poppies. The final few hours were boring, over the uninteresting road we had covered that same morning. Yuri was still going strong, and when we pulled into the parking lot of the Hotel Uzbekistan it was only six-thirty and still light. We unloaded the car, dividing the goods and making sure that we had everything that was ours. Yuri had been great. We talked at the beginning about giving him twenty dollars apiece, or the sixty that was the price we had agreed on. But we later decided among ourselves to give him thirty each, and he accepted the ninety dollars with his golden grin. It was the equivalent of nearly 75,000 rubles, many times his monthly salary. But in the terms of trade in this little transaction both parties had benefitted and we had received value for money. We had become friends and he and I nearly embraced when we shook hands. But it was one of those awkward moments when neither of us knew what to do and the moment passed.

So, we had done it. Anwar and Ludmila and the fat lady in purple, Svierta and Rahima and the blond at the bank—they had all done their best to thwart us. Maybe we had been lucky and we had not been stopped, like the Dutchmen. But we had gone to Fergana and back and they didn't even know it. We weren't about to tell them.

Home

The next morning at breakfast I spoke with an American professor from the University of New Mexico who was in Uzbekistan on a short-term assignment, teaching teachers of English. The complaints she heard were consistent and predictable: from the Russians, that they had brought civilization and progress to these people and all they got in return was ingratitude; from the Uzbeks that they had been culturally emasculated for the past seventy years and it was time for a change.

Our flight was at three o'clock and we had half a day to kill. We spent it making the familiar rounds. The cab driver on the way back to the hotel from the museum was a dark old Uzbek, but it turned out that he had been in the Soviet Foreign Service and spoke Arabic. He had spent eight years in the Yemen, Baghdad, and then as the first consul in Cairo. His two sons were in the University of the East in Tashkent. He used the Arabic word *mashriq* for the east. As it turned out, he wasn't a cab at all, but just driving around the city trying to earn a little extra money, and he seemed happy with the 200 rubles we gave him. In a different era, we might have had darker suspicions.

We checked out of the hotel and the bill was the usual complicated combination of dollars and rubles at different rates. The woman at the desk was new, at least to us, and we had to correct her calculations several times. She had a long nose and huge, luminous eyes and looked like she may have been Jewish or Armenian. We spoke in French:

Vous êtes Russe, madam?

Non, Uzbek, monsieur.

She spoke in a pleasant kind of singsong, and I fell into the rhythm myself. After we paid the bill she went away and I asked the other woman at the desk, still in my singsong French, where to buy a bolt of the famous Uzbek silk.

Parlez–vous Francais, madame?

English!!

She spat the word at me. Her rapid-fire directions followed:

> Take the metro to Navol station, two stops away. When you come out of the station, you will see a large commercial street. There are many stores where you can buy silk. But you must have coupons. Since you do not have coupons, you cannot buy silk there.

Seeing my obvious confusion, she added:

> Go out the hotel entrance and turn right. There are many stores nearby where you can buy silk.

Eventually, I bought the silk in the hotel shop. At 700 rubles, or about eighty cents, a meter, I couldn't go too far wrong. We paid Anwar for the van and took leave of our many Intourist friends at the hotel.

But they weren't through with us yet. The officer at check-in at the airport told us that our visas had expired and we had to have them renewed before they would let us out of the country. The next flight didn't leave until the following Thursday. We argued, saying that the visas were good on each subsequent return for three days, and we were only two days back from Almata. Then we became unpleasant. But he was obdurate and threw the documents back at us. So, Elizabeth and I stayed with the luggage while John went upstairs to see what Ghulam ed-Din could do. Meanwhile, the man from PIA asked what the problem was, as they were permitted only a few hours on the ground and they were going to close the flight in ten minutes. But, just then, John came back with the new visas. He had found Ghulam ed-Din's office packed with people, all with the same problem as ours. But the good man had cleared the decks for us. He threw everyone out and gave our passports his undivided attention. He renewed our visas in a matter of minutes, completing the formalities with the Foreign Ministry stamp, and wished us all the best.

At customs, they told us not to worry about ruble notes in denominations smaller than 1,000 and passed us through. However, the officer pointed in the direction of several carpets—*Tekke Bokharas*—just like the ones we had seen in the Museum gift shop, sitting on a shelf behind him. They were antiques, he said, and had been confiscated from other passengers. We gave him our best impassive, Bailey faces but Elizabeth's heart must have been in her throat. She had bought an identical one at an especially good price, since it had been torn on one corner and needed repair. But he didn't ask her to open her suitcase.

After the bags had been passed, we went to passport control. The line moved very slowly and when I reached the booth I learned why. The unsmiling officer took a leisurely, page by page stroll through my passport: Egypt in 1985, then Saudi Arabia, Kenya, Tanzania, Saudi Arabia again, Greece, Britain, Turkey, Egypt again, the UAE, Bahrain, Saudi Arabia again, Singapore, Australia. . . . Then he opened the supplemental pages and read on, French Polynesia, India, Oman, Pakistan, Italy . . . finally he stopped and tossed it at me and asked me to find it myself. He was looking for the Pakistani visa, and I showed it to him. He stamped an empty page, returned the document, brightened, smiled, and wished me a pleasant journey. It was an extraordinary performance.

We felt very Pakistani with our carry-on baggage: briefcases, backpacks, and packages of paintings, books, and maps. I still had my twenty-five-cent ceramic plate from Khiva, although I had been tempted to jettison it several times. The flight took off at three-fifteen and shortly afterwards we had our first airline meal in a week. We flew due south and after half-an-hour we saw the Amu Darya, or Oxus, curling like a giant chocolate-colored ribbon through the waste. At Termez we entered Afghan airspace and passed to the east of Mazar- i-Sharif. The weather was very clear and the country, in all of its vulnerability, lay spread out below. The Hindu Kush, or "Hindu Killer," marched away, peak after monolithic peak, to the northeast. Up until the latest round of fighting the currency markets in Kabul had been very sophisticated, the dealers calling on their cell phones every day to Hong Kong and other financial centers. Most of them had been Hindus, but now they were gone, shamelessly shaken down as they passed into Pakistan. The Hindu Kush had triumphed once again.

We gradually left the mountains behind, to be succeeded by the plains of the central part of the country. In the words of the *Gazetteer of Afghanistan*

> they . . . possess a well-merited reputation for bleak inhospitable, unproductive savagery. There is no more unpromising land in Asia than the wind-swept home of the Hazara tribes . . .

When we reached the vicinity of Ghazni, we banked left and headed for Peshawar. We came in low over the vale, and saw clearly what a highway the Khyber Pass represented. Actually, it was less a highway than a track, but it was the only track through the mountain fastness. We landed and spent about forty-five minutes on the ground, parked next to one of our old friends, an Il-78 from Uzbekistan Airways. At six o'clock we took off and the flight to Islamabad took about twenty minutes. We knew we were at home when we were the first off the plane, but somehow found ourselves at the end of the line at passport control. Everyone breezed through customs and we were tempted to make invidious comparisons with the countries to the north. But then, we reflected, no one was trying to smuggle drugs or himself *into* Pakistan.

So, Central Asia revisited had not been the cultural banquet of the first trip, but maybe it was a better measure of the temper of the region. It was not about the sites, and we saw hardly anything older than the eighteenth century. It was all about people: Alexander Akhrarov, Rahima, Hassan, Ghulam ed-Din, Svierta, Ludmila, Anwar Saeedov, the Reverend Kiel, Miriam, Deena, the massive lady in the purple knit dress, Rahman, Lucy, the entrepreneur, and Yuri. They were like people everywhere, most of them trapped in a system that stifled their better instincts. For all of the occasional unpleasantness, they were decent sorts. It would be interesting to see how they fared when—and if—the system changed.

of Ta'if and terrible rumor preceded them into Mecca and Medina. Again, it was Indian Islam that was loudest in voicing the call that the holy places be internationalized rather than fall into the hands of these wild men. But Ibn Saud was a statesman as well as a warrior and the *Ikhwan* were on their best behavior in the Holy Cities, albeit grudgingly. The Al-Sa'uds now pride themselves on their ability to manage the *hajj*, and the Saudis have probably replaced the Indians as the spokesmen for the Muslim World today.

So how has Jinnah's secular—albeit Muslim—state fared in the decades since its founding? The report card is mixed. In spite of a propensity for strong-man (or strong-woman) rule, natives of the subcontinent still speak—if such it can be called—on matters concerning the faith. Pakistan has shared in the radicalism that has overtaken much of the Muslim World after the Iranian revolution in 1979, often abetted by the strong-men themselves. It is increasingly an Islam of a populist sort and, in protest against alleged American involvement in the siege of the Grand Mosque in Mecca, a Pakistani mob burned down the American embassy in Islamabad that same year. The voices of moderation are increasingly drowned out on Friday by those of the mullahs. One western invention that the mullahs *have* accepted is the loudspeaker, and in Pakistan this gives them extraordinary access to a population that is largely illiterate. The word "mullah" is loosely used when describing the phenomenon of clerical control of the masses. A Persian-English dictionary defines the word as "a schoolmaster, a doctor, a learned man, a judge, a priest," and derives it from the Arabic triliteral whose root means, among other things, "to spread, to fill." It is the active verb in the phrases to "fill the air with complaints" or "voice loud laments." It is probably this sense, unintentionally, in which it applies to Pakistani mullahs. The decibels on Friday are deafening. Illiterate Pakistanis are dominated by the mullahs in the same way that the Irish were once priest-ridden.

In 1960, the population of Pakistan was only 45 million. By 1995 it had grown to nearly 127 million, an annual rate of increase of 3 percent. And there were already too few jobs for the young entering the workforce. By almost any measure Pakistan was a miserably poor country. There were still far too many illiterate and dispossessed and, in spite of pockets of affluence and accomplishment, it always seems to have been that way. Zulfikar Ali Bhutto, for all of his Berkeley education, his populism and Shiism, was at heart a feudal Sindhi landlord. His daughter Benazir, for all of her membership of the Oxford Union and reputation in the West as an enlightened "Daughter of the East," remained a feudal Sindhi landlady to the end of her days. Official figures such as per capita GDP were suspect, given the strength of the unofficial economy in Pakistan, and westerners were not well placed to judge, occupying as they did a visible but unimportant place in the economy, located somewhere between the native wealthy and the great unwashed masses.

Much of the fiscal problem in Pakistan probably came from under-reporting of income and inefficient collection of taxes. For the working poor the amounts were small, and the "influentials" did whatever they could to avoid liability. Tax evasion, especially among the upper classes, was habitual and most tax was probably collected from the small middle class. It was reported that the default rate in consumer debt in the United States in the mid-1990s was 5.9 percent. That would be unthinkable in Pakistan, except at the very highest levels. In a largely cash economy there was little consumer debt and, so, little danger of default. The other side of the coin was that without consumer debt, the capacity of the consumer engine was not as great.

The level of crime, or at least of burglaries, seemed high in Pakistan if the newspapers were to be believed. They were full of reports of "dacoities," a term last used in Britain during the reign of Queen Victoria. We recognized it from a reading of Kipling or Dickens. But behind the quaint language there was a serious problem, and the situation in Sindh was no laughing matter. There, with the general availability of arms during the Afghan war, dacoits held up trains using rocket launchers. Serious ethnic differences still plagued the province, with its Sindhis and Muhajirs—or those who had relocated from India after partition—and gangs worked off old scores by the dozens in Karachi. The wars in Afghanistan had another unfortunate effect on Pakistan. In the interest of keeping India from influence in Kabul—which would lead to the Pakistani nightmare of a hostile country on both its eastern and western borders—Pakistan was a meddlesome player in Afghanistan's wars with an interest in keeping the already chaotic post-Soviet period in its by-now normal state of chaos.

But for all of the poverty, corruption, and violence that had turned it into an economic and social backwater, there were pockets of excellence that made Pakistan an enduring enigma. The Pakistanis were the nearest things to workaholics in the Muslim World and privileged young Pakistanis were accepted at the best universities in the United States and Great Britain. They were also exceptional athletes. Pakistan may have won only one bronze medal in the 1992 Olympics—a source of national shame—but it was in a major sport, field hockey, and they won gold in the same event in 1984. They were the current world champions in cricket. And then there was the phenomenon of the Khans in squash. Jehangir was getting old, but Jansher had seamlessly stepped into his place and was easily the best in the world, on a different plane from everyone else. He was a brilliant shot-maker, but what really made him great was *work*, what the Pakistanis called "fitness." We thought of it as a western trait. For Jansher Khan, it was fitness, fitness, and more fitness. He had every shot in the book, but usually won by simply wearing down his opponent.

Unlike the situation in most of the developing world, the press in Pakistan was free, and the papers were fearless in reporting alleged corruption. In fact, the problem in Pakistan seemed to be one of journalistic responsibility rather than freedom. Of that, more below. The *Jang* group of newspapers, which included the Urdu daily of the same name as well as the English-language *Times*, was founded by Mir Khalil ur-Rahman. He was revered as a kind of secular saint in Pakistan and papers carried tributes for months after his death in 1992. The editor of the *Times* was a woman, and the paper was full of what might be called "women's issues:" the place of women in Islam, spousal abuse, and rape. But they seemed to be aimed at the foreigners who were its primary readership, and it was reminder of the foreign consuls who constituted enlightened public opinion in nineteenth-century Istanbul. All the talk in the world was not going to change an impulse as deeply embedded in Pakistani society as the treatment of women.

Napier had conquered Sindh in 1843 and was, incidentally, the author of one of the wittier cables in history when he allegedly minuted London the Latin for "I have sinned." A fiery Scot, he administered the province with a western sense of rectitude, and hanged all the Sindhi perpetrators of honor killings he could lay his hands on. But the killing of women for real or suspected infidelities has persisted to the present day. And we were mistaken if we imagined that Pakistani women were natural allies in our efforts to change local customs. Women were often more resistant than men to foreign dictates and one Pakistani woman recently objected, stridently and publicly, to lessons in morality coming from a people who hadn't yet learned to wash their bottoms. She was referring to the western preference for paper rather than water after use of the toilet.

But there was a limit to what could be said. A poem, published in the English-language *Times*, provoked a constitutional crisis and even drew the Americans into the fray. It was written by Youssef, an old man whose had lost his life savings in the collapse of Taj, one of the cooperatives that catered to the small investor. The cooperatives appeared to be simple Ponzi schemes, with dividends paid out of current cash flow, the rest being used to fund the lavish lifestyle of the managers. This poem, however, seemed to go beyond even the liberal conception of press freedom in Pakistan. It was written in Urdu, buried innocuously on an inside page of the *Times*. The paper fired the staffer who let it pass, and issued an apology a few days afterwards. But the damage was done, and the author and the editor of the newspaper were charged with sedition by the government. The charges were dropped a week later, but for a while they were the talk of Islamabad. The Americans weighed in with a statement by the ambassador that we did not favor suppression of a free press.

The poem was a call to violence and overthrow of the ruling regime. The word "*mian*" was an Urdu honorific, and it was used sarcastically in the text to refer to the Prime Minister, Nawaz Sharif. It called on the chief of the army staff, Asif Nawaz, to lead the charge. He later died, at the age of fifty-five, after a morning jog and his wife had filed charges alleging that he was poisoned. An investigation was underway. A girl in the office made an English translation of the poem, and at first it was loose and referred in general to "corruption." A later version was more literal and colloquial and spoke of "Lootistan." That said it all: Pakistan was "the land of loot." The fat were getting fatter and the little man was being crushed under a heavier burden with every passing day.

In Arabic, the country was called "Bakistan," speakers of that language not generally being able to pronounce the "p." It was a small measure of revenge for Urdu speakers. There had been a recent book written by an Arab, *Whatever Happened to Bakistan*? It chronicled a discussion among a group of non-Indian Muslims and was a combination of a question and outsiders' lament for the squandering of the promise held out to the faithful everywhere. In spite of its bright people, exceptional athletes, press freedom, and elections that actually turned out sitting governments, Pakistan didn't work very well. It was a dysfunctional country. The dream of Jinnah had somehow gone wrong, and no one knew how to put it right.

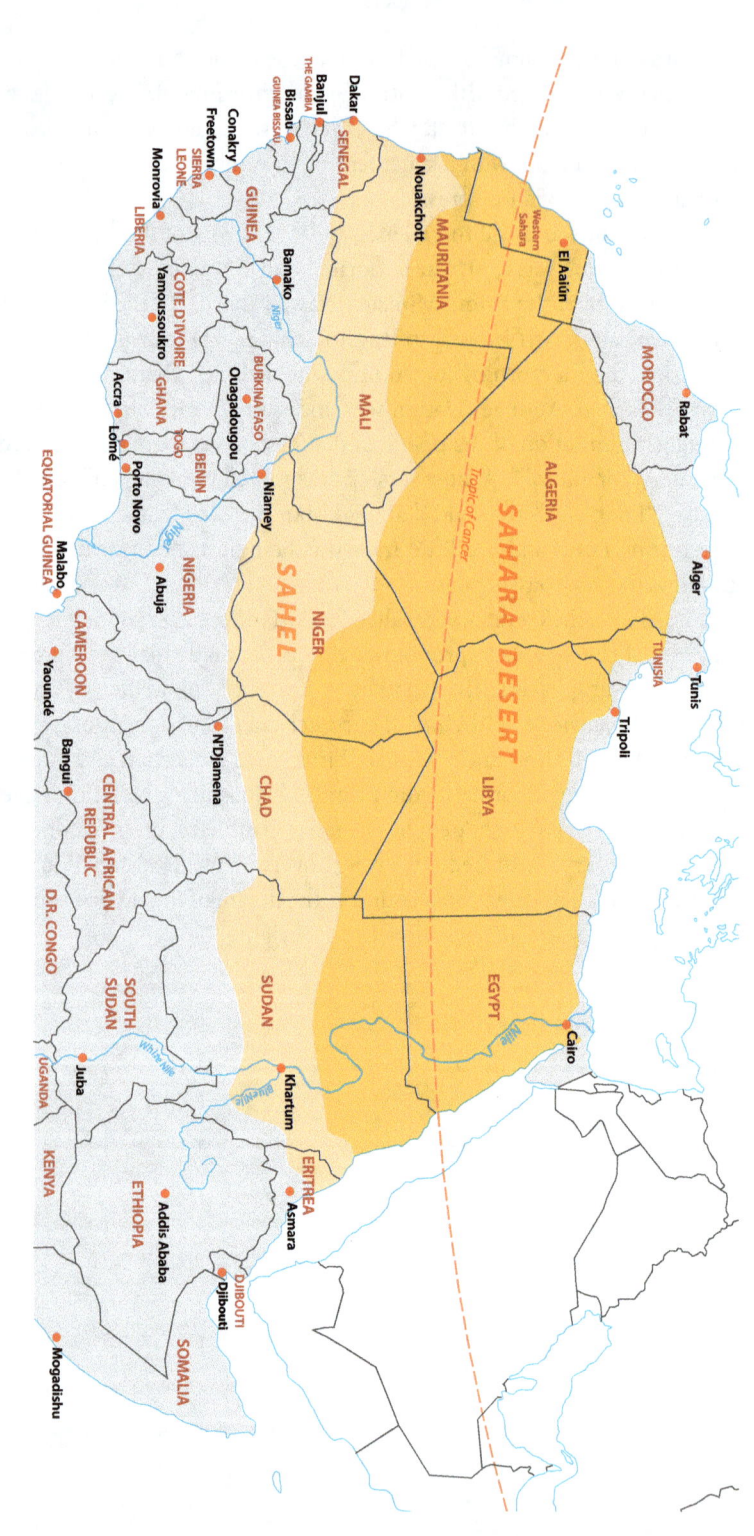

16

Paris Interregnum

IN LATE 1994 AS the Afghan program wound down RONCO was awarded a contract by USAID to provide assistance to Niger in old French West Africa. The country had a history of chronic famine, punctuated by military coups, and the hope was that the vicious cycle could be broken by a more systematic approach to management of the food-security situation. The award was surely based in part on RONCO's work with the Afghans, another people subject to chronic civil strife. Over the last several years of the project in Pakistan the company had developed expertise in demining, which would later make it one of the premier humanitarian and commercial mine action, ordnance disposal, and security companies in the world. But all of that lay in the future as I spoke with the home office about this new project. It was a more traditional institutional development effort and I had helped to write the proposal. I was bid as the project manager.

It would be introduction to another country. But there was nothing new about that. In years of postings overseas there were always surprises, most of them pleasant. Niger regularly placed among the poorest countries in the world. In addition to food shortages the vulnerability to drought and desertification, rampant corruption, and fluctuation in the price of uranium, its only real export, all contributed to the calamitous situation. After Chad, it was the second largest country in West Africa, consisting of some 1.3 million square miles of mostly desert and Sahel, with a habitable fringe along the Niger river in the south. To the north, from Mauritania in the west to Eritrea in the east, lay the broad band of the *Sahel*. *Sahel* was an Arabic word that meant "coast," but here it referred to the coast not of the ocean but of the desert. Beyond it lay the great expanse of the Sahara, *the* desert of which all others were just pale imitations.

The country was also Francophone. That meant that when people weren't speaking Hausa or Djerma, the two major language groups in the country, they spoke French and it was the official language of business and culture. French was also used by the European aid agencies that were a fixture in the country. That placed a premium on being able to communicate in the language, and my two years of French at Berkeley would be put to the test. I had years of experience as a translator from French to English, including three volumes of Niebuhr's *Travels in Arabia* and *Description of Arabia*. But reading and speaking were very different things. I hadn't spoken French in years and, as preparation, that meant immersion in a Francophone environment. So, I spent a couple of weeks in Paris refreshing my language skills, such as they were. But it was too short a time to do much more than expose the gaps in my knowledge. And, in some respects, it was the worst possible preparation for Niger.

I flew PIA from Islamabad to Karachi and Air France from Karachi to Paris. I had reservations at the hotel Raspail Montparnasse in the 14th arrondissement. It advertised itself as "a charming Art Deco hotel . . . with 38 rooms . . . in the heart of Paris's left bank." It was also only ten minutes from the Montparnasse metro station, important since I had two monstrous bags into which I had packed everything that I thought might be useful in launching a new project. With the bags, the advertised ten-minute walk seemed much longer. But the Respail was welcoming and everyone was pleasant and always helpful as I struggled to refresh my knowledge of French. The desk-clerks occasionally completed my sentences for me.

The Respail was also a six-minute walk from the Luxembourg Gardens and not much farther from the Louvre and Notre Dame. And Paris probably had more in the way of cultural diversions than any city in the world. So, I fell into a pattern of left-bank peregrinations during the day, interrupted by a short course in conversational French, and occasional visits to bookstores. Quality paperbacks were a French tradition and I found *L'Exploration du Sahara* by Jean-Marc Durou, the only book I bought in the fourteen months in West Africa. It was an excellent primer on the history of the area.

Durou told the story of the exploration of the Sahara, from antiquity through the Middle Ages and the initial Portuguese contacts with the continent. But where the Portuguese of the fifteenth century had sailed down the west coast before rounding the Cape and opening the maritime road to India, European exploration of the Sahara was largely a nineteenth-century, and land-based, phenomenon. Previously described only by Arab and Sudanese travelers and explorers, the Sahara, or great interior ocean—*as-Sahra al-Kubra* in Arabic—would remain largely an unknown to Europe until the greater scientific rigor of the late eighteenth century opened a new chapter. Celebrated names in the exploration of the continent, principal among them James Bruce and Joseph Banks, joined together in 1788 to form the "Association for the promoting of the discovery of the interior parts of Africa." If this phase had a distinctly Anglo-Saxon flavor, the next century would witness an effort that was at first German and then, more particularly, French.

French probing to the south began early in the century. But conquest of the interior really only began in 1852 with the occupation of the oasis of Laghouat, 400 km south of Algiers, capital of *Al-Jaza'ir al-Fransiyah* or French Algeria. This was followed shortly thereafter by Mzab, 200 km further south, and then Ouargla, another 150 km to the east by south. These desert oases were still over 1000 km north of the border with present-day Niger. It would be another 500 km from that border to the southern limit of the Sahel. In this great expanse of desert that meant contact—and conflict—with the Tuaregs, Arab tribes that occupied the desert regions and saw this advance as a threat to their traditional caravan trade. Outside factors intervened to accelerate the French effort. The humiliating defeat at the hands of Prussia in 1870 led to domestic pressures to retrieve the country's honor and the push south continued with even greater vigor. Widespread public support was an important factor, in spite of local resistance and the massacre of a French expedition in 1880 by the Tuaregs.

At the Berlin conference of 1884 fourteen European nations agreed on, among other weighty matters, the principles governing the penetration of sub-Saharan Africa. The "scramble for Africa" was on and in 1890 England and France jointly recognized a French area of influence to the south of its Mediterranean possessions, from Sai on the river Niger nearly 2,000 kilometers eastward to Lake Chad. The decade also witnessed a series of military victories that cemented French control of what would become its West African colonies: they were Mauritania, the French Sudan (today Mali), Niger, Senegal, the Ivory Coast, Dahomey (today Benin), Guinea, Upper Volta (today Burkina Faso), and French Togoland (today Togo). Mauritania, Mali, and Niger were mostly desert or Sahel. Interestingly, the tribal areas in Niger were treated differently from the more settled areas and were under the direct control of the military. Shades of the Northwest Frontier Province in Pakistan.

The federation of *Afrique occidentale française*, or French West Africa, with its capital at Dakar lasted from 1895 to 1960. Since independence in the latter year, Niger had been wracked by chronic famine, unrest, and military coups. Public pressure had resulted in multiparty elections in 1993 although political infighting led to the inevitable counter-coup in 1996. In this short hiatus, the American aid effort was launched. But we were stepping into a minefield and, as we will see, the project was not destined to last.

In the end, after fourteen months in Niger, my spoken French was serviceable, almost as good as my Arabic. But it was never the same thing. Arabic had been a constant adventure, learning new words and colloquial expressions and testing them on an always-appreciative audience. That was the difference: an American who spoke Arabic was a phenomenon and people would actually thank me for taking the trouble to speak their language. But an American who spoke French was just another inadequate speaker of that dowager queen of languages.

17

Cherif

On Saturday I went to see Cherif off on his trip to Japan. It was early May 1995, a weekend, and I really didn't have to go to the airport. But it was the courteous thing to do and courtesy was an important part of the business culture in Francophone West Africa. He would have done the same for me. It was also an important part of building the trust that was necessary if he and I were to work together effectively. He was the permanent secretary of the *Système d'alerte précoce,* or SAP, in Niger, the disaster relief organization attached to the prime minister's office, and my direct counterpart.

Oddly, Arabic was one of the avenues to our shared confidence. I don't know why it should have been so important to an African Christian. But it was, and we often talked about etymology and the relationships between the three languages in which we conversed, French, English, and Arabic. Arabic provided many of the words in Hausa, one of the major dialects of Niger, spoken by 60 percent of the population and supplying, among other things, all the numbers above twenty. Cherif and I spoke mostly in French, although he was keen to improve his English. His being a Christian was odd, especially in so sensitive a position in an overwhelmingly Muslim country. He was, in effect, the economic advisor to the prime minister. But maybe his religion provided some insulation against party politics and political pressures.

Those pressures were very familiar to Cherif. Disaster relief was the only game in town in Niamey and the donors—the French, the Germans, the Americans, the European Union, and the usual collection of NGOs—ruled by *diktat.* In addition, aid was politicized internally by the prime minister who didn't believe in free food, even when it was the only option during a famine; by the local *commerçants* who worried about its impact on the market; and by the government *fonctionnaires* who went public with inflated demands, believing that if they asked for twice what they needed they might get half. The tactic backfired. The donors said the numbers were worthless and often gave them nothing. Cherif and I would sit in his office and commiserate at the end of the day. Fatigue was etched in his face. His phone constantly rang, and it could be anyone from the prime minister with a global problem, to a *sous-préfet* haggling over lodging for consultants. Like every *patron* in West Africa, he was expected to solve all problems.

His office was standard third-world issue: broken furniture, cluttered desk, lopsided bookshelves stacked with consultant reports that nobody read. There were leaks in the roof and, in the violent storms in the Sahel this led to water intrusion. The water left irregular brown stains on the walls and the carpet and an unpleasant odor in the air. We agreed to renovate the SAP offices but in a year, they would have reverted to type. The mess on his desk was a little emblem of his mind, with old letters, dog-eared files, bits of paper, and dated magazines. But amid the clutter there would be his latest purchase from Paris, a text on food-security in the developing world, or an economic analysis of apartheid. It could be in English or French. With all the everyday demands on his time, he would suddenly brighten and talk animatedly about "public goods" or economic theory as enunciated by a former professor. In fact, he was an academic, not a manager.

He had a doctorate in economics from the Sorbonne and a first-class mind, with the facility of those educated in the French system to summarize quickly and effortlessly. Someone said it was the result of having to write an essay every day. Whatever the reason he always got to the heart of the matter in our plenary sessions. He gave a very positive spin to the food-security situation in Niger in general, and to our project in particular.

Cherif arrived at the airport late and hurriedly began the departure formalities. He was a small man, about five-feet seven, with a little paunch. His face was very round with just the hint of a mustache and he smiled easily. He was dark, but not the black of some Africans. About five minutes later his wife arrived, having parked the car. She was also small and very pretty, as sharply featured as he was round. They were both about thirty-five. She smoothed the collar of his pink pullover and kissed him tenderly before he left for passport control. There, he fiddled under the portrait of Mahamane Ousmane, the President of Niger, while they examined and then stamped the document. He hurried back briefly to press my hand and assure me that all outstanding project matters had been dealt with. Then he disappeared into the departure lounge, off to Yokohama to deliver a speech at a United Nations conference on disaster prevention. The scene was oddly touching and I was struck with his vulnerability and that of his country. As usual in Niger, it was not long in manifesting itself.

The airport was the usual developing-world showcase facility gone to seed: clocks that didn't work, a newsstand selling month-old copies of *Time* and *Jeune Afrique*, lounging clusters of taxi drivers, and an arrival and departure status board that bore little relation to reality. Since there were only a few flights into or out of Niamey, even on a busy day, it was academic anyway. I could generally gauge the time to leave for the airport from the sound of the plane I was meeting as it made its final approach over the city. The stubby Air Afrique A300 Airbus was probably coming from Paris or Dakar and we would see it land from the second-floor observation platform. It would taxi to the terminal building and we watched the passengers as they came down the accommodation stairs, looking for a friend or relative.

This time, as I drove away, I saw a giant white cargo plane on the tarmac with what appeared to be a Russian flag painted on the tail. It looked like the Antonov An-124 I had seen in Uzbekistan the year before. And so, it was. It was slightly larger than our C5, and so the largest aircraft in the world. In town, I stopped at the Gaweye for a beer. The Gaweye was the five-star hotel in Niamey and an international meeting place of sorts. This afternoon there were three white men at the other end of the bar. One asked me in English if I spoke French since they needed an interpreter. They wanted to know if there was a sauna in the hotel. After we established that there was not they asked me to join them for a drink. They were part of the flight crew of the Antonov: Vladimir, a colonel, Yuri, a major, and Sergei, a captain. They had just delivered a planeload of arms—"no secret" said Yuri—and they would leave when they had refueled: "Ve need vun-hundred fife tons of aviation fuel." But it was the *hajj* feast, called *tabaski* in Niger, and no one was working. The men were all from Moscow and had been in the bar for several hours drinking boilermakers, whiskey with a beer chaser. The whiskey had to be Johnnie Walker Black Label, although the beer was the good local brand.

So, we shook hands all around and I had a couple of boilermakers with them. Yuri was the translator. He had been to airshows all over the world and was wearing a sleeveless T-shirt with "California" stenciled across the front.

> I haf been to Texas, Seattle, Salinas, Harrisburg, and Kansas. American people are very good and very hospital. And gorls in Salinas are like gorls in Moscow. Only two places in vorld are gorls like that, Moscow and Salinas.

We talked about our two nations and how the cold war was over. We agreed that it was the politicians who made problems and that no one wanted war. Vladimir had also served in Vietnam, so we drank a toast to old times and future friendships. Then we discussed the value of the ruble and the situation in the former Soviet Union. They maintained that it was not as bad as everyone said. I was sure it was not for them, with the chance to travel and access to hard currency.

By now the boilermakers were beginning to tell and Yuri was slurring his words:

> Ve do not vant varr. Amerrican people are very hospital. Ve only vant to drink whiskey and fuck. How you get gorrls here? I haf family in Moscow, but I am man, you understand. If Amerrican C5 come to Niger, Amerricans fuck all Niger. Russians fuck Niger and all neighboring countries.

Uproarious laughter. I left them negotiating the bill with the bartender. They wanted to pay with crisp new US $100 bills, of which they appeared to have an endless supply.

Later that afternoon in my little pool, I reflected on what I had seen that morning. There was a growing food crisis in the country. But the prime minister and the director of cabinet were in Mecca for the *hajj*. The permanent secretary of the disaster relief organization had just left for Japan to make an academic presentation on the subject when the real thing threatened his country. And the Russians were delivering arms in exchange for the hard currency that was needed to buy food. But in a chronically food-deficit country like Niger, there was always a question as to what constituted famine. And there were political problems of food aid, with the French—prickly as always—resisting the lead of any other donor in this, their private preserve. As far as I was concerned, we had to move at the speed of the client. That was what these institutional development projects were all about. If it were simply a matter of feeding people, we would bring in the American army and do the job ourselves. But that wasn't the purpose of the exercise.

I had just begun to congratulate myself on having built some bridges to the client. I was quickly brought up short. One of the team arrived with the news that a USAID project officer had played tennis with the American ambassador the day before. Afterwards, over drinks, the ambassador had not minced words: there was famine abroad in the land, there were four highly-paid, disaster-management consultants in the country doing nothing, and what was USAID going to do about it? He himself would go north on Monday to assess the situation first-hand. So, we had the impossible situation of an ambassador micromanaging a USAID project, calling the mission director or one of his minions into his office on a daily basis to provide updates. He didn't understand our project and didn't want to. He just wanted results. He told a USAID group that they had a year to "turn this country around."

So, I kept hearing, at second hand, what he thought about us, the projects we were implementing, and the amount of money we were making. I tried at one point to give the deputy chief of mission a team briefing, a straightforward explanation of what we were doing and what our constraints were. But he blindsided us by reporting to the ambassador that one of the team said something that might have been construed as critical of American food policy. The mission director was hauled in shortly thereafter to explain himself. I, of course, was summoned by the director to explain myself. This was ludicrous and I wrote a strongly worded but polite note to the director saying so. It was the kind of pressure we were all subject to on a daily basis.

The ambassador tried to personally organize the donors and weighed in with a heavy hand. He would show up at donor meetings, the only ambassador in attendance, and browbeat everyone present. He tried to orchestrate meetings and agendas and it soon backfired. The French, always suspicious and jealous of their prerogatives, particularly here in West Africa, announced that they would not operate under these conditions and would go their own way. What little cooperation there had been among donors evaporated.

It was useless to argue that the ambassador didn't understand the project; that "disaster management" was not our brief; that we had tried to go into the field and had been forbidden to do so by the client; that our own plan had been rejected by USAID. As for "doing nothing," we were just getting started and put in long hours, renovating an office, moving into houses, advertising and hiring local staff, drafting their contracts, procuring air-conditioners and Toyotas, conducting workshops, preparing work-plans, dispensing cash, and designing the system for the client's fund.

No, we had a problem. Not the least of it would be protecting Cherif from the fallout. It wasn't long before I had developed more sympathy for him than for the bureaucrats at USAID or the embassy. He may not have been much of a manager but he was in the trenches every day, something the conceptualizers were not, and I grew to like and respect the man. More immediately, we had a classic scoop: "Niger starves while high-priced American consultants recline in swimming pools." I thought about suggesting that the ambassador give up tennis until Niger was food-secure. At that rate, his game wasn't going to improve much.

18

Demilunes and Looney Tunes

PART OF THE PROBLEM in Niger was the natural antipathy between USAID and the State Department. USAID seemed to be rather despised by the diplomats, and the comment by a political officer in Pakistan had been typical: "I thought all USAID employees came equipped with an Oriental wife." Even though everyone in Niamey—both USAID and State—seemed to have come up through the Peace Corps, the common bond didn't seem to matter. The deputy chief of mission was supposed to be a reasonable man and a buffer between the ambassador and USAID. But something about him reminded me of a little sailboat: too trim and prim, too well organized. I first met him at an embassy cocktail party where he asked a few questions but didn't pay much attention to the answers before tacking away to play the crowd like a politician. It was said that he was on the fast track and he looked the part, like an admiral's aide in the Navy, although the State Department was not the Navy. Beneath the bland exterior, he struck me as crudely ambitious. But the judgment was probably too harsh. Niamey was no place for ambition and he probably had as much trouble with his boss as everyone else.

There was also something incestuous about the American assistance program in Niger. That was because the USAID and Embassy offices in Niamey were in the same compound and there was an even greater insularity about them than in other countries. The problem was heightened because Niamey had such a small American community. Everyone seemed to know everyone else, not to mention everyone else's business. You could lead a very comfortable existence in Niger seeing very little except your home, appointed with the standard USAID furniture allowance, and the inside of the compound. There, lunch could be an inexpensive and filling meal taken with other USAID and embassy people, talking shop in the recreation-center cafeteria.

There was nothing wrong with that. Americans overseas were no different from other people, wanting to eat familiar food in familiar surroundings in the company of their own kind. But the bureaucracies we created to administer the aid acquired lives of their own and the bureaucrats sometimes forgot that the beneficiaries were supposed to be the people in the countries where we operated. The systems we put together were top-heavy with management, and maybe it was that Niger seemed so small and the needs so patent that the management overlay looked so large. RONCO had won this project largely on the strength of its work with the Afghans, another people under chronic stress. But the two countries were really as different as night and day.

Food was everything in Niamey: if it rained the Nigerians ate, if it didn't they didn't, although if it rained too hard they also didn't eat because then the rice fields would be flooded. It didn't take much strategizing to see that. But we still created elaborate programs with abstract goals and performance matrices and pretended that the system was efficient. The tendency to see projects as intellectual exercises was probably natural. The direct-hires wrote project papers with an eye over their shoulders at congress or some other watchdog, ensuring that the goals were clear and that sustainability and accountability were incorporated in the design. But, in the process, they made demands on host governments in the form of conditions precedent that often had legal, even constitutional, ramifications that no one had clearly thought through. In many cases, the host government had not been consulted beforehand, and so never understood them. Ministers would be called in, generally at the eleventh hour, and invited to sign the agreement if they wanted the money. They did, and so they signed. But they really didn't understand the implications of the documents they were signing.

This project was a hybrid, having been cobbled together by a project officer who was long gone and a general development officer who was about to follow. The GDO, a Peace Corps veteran and a political appointee from the Reagan years, was maneuvering, increasingly desperately, to cover her tracks before she left. She was full of ideas but utterly thoughtless. She had no sense of priorities: everything was equally interesting and she would feed me articles on the use of natural fertilizers in China, or the techniques of gender disaggregation in Africa. She was a regular attendee at the briefings in the USAID conference room on everything from natural resource management to female circumcision. Her attention span could be measured in nanoseconds. She would be talking about high level disaster management and suddenly turn on me with a question as to what I was doing about finding her cook a job. Like everyone else on their way out, she was trying to ensure places for her domestic staff.

As usual in these overseas undertakings the project was staffed by a group of expats that could only loosely be called a team. It led to our own problems with implementation. We fell into two camps, the doers and the conceptualizers and there were two of each. The doers wanted to get on with it, while the conceptualizers wanted to surround the problem with an intellectual construct and not move until it had been satisfactorily defined. Since a clear definition was almost always impossible given the information available, it was a recipe for doing nothing, and that was deadly in this environment. It didn't help that the evaluation specialist was responsible for monitoring the work of the disaster specialist, and the two soon developed a dislike of each other that bordered on the pathological. Part of the problem was the way project teams were staffed. Most often we had never met each other or the people who hired us, who were frequently from different companies. Then, we were thrown into the breech in a developing country with two difficult clients, USAID and the local organization, and asked to behave like a coherent whole. Even with the silly little team-building exercises, it never really worked out that way. Eventually it seemed that what we needed in Niger was not team building but—like in draw poker—a whole new hand.

Meanwhile, our client was woefully unprepared for us and for the project. That was not surprising since the government of Niger had not been consulted during project design. Our contract stated that the conditions precedent would be met before we arrived. But they were not and we faced a long, tedious process of negotiation before we could begin to be effective. After an initial recognition that she had dropped the ball, the GDO now suggested that it was *our* fault. As a remedy, I was supposed to organize community workshops throughout Niger to develop a national consensus on disaster management.

Another goal of the Mission was to push the money through the pipeline and that created a tension with the conditions precedent. Too often the host government pretended to conform and USAID pretended to be impressed. That allowed disbursement to continue while this "progress" was being made. In the design papers USAID demanded the undoable, contractors promised the impossible, and it was up to the people on the ground to discover what could actually be achieved. As a general rule of thumb, the narrower the focus the better the chance of success, and some useful things were undoubtedly done in overseas projects.

The people who wrote the project papers spent days at USAID presentations with like-minded people, often TDYers (temporary duty staff), discussing such abstruse subjects as the influence of non-farm, traditional income on local consumption habits. They wrote things like:

> ... approaches to strengthening drought coping strategies have not based themselves rigorously on a zonally differentiated economic analysis of income and asset maximization strategies according to different drought incidence conditions.

They didn't call economics the dismal science for nothing. The target population of the study was necessarily small in Niger and, at the end, after everyone had asked pertinent questions and looked thoughtful, the presenters extrapolated from the particular to the general and congratulated themselves on the pertinence of their conclusions. These kinds of sessions were always exciting, at the cutting edge of the nascent science of development But, there wasn't an intellectual meal for a hungry man in the entire portfolio of USAID Niger. What was needed was less intellectualizing and more doing, with an emphasis on blue-collar projects that spent the money and helped the people.

Some presentations were more interesting than others. One TDYer, in spite of the fact that he spoke no Hausa or French, spent three weeks touring the country by taxi. He even flew with a French nuclear scientist to the uranium mines at Arlit in the middle of the Sahara. The mines would later be remembered for the discredited story of Saddam Hussein's attempt to buy uranium there. But the plane couldn't land because the airport was under siege by the Tuaregs. The TDYer's own story sounded more implausible with every new detail, but it all seemed to be true. His first wife and son had been killed in an automobile accident and he married a second wife who had been a thalidomide baby, with little flippers for arms. They had adopted two children as infants, both of them black girls and both severely compromised *in utero* by alcohol and crack cocaine. After long stays in the hospital the girls were released. The TDYer had rehabilitated them on fish oil and fish meal. On this regimen, both had made startling recoveries. They were now six and eight years old.

There was a scientific explanation for all of this and he was a proponent of fishponds as an answer to the problem of protein deficiency in Niger. He worked closely with Peace Corps volunteers. Some of the flavor of his presentation appeared in an extract from his final report:

> As we slowed to enter this village on the metal road, I was struck by the obvious health of the children playing near the road. Chronic malnourishment showed no signs, in even one child. Just as I was about to inquire about the great wealth of this

> village, I saw the reason: a deep pond, not 100 meters from the road dominated the village.
>
> The presence of blue-green algae could be confirmed from the road, and a glance at the incoming water channel confirmed a huge population of Talapia (Nilotica) and a larval eating cichlid, possibly an Acquidens or Steatogranus. Upon examination and interrogation, the children eat all the fish they want and chew continually upon the inner membranes of the camel's foot seedpod. Thus, their extremely good health.

He had first seen the beneficial effects of fish when, as a young man in the army in World War II he had helped open the death camps in Germany. The survivors seemed to have lived on dried fish and little else.

But fish weren't the only arrow in his quiver. He also spoke of breaking the hardpan, "nature's way of allowing the soil to regenerate itself." The favorite technique was demilunes, which

> ... trap wind-driven biological debris, impede wind erosion, trap flowing water, and encourage reforestation and the reemergence of Sudan grass, Acacia hulio, and other desirable plant life.

And there was much more. We felt that we were in the presence of some latter-day Buckminster Fuller, with a new and different way of looking at almost everything. It sounded plausible enough, this recipe for turning a chronic food-deficit country like Niger into a protein-surplus one. However, nobody knew enough to know whether any of it made any sense.

19

The Project

WE WERE UP EARLY and on the road to Ouallem, north of Niamey, where we were implementing our first project. The vehicle was a big Toyota Land Cruiser, a 4x4 with an extra fuel tank and extra spares. We had just placed an order for three more and it wasn't hard to see why we needed them. The roads in Niger were mostly dirt with a washboard effect, and the cars took a terrible pounding. At first the driver took the bad parts too fast and we slowed him down. But still, the scenery of the Sahel flew by. The Sahel was the broad band of sand and scrub that ranged from about ten to fifteen degrees, north latitude, and stretched five thousand miles from Senegal on the Atlantic to Eritrea on the Red Sea. Unfortunately, with the revolt of the Tuaregs it was now off-limits to foreigners. They wanted their own country. Here, there were occasional acacias and thorn trees with camels cropping the lower branches. The color of the sand ranged from grey-brown to pink, and there were mesas and black patches of lava that had survived the erosion that was the general rule. We passed flocks of goats and two-tone sheep, exactly half white and half black with the vertical demarcation across the abdomen. An Abyssinian Roller streaked by, a brilliant turquoise body with royal-blue wings and a long tail.

The disaster specialist and I were in the car. He had designed the project and it was probably a carbon copy of countless others he had implemented over the past twenty years. He was also a Berkeley graduate, an old Africa hand, and a pro. When the canal into Timbuktu had been opened several years before he had managed the project. He was rock-solid in his knowledge of financial accountability, which made my job easier. But he needed a disaster to make him happy and when there was none at hand, he manufactured one. When my household shipment, containing artwork, valuable books, Persian carpets, and computer files, was delayed in Lomé, Togo he provided regular updates, each more alarming than the one before. Nothing survived a day in the port of Lomé and unless I flew there instantly there would be nothing left to claim. The shipment eventually arrived intact, but not before I'd passed a few sleepless nights.

With this project, we'd made a conscious decision to work closely with the government *fonctionnaires* and it was a bit of a risk. They were paid irregularly and many civil servants—in customs, water, power, and electricity—had been on strike since our arrival three months earlier. But we were supposed to be promoting institutional development and involving them was the only way to make it happen. So, everything in the project was carefully laid out: cash box, signed project proposal in multiple copies, receipt form, expenditure forms etc. But I still felt a little pang as we turned over CFA 2,668,350 in cash—about $5,000—for safekeeping to a representative of the Post Office department in Ouallem. The office was filthy and cluttered and he brushed away the dust on the desk so we could review the documents. He was a small man and looked to be about fifty, given the white in his black hair and beard. As we counted out the cash he put on his glasses and, after a short hesitation, signed the receipt. I don't think he was any happier about the money than we were. I had been to countless meetings like this in Upper Egypt, or Saudi Arabia, or Chaman on the Afghan border. But it was always different the first time in a new country.

Our next stop was at the office of the *sous-préfet*, in a typical mud brick building in the center of town. It differed from the others only in the Nigerien flag flying from the staff overhead. The *sous-préfet* himself was in Niamey, so we dealt with his deputy. That done, we went to the offices of the *Système d'alerte précoce* (SAP) for a general meeting. But the word hadn't gotten out and we spent the next half-hour driving around town collecting the participants, representatives of the ministries of Plan, Health, Agriculture, Livestock, and Environment. As we left the building a woman who had been burned in a domestic fire was being loaded into the bed of a pickup truck. This was one of the poorest areas of Niger, and Niger was one of the poorest countries in the world. Starvation supposedly threatened, but from the look of this woman they still had enough to eat. She was large and several men struggled to lift her into the truck. Her breasts were full and round, not the empty sacks we sometimes saw in Africa. I noticed them because that was near the area where she had been burned. Under one arm and across her back the skin was pink where the outer layer had blistered and peeled away.

Eventually the last of the *fonctionnaires* drifted in and we began the meeting. The office was not air-conditioned. It was only nine thirty in the morning but it was already hot. The rains in the Sahel were torrential in the early spring, with high winds and dust. Water had leaked into this office when it rained and the walls were streaked with muddy trails. It smelled strongly of stale urine. A desk and a collection of miscellaneous chairs, most of them broken, were the only furniture in the room. The flies were already a plague. But the meeting began, as usual in these Francophone countries, with an impressive display of protocol. The participants were greeted formally and I was introduced as the *grand patron* from Niamey. A short *précis* of the project followed, during which several of the men attempted to interrupt with questions. They were told to wait their turn. The meeting was chaired by Abu Danguiwa, the *agro-pastoralist* and SAP representative from Niamey, and he was a stickler for order. Many of the men in the room had discolored teeth and gums, but Danguiwa's teeth were sparkling white and his gums were the pinkest I ever saw.

After the presentation, the discussion became a free-for-all. Maybe it was because of that French tendency to interrupt, or just talk by one another. Here, all nine men in the room were speaking animatedly, and all at the same time. The characteristic *patois* of the Sahel filled the room, and as the decibels rose we also rose and left. This was their show and they would eventually settle it among themselves. They were arguing whether the Ministry of Agriculture or the Ministry of Environment should be responsible for the project. It was a land reclamation project and that suggested Environment, but the land being reclaimed was agricultural and that meant Agriculture. It was a typically abstruse French argument and we didn't much care which way they decided.

So, we drove out to the village, Santigui, where the project would be implemented. It was food for work (FFW) and each of the villagers would be paid five kilograms of millet per day. I had signed a check for OPVN, the government grain organization, the day before for about $10,000 worth of grain. It was already in the local warehouse. What we brought to

Woman, Santigui, Niger

the party, in addition to the money, was the ability to do this kind of thing quickly. Moving an invoice through the government system could take weeks. We did it in a day. The villagers were mildly curious when we arrived, two white men, generally harbingers of something good, or at least of interest to them. This was not Somalia or Ethiopia, and we saw no living skeletons, but they were supposed to be consuming their remaining margins and eating their seed corn. This was critical since they would have to plant soon. But we saw women pounding millet—men never did this kind of work—with long wooden pestles in wooden mortars made from hollowed tree trunks. Village women had calloused hands and highly developed biceps. One woman examined my hands, feeling for rough spots, and finding none just laughed.

Driver, Santigui

Then they sent for the village chief and he arrived, looking expectant. He spoke only Djerma so the driver interpreted for us. Yes, they had heard of the project and knew about the ration, and yes, they could use the food. We told them that work would begin in a week. It was a typical village scene: naked infants and half-naked kids dressed in ragged hand-me-downs from Europe or the United States. Used clothing was a regular business in Niger. It arrived in huge bales and then was sorted and washed before being sold. The middlemen made all the money. There were long-sleeve shirts and short-sleeve shirts and many T-shirts with logos like "Mount Holyoke," "UCLA," or the "Chicago Bulls." The Bulls were a favorite.

The situation here was interesting because the prime minister would be launching a general plea for food aid today in another village to the east. Every time the word "famine" was uttered there was pressure from the American ambassador to do something. We would have to see what the fallout from this latest speech would be. But here in Santigui, where there was supposed to be severe stress, the people looked healthy. The kids didn't have the orange tint to their hair that was a telltale sign of vitamin deficiency. And if someone were to measure their biceps—a favorite technique of health surveyors—I was sure they would find them within the normal range.

Afterwards, we drove back to the center of town and stopped for a Coke. The houses were all mud brick with a little hole near the ground level, through which the sewage emptied into the main street. It was not uncommon to see children, and occasionally adults, defecating in public. The Coke was good, sweet without too much fizz, like everywhere else in the developing world. Then we went back to the SAP office. The commotion had died down, everyone finally agreeing on the Ministry of Environment as the project manager. That had been our bet. Then, we hurtled back to Niamey with the assistant *sous-préfet* as a passenger. We were back in the office by noon, feeling like we had done a good bit of work that morning.

But in Niger we had learned to take nothing for granted. Each little success made us better able to deal with the nay-sayers. This was a little success and nobody could take it away from us. But there was still the prime minister's address later in the day. Then, it would be the ambassador.

Kids, Santigui

20

The Bulletin

SLAP! "F*INIS PAGE DEUX. Quelques observations au page trois?*" We were assembled to review the *Système d'alerte précoce* monthly information bulletin. It was, in theory, an important document, giving the latest status on the situation in Niger, a country plagued by chronic food shortages. The meeting included representatives of the ministries of Agriculture, Plan, Health, Commerce, Livestock, Social Affairs, and Communications. They were in addition to the SAP permanent secretary and his staff, an *agro-pastoralist*, an *informaticien,* and a secretary. It was almost five o'clock, or 17:00 in the French system, and we were just getting started.

Unlike the government employees who took a siesta from 12:30 to 15:30, we had already put in a full day. This meeting didn't start until 16:40, although it was scheduled to begin at 16:00. We were the only ones there at 16:00. It wasn't the permanent secretary's fault. He was probably on the phone with the prime minister or the director of cabinet, absorbing his daily tongue-lashing. He and I often commiserated on the pressures of the job and he confessed that he spent sleepless nights over the food situation. He said he was *nerveux*. But even allowing for these pressures, or maybe because of them, he brought his own domineering style to the meetings. He conducted them with a combination of a very French and professorial tendency to lecture and the unpleasant habit of barking at anyone who questioned his decisions. The first trait was probably the product of a French academic background and a PhD in economics. The second was all his own. Everything was in French, of course, his delivery slow and methodical with the words chosen being very commonplace. At least it made the proceedings easier to follow.

He was a small man and a Christian in an overwhelmingly Muslim country. I didn't know what, if anything, that meant. The Nigeriens didn't seem to pay much attention to religion. He smiled easily and engagingly and, at his best, he was a very pleasant man. But when he was crossed, his countenance darkened and he betrayed considerable repressed anger. This was probably the result of years dealing with European donors who held all the cards and simply imposed their will. Whatever the reason, he lectured without stop in a flat monotone, the degree of emotion rising with the importance of the subject. When he wanted to make a point, the decibels rose and he imposed his ideas by dint of sheer verbal force. He would *not* be checked and had the very French habit of interrupting everyone else. I had seen him go on like this for hours at a time.

He led with a kind of sham collegiality, making a show of involving his staff in all but the important decisions. These, he reserved to himself. In fact, this meeting was a textbook study in how *not* to manage. We began the discussion on the subject of the cover of the bulletin, and he asked for comments from the group which had eventually drifted in piecemeal, the last one arriving an hour after the scheduled start. The man from the Ministry of Health made the reasonable comment that he thought the emphasis was misplaced, that the SYSTÈME D'ALERTE PRÉCOCE should be in lower case letters and the name of the bulletin in upper case, instead of the other way around. Innocently, I seconded the motion and it was carried by voice vote.

I say by voice vote because this agonizing review of all eighteen pages of the document, sentence by sentence, paragraph by paragraph, page by page, occupied us for the next three hours. Everything was done according to Robert's Rules of Order. When we had finished with a page, the permanent secretary would ask for further comments before slapping the table with a loud bang like an auctioneer: "Going once, twice, three times, sold to the man in the back row." That was the signal that the page was finished and we could move on. It was a sham because nothing important was decided by vote. And we discussed everything except the relevance or utility of the information, spending fifteen minutes deciding whether Roman numerals should be followed by a period or enclosed by parentheses. Finally, after asking whether anyone objected to substituting a period for the parentheses—it was *his* idea—he ruled that a period was appropriate. SLAP! *Finis.* Next page. Unfortunately, it was only page two and we were already thirty minutes into the meeting.

And so, it went for the next several hours. At one point, I offered a suggestion that I thought would make the information more useful to a decision-maker and was sternly rebuked for my pains. The other American present confined his remarks to the observation that "Zinder" was misspelled. Outside, the sky darkened and I soon saw my first storm in the Sahel. It was like a summer storm in Arizona. The wind picked up and blew the fine, pink sand in swirls and eddies, and then the rain came down, first in large drops and then in torrents, the dirty water running down the window panes outside. By the time the meeting ended so had the rain. Inside, we droned on and on and my attention drifted. In meetings like this there was always one individual with an arsenal of superfluous points to make, or errors to correct. We would all wait, hoping that page seven or eight or nine would be accepted, waiting for that SLAP, when the man from the Ministry of Agriculture would make another vacuous comment or notice another typographical error. If the point was unimportant it would be discussed at length. If it dealt with something substantial, the fire would be kindled, the voice would take on an edge, and the lecture would start. It always began with "NON...."

The permanent secretary referred to himself in the third person as the *rédacteur en chef* or "editor in chief." One man across from me had sunk almost out of sight in his chair and, after two hours, his feet were nearly touching mine under the table. Just as we thought we were finished with page fifteen, waiting for that SLAP, he roused himself and made his sole contribution of the afternoon. That set off another lecture. The permanent secretary hectored his own staff, reducing the *informaticien* who had put the bulletin together to sullen silence, weary of trying to defend himself. The *agro-pastoralist*, an older man who knew the ropes, simply giggled when he wasn't making an occasional pedagogical point.

On and on it went. SLAP! The voice. Lecture. Question. SLAP! These were *fonctionnaires*, consummate bureaucrats, talking about periods and parentheses when parts of the country were on the verge of starvation. It really wasn't their fault. Most of them were young and doing what came naturally to bureaucrats. And the attempt to involve them, however superficially, in the decision-making process was not bad. But the effect was deadening.

They were different from the private sector in Niger, and every time we dealt with private contractors we wondered what we could possibly teach them. They had interesting names like Abdou Djibo or Odah A. Hyacinthe. They were hungry, like everyone else in the country, but prepared to do something about it. If we asked them for a pro-forma invoice they produced it in a matter of minutes. When we pointed out errors they corrected them or wrote them out again and again until they got it right. One difference was that they were paid regularly, unlike the *fonctionnaires* whose pitiful salaries were chronically months in arrears. But there was still something that set them all apart. To my initial surprise, they all spoke French although I don't know what I expected in a Francophone country. But this was the idiom of international diplomacy and I remembered the guy in the navy who, on a port call in Nice, couldn't believe that the little kids in the street were speaking *French* for chrissakes.

Afterwards, I thought that one of our contributions would be to introduce a little organization into these meetings. Maybe one day the suggestion that we make the monthly review more brisk and businesslike might bear fruit. The permanent secretary was, for all of his pedantic leanings, a smart man and a quick learner. But he was a bundle of contradictions, as was his country, and a meeting later in the week would epitomize them all. The meeting was with the former Nigerien foreign minister, who had also been ambassador to the United States. He was a personal friend of the permanent secretary and it had been suggested that he could help with the conditions precedent. When we called at his home in the *Ancien Plateau*, the two greeted each other warmly and it was clear they were like father and son. The older man was occupied with another visitor when we arrived, so we moved past a stuffed hyena into a second reception room filled with the bric-a-brac of years of international postings. A servant offered coffee while he completed the other meeting.

The ambassador was a natural aristocrat, of medium height, very thin with fine features and white hair. He listened carefully, punctuating Cherif's tale with an undercurrent of understanding: *"tout à fait, tout à fait."* This was little more than a courtesy call and not much of substance was discussed. But it held promise for the thornier institutional issues we faced. He walked us not only to the door but also to the gate, and, finally, to the car, where he and Cherif took affectionate leave of one another.

This was a different, and higher, plane than the one we normally occupied. But it showed how small a town Niamey was, how concentrated was the elite, and what an extraordinary phenomenon Africa was. The gap between His Excellency and the scenes at the *petit marché* seemed too wide to bridge. *Suqs* in the Arab world were interesting collections of sights, sounds, and smells. But an African market contained sights, sounds, and smells that were always unforgettable. The *petit marché* in Niamey was across the street from the Score supermarket and the contrast between the two couldn't have been greater. It may have only been fish, meat, vegetables, and fruit for sale but there was something almost savage about the bush meat, the dismembered animals, the pervasive odor of decay and defecation, the constant bustle, the brilliant colors of the women's dresses, and the unfathomable thoughts behind the men's eyes whose whites were yellow.

Then, too, there was something about the effect of French culture, however superficial, in these Francophone African countries. American blacks set the tone in our popular culture. But in Niger they seemed out of place. At a mixed party, the two cultures clashed. The Americans would arrive, featuring dark glasses well after nightfall, sleeves cut away to reveal their biceps. They would be greeted by other American blacks:

Hey bro, how it *is*.

Hey man, kiss my ass.

The Nigeriens, meanwhile, would greet each other with a courtly "bonsoir monsieur" or "enchante'" or "excellente soirée." It was more than language, but it was difficult to know how deeply the acculturation went.

21

Foreign Service Nationals

They were called "foreign service nationals," or FSNs. Technically the term applied only to the locals who worked for USAID or the embassy. But I have also used the term for those who worked for us, even though they were as different from government workers as employees of a private company were from the people in the post office. They came in different sizes, shapes, colors, and genders and were often the glue that held overseas projects together. They were sometimes better educated and more cultured than the expatriates they served. What they most often lacked was a grounding in management skills, which was why we were there. Management meant decision-making and, almost by definition, all decisions were bad. It's just that some were worse than others. In the developing world decisions were to be avoided, and that's where Americans came in. We tried, with mixed success, to be straightforward and incisive, setting an example of good management practices. The skills needed constant honing and, if we did our jobs right, we helped the FSNs to become better managers. Some were eager students and I especially remembered those who learned from what we had to offer. There were many who taught me a few things as well.

Those mentioned here are mostly men because we worked in Muslim cultures where women supposedly lacked opportunity. But the rule was far from invariable. We knew as many women telecommunications engineers in Egypt as men, and they included most of the few good managers we worked with. This short list includes an Afghan, two Pakistanis an Egyptian and two Nigeriens. They are singled out not because they were the only ones, but because, each in his or her own way, was outstanding. I could probably add as many more if the field were widened to include the clients, the local organizations we worked with.

Sefatullah

The first was Sefatullah, a Pashtun from Kabul although his mother was a Tajik, another large ethnic group in Afghanistan. He was working in Islamabad for an Afghan NGO and we hired him to be the financial and administrative manager of the Mine Dog Center, or MDC. Unlike some of the other organizations under the demining umbrella, we insisted on strict financial accountability. The United Nations seemed to be a particular offender. UN managers would fly to Herat with gunnysacks full of *afghanis* that had been changed in the local market before the bills were paid. It left scope for irregularity. We knew that when a team of dogs and handlers was deployed for two months at a time into Afghanistan, accountability was a relative term. Receipts were religiously provided for every expense they incurred, from firewood to the often-outrageous charges for pulling a vehicle out of a river in spate. They were almost always from the same receipt pad given to the set leader, so we knew that he had probably written them himself. The Afghan who provided the service didn't come equipped with a cash register and probably was illiterate anyway. But we still checked all the receipts for reasonableness and disallowed those that appeared to be bogus.

I say "we" but it was really Sefatullah who took the tough decisions. He first impressed me when he was asked to describe, in "play-script" format, the procedure for hiring a new employee at the MDC. Since he would also be the administrative manager, this was important. He completed the task with rare zeal. It was a characteristic of Sefatullah: give him two tasks to complete by the end of the day, and he would have completed three by noon. It was not a matter of trying to impress us. It was simply the right thing to do. Having encouraged this characteristic in him, we sometimes ourselves fell short of the ideal in his eyes. The Afghans were as tough a bunch as ever came down the pike. But Sefatullah would take them on. He would send a receipt back to a set leader with the statement that he could either justify the cost or eat it. They would meet his high standard or answer to him. It was his courage as a manager that stood out.

Like almost everyone else in the program, he lived in one of the refugee camps near Peshawar. He had a wife and two small children and his salary, modest by our standards, meant that he could do things for his family that most Afghans could not. There was no question of meeting his wife. She was probably in *purdah*, although there was a surprising amount of good sense among the upper levels at the MDC. They were not Taliban zealots and just wanted to see their poor country return to some semblance of normalcy. Sefatullah was also evidence that, in the right setting, the Afghans could get along with one another. After we purged it of Punjabis, the MDC was a microcosm of Afghanistan, heavily Pashtun, but with a sprinkling of Tajiks, Hazaras, and Uzbeks. There were even a few mixtures, of whom Sefatullah was one. They worked well together and Sefatullah managed them all. He was also one reason why I would modify Will Rogers slightly and say that I never met an Afghan I didn't like.

Sayed

Sayed was also in the Afghan program, but he was a Punjabi. The larger program, of which the MDC was a part, acted as the procurement agent for USAID Afghanistan. We provided non-lethal commodities and supplies to the seven parties: *dal chana*, rice, wheat, chickpeas, fertilizer, trucks, computers, and pack animals. The program was staffed in Islamabad primarily with Pakistanis and Sayed was one of them. He was an accountant and cash manager and like most Pakistanis he was very good at what he did. The systems we put in place had safeguards within safeguards and we hired a team of enthusiasts to ensure that they worked. The experience was valuable later in West Africa.

But any system could be circumvented and if Pakistanis were good at what they did, they were good at circumvention as well. I think we kept them honest by paying them an honest wage, incidentally making them part of the small portion of the population in Pakistan who paid income taxes. But Sayed didn't need any inducement other than his own sense of right and wrong to walk the straight and narrow. He was honesty personified. I always knew that his review would be done thoroughly and carefully. In the flesh, he was so thin as to be emaciated, like some of the men we would later see in the concentration camps in Bosnia. His metabolism seemed to be that of a humming bird. Every movement was complicated, as if designed to burn off excess energy. He perpetually wagged his head in that characteristic Indian fashion, and his signature was a frantic series of circles with the pen hovering in the air over the paper, warming up as it were, before descending to the writing surface.

He later left the project to work for a Pakistani construction firm in Ta'if in Saudi Arabia. He asked my advice on the move. We hated to see him go but wouldn't stand in the way of a better opportunity, and Saudi Arabia was still a land of opportunity for Muslims the world over. Maybe he could even make enough money to get married. I received several letters from him telling me about his new life. They all began "Dear Boss." Somewhere in the Hejaz that pen was poised over an invoice or bank statement awaiting approval. I hoped there was someone there to appreciate it the way I did.

Aamir

If Sayed was uncomplicated, Aamir was anything but. He was another Punjabi but his background was more fraught: his mother's family were Shia and his father's people were Wahhabi Sunnis. Sunni-Shia tensions were lethal in Pakistan and the mix probably made him cautious. The Wahhabi part was interesting. In Saudi Arabia, they would deny that there was such a thing: there were only Muslims, not Wahhabis. But away from that center of orthodoxy, things broke down. We even had an Abdel Mohammed in the dog program, the name a theological absurdity.

Aamir was the consummate professional. He was the data-processing manager on the project and the author of most of the systems we used. They were built on an Oracle database. We had other data-processing people, but too often they were the usual IT know-it-alls whose performance fell considerably short of the ideal. Not Aamir. If I asked for documentation of the payroll system he produced it, carefully prepared and bound in multiple copies. He thought logically and concisely and his English was equal to that of most expatriates on the team. The praise is perhaps too modest. Pakistanis generally wrote passable English, but his was free of the malapropisms that made it a constant adventure for a western reader.

However, Aamir was not without fault. As with most Pakistanis there was a darker side. The inferiority complex that was the most lasting legacy of the British in the subcontinent lay very close to the surface. And he was always looking for a complicated explanation when a simple one would do. When we closed the project the staff wanted their considerable severance pay in US dollars instead of rupees. They made Aamir their spokesman. We had always paid them in rupees—being required by the contract to do so—and intended to continue the practice. So, Aamir bore me a silent grudge, as if it were my decision alone that deprived him of the benefits of exchange appreciation. But even with the dark looks in those final days, the consummate professional still shone through.

Hanan

In Egypt, we sometimes found Copts to be more comfortable in English than the Muslims, and that placed a premium on them on the projects we staffed. Probably our outstanding local employee in ten years in Egypt was a Copt. Hanan was a medical doctor but, at LE 120 (or about thirty-five dollars) a month, she couldn't live on what they paid residents in public sector hospitals. So, she worked for us as an executive secretary. In that capacity she was invaluable, her English nearly as good as her Arabic and her efficiency beyond measure. That may have been because she was also a wife and mother and those roles always took precedence for a woman in Egypt. She could only work for us from eight in the morning to two in the afternoon in order to be with her children when they arrived home from school. But we paid her for the full day anyway. I am not sure that she consciously made up the extra hours. But if it was measured the way they did in the United States, she would single-handedly have raised the productivity level in Egypt.

If some of the staff knew Microsoft Office well, Hanan knew it better. When I complained about the latest release—and it was always like learning how to drive a car again, with the controls reversed, the steering wheel on the right instead of the left and the hand brake on the floor instead of under the dashboard—Hanan patiently learned the new system and, equally patiently, taught me. Whether it was Windows or Excel or Project she became an expert and we could always count on her for thorough and professional work. In her relations with the client—a mixture of ministers, chairmen, and secretaries—she always struck the right note, a combination of authority and respect. She was, quite simply, beyond valuation and when one of the expats suggested that the project should put her firstborn through college, he was right. Her children were, typically, being educated in the French system.

Hanan was not just a Christian, but in her quiet way a *believing* Christian. She had seen her redeemer and didn't need to advertise the fact. She and I would have periodic theological discussions but there was a line we couldn't cross. It was announced in Hanan by the raising of a single eyebrow and a look that said:

> Don't give me any of your Western latitudinarianism. I'm not interested in the difference between truth and fact. The Scriptures say that Christ will come again and that's all I need to know.

The eyebrow was enough. Religious differences had a lethal resonance in Egypt, for all of the surface calm. At one point, we hired a Muslim woman who refused to share the ladies room with Hanan because she was Christian. We fired the Muslima forthwith.

Guiry

USAID Niger employed the usual army of locals and one we noticed shortly after our arrival was Guiry Abdel Razzaq, the name itself that characteristic blend of Europe and Islam in Africa. He had helped us find houses by drafting leases, negotiating with landlords, and arranging alterations with local contractors. What we liked best about him was his attitude. Nothing was a problem for Guiry, just an opportunity, and he was always ready to get on with it. When we later looked for an office manager he was our first choice. Guiry knew that nothing in life was certain and that he would be trading a comfortable sinecure with USAID for the uncertainty of a project. But he wanted a challenge. USAID said that they would be sorry to see him go but wouldn't stand in his way.

So, we hired him at a healthy salary increase and he soon became our right-hand man. He was short, maybe five feet seven, trim, and very black. When he smiled, which he did often, it lit up the room. Like most Africans, he came equipped with several languages: Hausa, another tribal language, French, and English. He was especially interested in our work with the emergency fund, and would become the procurement agent when the fund got off the ground. We knew that it would be done thoroughly and professionally.

An incident occurred early in the project that showed Guiry's real mettle. One of the expatriates was ranting about some alleged inefficiency, and took his pique out on Guiry. The American, a white man of about Guiry's height, stood nose to nose with him, shouting imprecations. Guiry responded with his usual politeness. Another man, an African-American, witnessed the scene. He took a long pull on his imaginary pipe and gravely opined that perhaps racism was involved. He was looking for a racist under every bed. I didn't think racism was involved and neither did Guiry. In his case, I think it was because he didn't know racism existed. Anyway, he had better things to do.

He earned enough from us to marry and we were invited to the wedding. His wife was a teacher. He lived in the family compound in Niamey and had just completed his own detached house. The wedding began with a reception for the men at the house, with baguettes and *café au lait* in large saucers. Then we adjourned past the tin shacks on Tillabery Road to an open-air reception under a tent, where the families reenacted the agreement. Packets of betel nuts were passed out to the guests. It was a combination of poverty and gravity and color that will always represent Africa for me. When I left the project, it was with regret most of all for people like Guiry. He cast his lot with us and I seemed to be letting down the side. But I probably shouldn't have worried. There would always be a place for Guiry. He wouldn't worry about the small things because he would always have better things to do.

Mousa

The last of these employees was in many respects the most interesting. When we were looking for a chief accountant for the project in Niger, we were given Mousa's resume by the controller of USAID. We wanted a strong candidate and Mousa seemed to fit the bill. He was the former chief accountant at USAID, Yaoundé in the Cameroon. After the locals had plundered the United States government of several hundred thousand dollars, USAID closed the mission. Moussa was the man they assigned the job. He was also Nigerien, and when he happened to be in Niger on a visit, we arranged for an interview. The figure that appeared in the office that morning was extraordinary. He was light, almost *café au lait* in coloring, with straight, wavy black hair. I thought he might be Indian, since he also had a stomach. It wasn't just a stomach, but a belly beneath the T-shirt that was as round and smooth as a billiard ball, and he seemed to treat it lovingly, the way the Indians did.

He looked like he hadn't shaved in several days and the sparse half-inch hairs on his chin stood out. He was dressed in a T-shirt, wrinkled trousers, and a pair of flip-flops. But it was not the appearance that stood out so much as his manner. To say that he was laid back would be an understatement. His attitude seemed to be: "Here I am and if you want me, fine. If you don't, that's all right too." We swallowed hard and decided we wanted him. Afterwards I would regularly take him up on his appearance. He always improved, at least as long as it took for the whiskers to grow out again. It turned out that he was not Indian at all, but half-Tuareg. They were the nomads from the north and the Sahara, who once owned most of Niger and the people who lived in it.

Most of the Tuaregs in Niamey were *gardiens*. After losing their herds in the drought of 1973, they moved south and took odd-jobs guarding expatriate homes. They would greet us in the streets as equals. They seemed to be saying "We white men understand these blacks." They never did any real work, honest labor being beneath them. Not so with Mousa. He was self-taught in Windows 95 and soon improved the rudimentary systems I had designed. I don't think we ever had work enough for him, although he designed systems and forms and reports, and more reports and forms and systems. We paid him at the highest local rate in Niger, but even that was a step down from his salary in Yaoundé where he had been paid as an expatriate. When USAID sent an audit team for a week to review the system we designed for the fund, they passed it in a day. Most of the credit belonged to Mousa.

Shortly after returning to Niger he also married, in his case a second wife. For the wedding, he had a haircut and a shave and the belly was encased in a brand new *galabiya*. He wore a clean Nigerien cap, perched on top of his new-shorn head. He was about five-feet nine but the new wife was an amazon. She was very black, over six feet tall and statuesque, with great gaps between her front teeth. During the ceremony Mousa was his usual phlegmatic self.

He knew the meaning of authority and always called me "boss," the *patron* of West Africa. That wasn't because he wasn't capable of leading, but because there were headaches that came with the turf and Mousa didn't want any part of them. He would probably never be a boss himself. But technically he was the best FSN I ever saw.

22

Thanksgiving

IT WAS THANKSGIVING DAY in 1995 and a good time to take stock. If the project had been fully operational we would be working. But we were still struggling with the client and the conditions precedent and could miss the day without much loss of productivity. I had given the Baptist day-guard Danladi—literally "born on Sunday"—the day off. Bureima, the night-guard, had already left. Bureima was the only Muslim and the only native Nigerien among the household staff and he spoke only French in addition to his native Hausa. He was black as a ripe eggplant and kept a machete, a bow, and a quiver full of arrows to protect the house against *voleurs*. When someone tried to break into a villa down the street, the guard had shot him full of arrows. Bureima was quite prepared to do the same.

The day began inauspiciously with a flat tire. I intended to do an early-morning walk around the rice fields of Kolo, on the other side of Niamey. Richard, the Ghanaian Baptist cook and houseboy, had already padded in with my first cup of coffee and would have juice and cereal ready when I returned. If this had been a Sunday, Richard and Joseph, the yard- and pool-man, would have been off to church where Richard sang in the choir. I gave him a beige suit I had made in Egypt and he looked very smart. Both would have promised to pray for me. They regularly read the Bible and punctuated their conversation with pious ejaculations like "By His grace," or "If God wills." It was all very natural and unaffected. The religiosity didn't keep Richard from bringing his girlfriend to spend the night in the servant's quarters attached to the house and he introduced her to me the next morning as his "lover." I had been advised that this was a no-no in Africa and sent her away. Richard always called me "master." I sometimes had to be severe with him but he was an excellent cook and ironed beautifully.

Outside this morning, Joseph told me that we had a "puncture" and this required a change of plan. Joseph was a graduate agronomist and an expert in the flora of West Africa, particularly of his native Ghana. He regularly lectured me on the Latin names of the trees in the yard. After the rains this year, the heaviest in the Sahel in forty years, the yard looked like a tropical rain forest with frangipani, flamboyant, and bougainvillea, mango and papaya trees. The wide, fern-like leaves and red flowers of the flame trees reached almost to the ground. Joseph's green thumb also meant that it was full of flowers. It had been a wasteland when I moved in but Joseph and the rain, together, had restored it.

The little swimming pool had been peeling and full of trash but Joseph cleaned and painted it, and now kept the water at just the right pH balance. It was too small to swim laps but it was cool and inviting when, as Joseph put it, I wanted "a bath." I had already needed it. The rainy season in Niger was followed by a period of intense heat and in March the thermometer approached 125 degrees Fahrenheit. It was so dry you never knew you were sweating: the moisture evaporated so quickly that it didn't wet your clothes. We had to drink at least three liters of water a day to avoid dehydration. Joseph was currently reading the memoirs of Charles Colson and he talked knowledgeably about many matters beside agronomy. Shortly after we came I gave him the bicycle we had shipped from Pakistan and he said "God bless you." Then, Bureima wanted a *velo* as well and I had to tell him that I was not *père Noël*. In Africa, it was thought that the *patron* could do anything, and in a way, I suppose they were right. When I left Niger, it was Joseph, not the younger Richard, who was most affected, breaking down in miserable, throat-catching sobs.

There was little of the Indian concern with caste here—inside men doing outside work or vice-versa—and Joseph and Richard set to work with a will. After removing the tire, we took it around the corner to a little commercial area of tin shacks to look for a tire-repair shop. It was not far from the convenience store I used when I didn't want to go downtown to Score, the French supermarket. The store was a kind of Nigerien 7-Eleven and, like many businesses in Niamey, it was owned by Lebanese. I later learned that most of them were Shiites from the south of the country. All the stationery stores, most of the fabric shops, and several restaurants were Lebanese-owned, although the best restaurant in town was run by an Italian who had relocated from Agadez when the Tuareg revolt broke out. This store carried a good selection of household staples. I occasionally spoke Arabic with one of the sons of the owner. He was tanned and at first I asked him if he was Tuareg. He was offended but eventually got over it.

When we found the repair shop the boy inside was asleep under what looked like pieces of heavy butcher paper. We called and he stumbled outside tucking in his shirt. It was a "Chicago Bulls" T-shirt. The rest of his dress consisted of filthy brown trousers, without shoes. He set to work and for the next half-hour I absorbed the early-morning rhythms of life here in the big city. The sights and especially the smells reminded me of somewhere I couldn't quite place, and then I remembered it was the lower slopes of Kilimanjaro six years before. But I didn't get out much in Niger, except for the office and walks in the rice fields.

It was a sobering admission and one of the reasons I was not happy here. To an unusual degree, the house was an oasis. An eight-foot wall surrounded the yard. The gate was locked and the day- and night-guard were there to keep out intruders, which they very effectively did. Inside, the house was light and airy, all whitewashed walls and white tiles on the floor, with plenty of room for pictures and carpets. It was the former residence of the Egyptian ambassador and probably our nicest house in twenty-five years abroad. It had American touches with appliances from Sears, including washer, dryer, refrigerator, and freezer. The freezer was so big that I shut it off. The library was well stocked with books on the Arab world, the Indian subcontinent, and Central Asia and maybe that was part of the problem. I was in West Africa and there was nothing to buy in town except a few overpriced coffee-table books and a selection of *policiers* in French.

A regular routine was a visit to the bookstore on Saturday morning followed by shopping at Score. If I was lucky the Thursday *Air France* flight from Paris would bring a recent *International Herald Tribune* (*IHT*) and the latest *Newsweek*. Then, I ran the gauntlet of beggars and lepers to Score to lay in the next week's supply of beer, wine, meat, and cheese. In Score, there were *marrons glacés*, various *pâtés*, smoked salmon, and a selection of French wines that cost the monthly salary of one of the *fonctionnaires* we worked with. That was if they were paid, which was infrequently. Ham was about twenty-five dollars a pound and the man behind the counter sliced it wearing plastic gloves like a proctologist. The meat and fish were local. The Nile Perch—big fat filets—was very good, but the beef was so tough as to be almost inedible. There were also less expensive items like canned *cassoulet*, cheeses, and good millet bread.

They also carried French and Spanish jug wine. I always bought the jug wine. Even so, a trip to Score generally set me back many thousand CFA's, or francs issued by the *Banque Centrale des États de l'Afrique de l'Ouest*. And this was after devaluation, so those of us with dollars were getting everything at half the old prices. It didn't seem fair. I bought bread at the bakery. There were the usual complaints that the French had introduced wheat—expensive and unnecessary—into these African countries where millet and sorghum were the traditional grains. It was probably true. But the baguettes in the little bakery were the equal of those in Paris. The clientele was mainly Nigerien.

Afterwards I read the *IHT* and *Newsweek* from cover to cover, including the advertisements. This routine took about five hours, door-to-door and page-by-page. The news was often depressing. The week before there had been an article in the *IHT* about a drunken Russian officer in Chechnya and it was a reminder of *The Hidden War*, a Russian journalist's account of their war in Afghanistan I had picked up in Quetta. The book was very Russian, full of half-baked philosophy with every conversation bearing a heavy weight of existential meaning. Interestingly, one of the generals fired by Yeltsin for opposing the war in Chechnya was the man who presided over the withdrawal from Afghanistan. This seemed a repeat of the crude tale told in *The Hidden War*, of the poor brutalized Chechens and the sad-sack, under-trained, and under-paid nineteen-year-old Russian conscripts thrown into Grozny.

That left the rest of the weekend for more serious reading. But I could take only so much of Fernand Braudel's very French thoughts on the Mediterranean. In Niamey, we were only a few hours by Royal Air Maroc from Casablanca and an hour further from Spain. But I never made it to Morocco or Spain, or anywhere else, in my fourteen months in West Africa. Then, there was always Richard Burton's footnotes and terminal essay in the sixteen-volume *Thousand Nights and a Night*. Before coming to Niger, I had bought a copy of his *Wanderings in West Africa*, thinking it would tell me something about the people and give me a lift, as Burton generally did. But the *Wanderings* were just an account of his journey by sea from Liverpool to Fernando Po in the Bight of Benin where he was posted as British consul. There were stops along the way, but nothing in the Gold Coast, the Windy Coast, the Ivory Coast, or the Slave Coast pleased him. It was all low-lying, feverish, fetid, and corrupt, Africans with an attitude, tainted by their exposure to the white man when they weren't being their brutish selves. The book ended after 600 pages with his arrival in "this very abomination of desolation," "the white man's cemetery," where he felt "uncommonly suicidal." So much for light reading.

There was a fairly wide selection of material in the community lounge at the embassy and it helped to pass the time. It included everything from *Penney's* catalogues to the *New York Review of Books*. I had last read the *New York Review* at Berkeley and it was heavily academic and leftist with contributors like Noam Chomsky and protest pieces on the Vietnam War. It was still rigorous but seemed less leftist, and a typical issue might have articles on the Jews and the African slave trade—they were just as guilty as everyone else—a chronicle of the re-education horrors in Vietnam after we left, or pieces on writers like Doris Lessing or Laura Ingalls Wilder.

There was a video shop at the embassy and I generally watched a couple of movies over the weekend. That accounted for a few more hours. There were some pleasant surprises but most simply passed the time. Then, I would count the books in the bookshelf or, lying on my back, the number of circles in the cast, recessed ceiling. There were a hundred and fifteen books in the bookshelf, unless I had removed one recently. It was an average of just over twenty-eight per shelf but there were several ways to count: straight count, by color, average per half-shelf, deviation from the average. Depending on where I was in the room the number changed because some books would be hidden by the doors. There were always 288 circles in the ceiling, but there were many different combinations: straight count, 8 x 36, 3 x 96, 6 x 48, 12 x 24.

It seemed that Africa was not my thing. The anthropologists and sociologists I worked with talked fondly of this village or that market, how Lomé had changed or how St. Louis in Senegal was not what it used to be. But I had none of these props to lean on. The project I headed could almost be reduced to one word: millet, although everyone said that the obsession with the cereal balance had to end. We were supposed to solve Niger's food problem. Rain-fed millet was the key and the recent rains had saved the season and, temporarily, our skins. They also, incidentally, caused heavy flooding and in parts of Niamey there were reaches of standing water that looked navigable. Coming back from a walk one evening I attempted to drive through a large pool with a heavy sewage content and had stuck. Two wheels and then four wheels wouldn't free the car, a big Toyota Land Cruiser, and the rocking motion only got us in deeper. A crowd of about fifty people gathered and witnessed the scene before someone suggested that for CFA 5,000 they would help. So, they waded into the muck and a combination of four wheels and their muscles finally freed us. I gave the 5,000 to the most aggressive man and chalked it up to experience. The Nigeriens, incidentally, appealed to the international community for assistance and this time most organizations came through. The United Nations gave $250,000, including a check for $80,000 for blankets. Our counterparts didn't know what to do with it. They were afraid that if they deposited the check it would be diverted by the government to some other use. The new permanent secretary of SAP, a woman, simply shook her head. "*Pauvre Niger*," she said.

I regularly put in long hours. But it was stress, boredom, and the strange effects of anti-malaria prophylaxis, not overwork, that were the real problems. I had an intermittent low-grade fever for most of the time I was in

Niger. I probably didn't have malaria but what all Americans in Africa had, a healthy fear of it. Some strains had crossed the blood-brain barrier and cerebral malaria was not the slowly wasting disease that afflicted as much as 80 percent of the population of the continent, but a killer in as little as twenty-four hours. In overseas postings to Egypt, Saudi Arabia, Oman, and Pakistan there had always cautions about malaria. We didn't pay much attention. But in Niger prophylaxis was mandatory. So, we took either Mefloquine once a week or Doxycycline, a broad-spectrum antibiotic taken once a day at a low dosage. The Mefloquine had unpleasant side-effects. It was not recommended for anyone with a tendency to depression. And even for those without the tendency it produced irritability, fitful sleep, and strange dreams. The Doxycycline, when taken at a low dosage, could mask an infection that may have been the real problem.

I had several episodes overseas that were attributed either to malaria or to a suspicion of the disease. The first was in Egypt where in the early 1980s I developed a high fever followed by teeth-rattling chills that had me shaking in the bed until it shook sympathetically. The lab drew blood and found no conclusive evidence of malaria: none of the parasites were "manifested." But they found nothing inconsistent with the disease and that, coupled with the other symptoms, led the doctor to a diagnosis of malaria. Later in the early 1990s in Pakistan there had been another, more violent, episode, a fever of over 104 degrees and then chills and sweats so heavy that I was soaked to the skin. But it was followed by the onset of giardia and I attributed the symptoms to that.

In Niger, it was more than an episode. Where the first two had been isolated incidents, here it was a chronic feverishness and fretfulness that lasted for months on end. Burton may have put his finger on it:

> The great gift of malaria is utter apathy, at once its evil and its cure, its bane and its blessing. Men come out from Europe with the fairest prospect, if beyond middle age, of dying soon . . . No one intends to stay longer than two years and even those two are one long misery.

A persistent low-grade fever was never enough to keep me from work but left me listless and apathetic. I hadn't missed a day's work because of sickness in fifteen years overseas. But after a few unsuccessful attempts to diagnose the problem, I began to feel like a malingerer. My temperature was normal in the morning but by noon it had risen to around 100 degrees. I was out of sorts. But the blood work found nothing and I eventually stopped going to the health unit. I changed from Mefloquine to Doxycycline and then back to Mefloquine. The Mefloquine was toxic. I had crazy nightmares and sweats.

The closest I came to a diagnosis was a visiting doctor's conclusion that I wasn't happy in Niger and that my body was trying to tell me something. I didn't see the connection. But the fever disappeared when I left Africa.

Meanwhile, the boy finished repairing the tire. He used a combination of tools that, for sheer ingenuity, rivaled anything in the developed world. Nearby, a fat woman was frying millet pancakes on a three-foot skillet into which were set little pockets for each pancake. They were good, and a variant on Richard's cereal. Half-naked children, wide-eyed, wandered around us. I realized that in nearly ten months in Africa I hadn't heard a child cry. The shops were on Tillabery Road and the morning commute pulsed by. There were Europeans in big Toyotas and Africans in little Peugeots and an occasional Deux Cheveaux. Europeans in Africa looked dissipated, all the men like alcoholics and all the women like whores. The traffic laws were odd. No one paid much attention to traffic lights, probably because the colored reflectors were broken and lights were not red or green, only the naked bulb shining where the color should have been. But everyone, on pain of the severest penalty, had to use turn signals, even several times in the middle of a roundabout. The law also required everyone on a motorcycle to wear a helmet and some complied. The variety was interesting: real helmets with visors, football helmets, equestrian riding caps, fiber helmet liners, even calabashes or gourds. The tire repair cost 600 West African francs, or about $1.20 and I gave the boy an extra 100 francs. He seemed satisfied.

Afterwards, I had my walk by the Niger. The course was a four-mile trapezoid. It was still early enough to be cool and the great river looked placid and inviting, with just the hint of a ripple on the surface to show that it was moving. The flow was about five mph, which I knew because it moved a little faster than I did. The river was still high, covering areas that were being plowed four months before. It was maybe a quarter mile across. The shoreline was covered with lily-pods and, not surprisingly, birds called Lilly Trotters. There were also Mourning Doves, Senegal Coucals, Long-Tailed Wydahs, Green-Backed Herons, and Abyssinian Rollers. Flocks

Planting rice, Kolo, Niamey

of Sacred Ibis would come later in the year after the rice harvest. The Sacred Ibis had a black fringe on its wings and tail, and they had been preserved in Egypt in Pharaonic times. Several million mummified Ibises were found at Saqqara, each in its own individual pot. But they were long gone from Egypt. This morning I also saw a pair of rare, rose-cheeked cranes. They mated for life and there was something touching about them as they moved around together. They would be in a field, eating together or in a tree a half-mile away, resting together. Maybe I noticed them because I was alone in Niger. Martha was with Laura in Pakistan, teaching at ISI while Laura completed her senior year in high school. They visited at Christmas, flying from Karachi via Dubai where they bought a large CD player, shepherding it through several customs authorities along the way. Martha was her usual omnivorous self abroad, absorbing the local color and becoming an expert in Nigerien jewelry in a matter of days.

Here, in the middle of the river was a dark shape, apparently a hippo. A man stopped me and pointed it out. It was the first hippo I had seen in Niger, the others having moved either up or down the river. On the other side were the pink plateaus of the Sahel, tufted with green and reflected in the glassy water of the stream. Close by the shore there would be an occasional *piroque*, or dugout canoe. Two turns around the fields, perpendicular to the river and then on a parallel levee before doubling back over the same ground again, was just about four miles and an hour's walk. The millet and sorghum, both in ten-foot stalks that looked like corn, had just been harvested and, thanks to the rain, this year's had been a bumper crop. That would give us a little breathing room before the next crisis. The rice was about

Rice paddy, Kolo, Niamey

eighteen inches high and it would be the second crop this year. It was very green and would be ready in another month or so, although some fields lay fallow and one was being plowed by a man with a team of oxen. The fields were full of frogs and, if this had been evening, their calls would accompany me around the course. This morning they were silent but many of the stalks were bent over with the weight of Yellow-Fronted Canaries. Great White Egrets wandered gravely over the levees.

Kids were catching little fish and roasting them over fires of sticks and straw. I said *bonjour* and they replied *donnez-moi un cadeau*—"give me a present"—but we all knew it was just a ritual. Some said *courage* to this odd white man walking for no apparent reason in the fields. In the developing World, no one walked anywhere unless he had to. Others, little black bodies, were swimming in the river or in the irrigation canals next to the fields. Occasionally a young woman would be bathing in one of the same canals. It was surprising in this, a Muslim country. But it was Africa and Islam and Christianity had always taken their own African forms here.

On this Thanksgiving Day, my problems were trivial compared with those of people in Kigali or Sarajevo, or Grozny. But that kind of reasoning never worked. On a trip to Maradi, 300 miles to the east, I was looking forward to a change of scene. But it was 600 miles of sameness and I didn't take a single photograph. Eventually, both the disaster specialist and I would leave Niger, he to Addis Ababa and I to Cairo. When we left, the $10 million fund, the reason for our being, was still not in place. We had been very active in the early days, before the other team members arrived and were a bit of a phenomenon in the mission. We had rented an office and rehabilitated it, hired good staff, and tried our best with the client. When the money didn't come, we begged the loan of $100,000 from the USAID controller.

Piroques, Niger river

Although it was irregular, this loan against an uncertain future, he granted it. He had been a member of the USAID reengineering team in Washington and seemed to be the one in the mission most committed to change.

He was an African-American well over six feet tall and weighed about 300 pounds. He looked like an offensive tackle in the NFL. He spoke very little French and had no use for the African sense of accountability, or lack thereof. His own local staff didn't seem to understand him, or he them. But if it was a question of helping the people, he was ready to bend the rules. So, the disaster specialist designed a food-for-work project in Diffa, 600 miles to the east, near Lake Chad. It was a classic African project, planting trees to retard desertification and the people badly wanted it. The results were encouraging. But the ambassador dismissed it as "Peace Corps stuff" and we were back to waiting.

It might seem odd that I would want to leave the clean air, the whitewashed villa with its lush tropical grounds, the American appliances, the friendly little community, the good Nigeriens we employed, and the efficient household staff. Instead, there would be a city of fifteen million, the persistent odor of burning garbage, the dusty trees, elevators that didn't work, the awful Louis Farouq furniture in most Cairo apartments, and a difficult public sector client. I would be advising ARENTO, the Egyptian telephone company.

But at least I would be going back where I belonged.

The yard, Niamey

23

The Milk Run

Along with everything else in Francophone West Africa, the French seemed to have monopoly on air service. There was hardly a flight out of Niamey that didn't go through Paris, whatever its ultimate destination. There was a *Royal Air Maroc* flight to New York through Casablanca that was both inexpensive and allowed access to Fez and Marrakesh. But for points north and east, everything seemed to go through Paris. That meant *Air France* or *Air Afrique*, both operated by the French. *Air France* seemed to be in a class by itself as an international carrier: the service was excellent, the food was outstanding, and the traveling experience was always pleasant.

The comparison was particularly unfortunate with any of the American carriers. It was the difference between a company with a large government subsidy and employees with job security, and a company and employees that had neither. Everything on United or TWA seemed to say to the passenger: we are making money on you, but the margins are so small that we have to wring out all the fat. Air France was much more relaxed and it showed in the service. Unfortunately, it also showed in the bottom line. The cost per passenger-mile was three times that of an American carrier and the company was in receivership. It couldn't afford to provide this standard of service much longer.

However, there was one route from Niamey to the east that seemed to have escaped the long arm of the French. It was an Ethiopian Air flight to Cairo via Addis Ababa. Since Cairo was where I was going, it seemed worth a try. It turned out to be a milk run across the Sahel, via a catalogue of places you didn't want to visit. But it was an interesting odyssey and the perfect way to leave Africa, not by the high road but by the low road.

Leaving Niamey was a wrench. I had friends in USAID, with the client, and even on the team. I would miss Mme. Maimouna Mamadou, the new *secrétaire permanent* of the Prime Minister's disaster relief office. In the tyranny of the French language the position was masculine even though it was filled by a woman. I had written her a final letter, helped by the fluent French of one of the team members and the sentiments were heartfelt. She was an excellent manager, incisive and willing to take tough decisions. She was a reminder of Burton's dictum: "Show me ten men and nine of them are women."

I especially regretted leaving the Nigeriens who worked for us. I tried to assure them that my departure didn't reflect on the project or on their future. But it may have looked like I was bailing out at the right time. A few months later the army grew tired of the endless squabbling by the political parties and staged a coup. That was the end of the sham democracy and, ultimately, of the project. The locals were utterly cynical about the parties and the experiment in democracy. In one of the inconsistencies of Africa there were countless little newspapers hawked on the street—*quotidiennes* or *hebdomadaires* or *bihebdomadaires*, dailies, weeklies, or bi-weeklies—full of political philosophy worthy of a Jefferson. But everyone knew that the politicians were corrupt and the system was rotten to the core. To my driver democracy meant only that some people didn't wear helmets on their motor scooters. The army wouldn't have allowed that.

And at last, after all of the unpleasantness, I realized why some Americans came to Africa and never left. I seemed to be the only American in Niamey who hadn't been in the Peace Corps. The rest were all frustrated anthropologists or sociologists or development specialists who were drawn to the diversity of the continent, the stunning landscapes, or maybe just the primitiveness of it all. Ultimately it was the Africans themselves, with all of their contradictions, who made it worthwhile. The Ethiopian Air flight left at one-twenty in the morning and the man with the fluent French was there to see me off. He bought me a beer, and if there is any lasting memory of expatriate life in Africa, it is of the beer. Everyone drank, some to excess. A beer at sunset on the terrace of the Terminus Hotel, overlooking the great expanse of the Niger River, was reason enough for some to come to Africa. To them there wasn't anything better.

We boarded the plane just after midnight and it was good equipment, as they say in the industry, a new Boeing 767. I was carrying dollars for the family of the wife of a USAID project officer. She was Ethiopian and almost surreally beautiful, a reminder that the women from *al-Habash* were the favorite concubines of the Arabs. The couple regularly sent money to the family in Addis Ababa. They needed it. Ethiopia had been caught in the same time warp as Cuba, only more savage, and the experiments in social engineering by the Mengitsu regime had been genocidal. The family had survived, but just barely.

The crew were efficient and I had an exit seat with extra leg room. The in-flight magazine had an interesting article on the churches of Roha, to the north of Addis Ababa. After the meal, I slept briefly before the seat belt sign came on and we made preparations for landing. It would be Ndjamena, old Fort Lamy, in Chad. The civil war in the country had raged back and forth for several years and the Libyans had tried, unsuccessfully, to intervene. Finally, the French had come in and things were now relatively quiet. Both disaster specialists on the team had spent several years in Chad. Despite reports in the outside world of civil war and insurrection, life went on, even for the foreign aid agencies.

The Ndjamena airport was actually fairly modern. It was cleaner than the airport in Niamey, and we wandered in our transit limbo through the duty-free shops and then into the bar. The local beer was good. Back on the plane it was now 4 a.m. and we had about 1,700 miles to Addis. The flight path looked like it would take us over western Chad and then southern Sudan before reaching the Ethiopian border near Asosa. For the next three hours I slept, fitfully and not restfully, developing the usual kink in my neck from sleeping in an upright position.

After dawn, the highlands of Ethiopia spread out below. It looked green and fertile, but years of famine had made the country the largest recipient of food aid on the continent. That probably had more to do with the resettlement schemes and the disruption of normal trade and exchange mechanisms than any natural niggardliness of the soil. The plane circled and then landed after a long descent. The hills behind the city looked like the Berkeley hills as they climbed above the flat. All that was missing was the bay on the other side. The city lay at an elevation of about 10,000 feet and I thought it might be cool. But on this day in May at nine forty in the morning, it already held the promise of heat. But it was nothing like Niamey where even after the hot season in March and April, where the temperatures would reach 125 degrees Fahrenheit, it had still been over 100 when we left. Addis looked green from above. But on the ground, it was more brown than green and Bole International airport was dusty and showed signs of neglect. We collected our baggage and passed through customs.

Some of us were transit passengers and Ethiopian Airlines put us up for the night. The flight to Cairo would leave just after noon the next day. So, we waited while transportation was arranged. Then a bus took us to the hotel. On the ride in from the airport the destitution of Ethiopia became clear. Even here in the highlands where the green should have predominated, everything seemed to be a dusty brown. People's clothing was threadbare. The cars were a sign of how isolated the country had been since the revolution in 1974, models that hadn't been seen in West in years. It was like Cuba, or Syria in the 1970s where everything was either eastern-block or old. I recalled the cab I had taken in Latakia in 1975. It was a 1953 Chrysler and the owner had proudly thumped his chest: "My car, good car."

The Ethiopia Hotel was adequate. It wasn't the Hilton, but there was something about the atmosphere in these second- or third-tier hotels that made them more interesting. The rooms were barely functional, with peeling wallpaper and cheap particleboard furniture. The bathroom fixtures worked with a little encouragement. In the dining room the clientele was generally "dressed," the men in suits and neckties and the women in dresses. The staff wore white jackets with bow ties, although the jackets were dirty around the cuffs and the collars were frayed. It was like the Kenya Railways train we had taken several years before from Nairobi to Mombasa, where white-clad waiters still served on monogrammed linen and the utensils were heavy flat silver. But it was all badly gone to seed. There appeared to be a tradition of good service and people tried to do the right thing, but the reality fell considerably short of the ideal.

After checking in, I took a walk around the neighborhood of the hotel. There were beggars everywhere. Urban poverty in Africa seemed different from poverty in Europe or America. There, the cold, the white skin and lank hair, and the reek of alcohol and urine made it particularly depressing. The photo of the feet sticking out from under the sheets on a slab in a Moscow morgue said it all. The skin was pale and mottled and the hair was worn off the calves. Here, the beggars were dusty and leprous and often crippled or otherwise deformed. Their skin was gray and dust had turned the poll of their hair the same color. Maybe because it was different the phenomenon didn't seem so grim. There were a few shops that offered souvenirs, largely silver Coptic crosses. I looked at a few and decided to return later in the afternoon.

Lunch was curry with rice. There was also meat with the ubiquitous chips. Afterwards I had several errands. The first was delivering the consignment of dollars to Emenet's family. Rob had provided me with an elaborate set of instructions: directions from the airport to the city center, a note on the currency, a caution about walking around after dark, a series of names, telephone numbers, and a drop point. It was like something out of a novel by John LeCarré. I dialed the family's number and the telephone actually worked. I got a sister, and we agreed to meet at the hotel.

After I had given her the letter and money she showed me around the city. We took a cab up the hill. Addis Ababa seemed to consist of a series of plateaus and we went up to the second before turning and parking on a hill overlooking the sprawl below. She knew a jeweler and I saw many of the same Coptic crosses I had seen earlier in the day. I suppose I was given a special price. Anyway, the crosses were not expensive. I selected two old pieces, both badly tarnished. One was simple and the other was covered with elaborate filigree work. They would clean up nicely. But when they were polished, both exhibited a yellow tint. The silver was probably an alloy with a little brass or copper in the mix.

The second meeting was with the friend of a friend, a Brit who ran the Coopers & Lybrand affiliate in Addis. We arranged to have a drink in the hotel later in the afternoon and chatted about finance in the developing world. He insisted that this was his turf and the drink was his treat. He and his wife were entertaining a prominent local businessman for dinner that night and would I like to join them? So, I retreated to my room for a necktie and then we drove to his home where his wife was waiting.

She was half Ethiopian and half Greek and very pretty. She was also a jeweler and the house was the usual eclectic expat residence with good local art on the walls. After drinks we drove up the successive plateaus of the city. This time we didn't stop but went all the way to the top. The restaurant was the best Italian restaurant in town and it was very good. There was fresh *prosciutto* with melon as a starter and then a selection of pasta of various colors and shapes. It was all washed down with Italian wine, white followed by red. Afterwards came the salad, in the European fashion. The conversation was mainly about telecommunications and how the rates in Ethiopia were ruinous.

The Italian connection was interesting. Mussolini's invasion of Ethiopia in 1936 had been followed by a failure of nerve on the part of the international community. Haile Selassie had gone before the League of Nations with a plea for help. They had done nothing. But it was not the first Italian invasion of Ethiopia and Menelik II had defeated an Italian army at Adwa in 1896. Many Italian prisoners-of-war who returned to Italy did so emasculated, that being a tradition of warfare in Ethiopia. After the British put Haile Selassie back on the throne in 1941 he ruled until the revolution in 1974. It was said that Mengitsu had personally smothered him with a pillow in his hospital bed. The grotesque experiments in social engineering and the genocide followed.

But there seemed to be little residue of ill-feeling from the Italian attempts at colonization. Maybe it was because they were largely unsuccessful or because, even when successful, the Italian yoke had lain relatively lightly on peoples' necks. There seemed to be none of the feeling against the colonizer that lay close to the surface in India or West Africa. At any rate, it was a pleasant evening with good conversation and good food in one of the poorest countries in the world. There was none of the corrosive sense that, somehow, it was unfair that we should enjoy ourselves while others suffered. It was still Alan's turf and he paid the bill.

The odyssey resumed the next day. The plane took off just after noon and allowing for the two hours at the airport before flight time it meant a midmorning departure from the hotel. The equipment was the same Boeing 767 of the day before and the next stop was Khartoum. There were many Sudanese on the flight, the men in white with the characteristic headdress and the women swathed in layers of multicolored fabric. They were northerners, Arabized and chocolate colored, not the black of their brothers to the south. "Brothers" perhaps put it too charitably. Our houseboy later in Cairo was from Juba, 100 miles north of the Ugandan border. He was a Christian, central-African, and probably a Dinka. His family were scattered over refugee camps in the Sudan and a few were in Cairo. They had no love for the northerners who were intent on eradicating their kind. Unfortunately, even in the late twentieth century, their own slave hunters and warlords were as much a problem as the northerners.

From the air, Khartoum looked like a dusty warren, with geometric row after row of hovels set in the flat. I looked for Omdurman and the confluence of the White and Blue Niles, but there wasn't a noticeable difference in the color of the water. I also thought of the tomb of the Mahdi at Omdurman and of the death of Chinese Gordon. The slaughter of the Mahdists in 1898, like the French decimation of the Mamluks a hundred years earlier, was a function of European arms brought to bear against a primitive but courageous—and contemptuous—enemy. Churchill had been there and *The River War*, for all of its sonorousness, was a riveting account of the campaign. Kitchener's victory may have been a foregone conclusion and the casualties seemed to indicate a slaughter: an estimated 9,700 of the Mahdists killed, 10,000–16,000 wounded, and another 5,000 prisoners, against Egyptian casualties of twenty British officers and 462 men. But the Egyptians were at the end of a thousand-mile supply line and were outnumbered three to one. If the Dervishes had attacked the night before or concentrated their attacks better the outcome might have been very different and Kitchener's head might have joined Gordon's as a trophy of the Khalifa.

People who knew Khartoum confirmed that there was little there. One of our staff in Cairo had lived in Khartoum as the wife of a USAID project officer. It was the usual story of a little bit of America set down in the middle of Africa, Niamey all over again. There were cavernous refrigerators and freezers, washing machines and dryers, and a large consumables allowance. She and her husband had lived, alone, in a seven-bedroom house. It was the local landlords who benefited. She was Peruvian and had an incurable tendency to malapropisms, calling the city "Cartoon."

The Sudanese deplaned with their armies of children and we waited in the aircraft while they unloaded the baggage. The breath of the Sudan was hot when they opened the doors. Afterwards, we taxied back out to the runway and took off to the north. Then we turned nearly due east towards Asmara, Eritrea, our next stop. The civil war was won, and the Eritreans had achieved the independence from Ethiopia they had sought for years. All of our drivers in Saudi Arabia had been Eritrean. They were stateless, technically Ethiopian citizens but without passports.

Eritrea had supposedly done very well since independence. There appeared to be some hope for the Horn of Africa after all. The yearly revenue per telephone line in the country was about $800, triple that of Egypt's and we later used the number in an attempt to shame ARENTO into change. But the Egyptians objected to any comparison with people to the south. Or to the east, for that matter. To them the Saudis were still medieval and barbaric. I innocently told the story of St. John Philby's experience with the telephone in Jidda. He was the Marconi franchisee and had arranged for a recitation of the Qur'an over the instrument to prove to the *ulema'* that it was lawful. But the story provoked only a derisive snort from the chairman of ARENTO: how could I possibly compare Egyptians with such people?

After a brief stay we took off again, and headed west of north for Cairo, the final leg. It was about 1,200 miles. About an hour later we picked up Lake Nasser and its outline was just as it appeared on the map in the inflight magazine. Then the river disappeared as we took the direct route over the desert to the vicinity of Sohag. North of Assiut the Nile reappeared and was our constant companion for the next hour. Then Cairo appeared below, looking just like it had ten years before. From the air it looked like Khartoum, another dusty warren. It was always surprising how much green there was on the ground.

After landing we taxied for what seemed like as long as it had taken us to reach Cairo from Asmara, because we were directed to the old airport and the last parking place on the tarmac. There would be no descent through the articulated arm to the new terminal building, but instead a wait for a pair of buses. They made their slow way past Air Malta, Kazakh Air, Olympic, The Royal Jordanian Airlines, Aeroflot, Hungarian Airlines, Kenya Airways, LOT, and Yemen Airways to the old terminal building. This was the service entrance to Cairo.

Then there were the old time-consuming lines at immigration. I wasn't in a hurry, since the assignment was for two years and Cairo would still be there when I emerged. So, I was able to renew an old acquaintance with

Egyptian officialdom. You could be high-handed with authority, which never worked. Or you could watch the change in attitude that a select few words in Arabic produced. Even after ten years my colloquial Egyptian was up to the test. Then, there was the glint of recognition when they knew that you knew their game. If you had the time, it was even fun.

After I had collected my bags I ran the gauntlet of taxi drivers. They were scoundrels the continent over. There were no meters in the cabs, only cabbies intent on extracting as much as they could from often-gullible travelers. The first trip in an African city was generally an expensive one. It was then that I realized that I hadn't just arrived in Cairo. I really hadn't left Africa at all.

Glossary of Foreign Terms

Cassoulet	A rich, slow-cooked dish of southwest France
Chowkidar	A night watchman, from the Hindi
Dhobi	A washer-man or -woman, from the Hindi
Eid	A feast day or holiday, from the Arabic triliteral "to celebrate"
Ghosht	Flesh, meat in Farsi; a kind of stew
Halal	That which is permitted; often referring to food where the method of slaughter and preparation is specified; from the Arabic
Hazara	A Mongol people living in central Afghanistan; from the Farsi word hazar, or "thousand," since there were originally about that many of them
Hebdomadaire	A weekly, with bihebdomadaire a bi-weekly
Hizb	Party or faction, often political; from the Arabic
Jami'	A Friday mosque, from the Arabic trilateral "to gather, congregate"
Jangl	A wood, forest, or thicket; from the Farsi
Jerib	A patch of arable land; from the Arabic
Koochi	A vagabond, member of a wandering tribe in Afghanistan; from the Farsi
Madrasa	A school or place of learning; from the Arabic trilateral "to study"

Mali	A gardener; from the Hindi
Masjid	A mosque; from the Arabic triliteral "to prostrate oneself"
Mullah	A schoolmaster, doctor, learned man; from the Arabic
Nan	Bread, a loaf; from the Farsi
Pashtun	A people of southeast Afghanistan and northwest Pakistan; sometimes called *Pathan*
Patois	In French, a provincial dialect
Pilav	A dish of fish or meat served with garnished rice; from the Farsi
Piroque	A long narrow canoe of West Africa made from a single log
Policier	A detective novel
Qafila	A caravan; from the Arabic trilateral "to come home"
Riba'	Interest earned on invested funds, usury; from the Arabic "to grow"; forbidden in Islam
Riwaq	Literally "living quarters;" organization of students by nationality in Al-Azhar university in Cairo; from the Arabic
Sifarish	A commission, tip, or gratuity; from either Farsi or Hindi
Shalwar	Breeches, drawers; along with *Khamis,* the dress of Northwest Pakistan and Afghanistan, consisting of drawers and a loose shirt falling to the knee; from the Farsi
Sous-prèfet	In Niger a government functionary responsible for a sub-prefecture
Tajik	An ethnic Iranian people spread among Tajikistan, Afghanistan, Iran, and Uzbekistan; speakers of an archaic form of Farsi
Ta'liq	One of the standard Arabic scripts, literally "hanging;" used widely in Iran and Pakistan
Tonga	A horse-drawn conveyance of Afghanistan and Pakistan
Tuk tuk	A small motorized three-wheeler, widely used in the Indian subcontinent
Velo	In French, short for *velocipede* or bicycle
Voleur	In French a thief or swindler
Wadi	A dry riverbed or river valley; from the Arabic
Waqf	A pious foundation; from the Arabic

Zabiba	Literally a "raisin;" a rough encrustation on the forehead, formed from the repeated pressing of the head to the floor during prayer; from the Arabic

www.ingramcontent.com/pod-product-compliance
Lightning Source LLC
Chambersburg PA
CBHW062014220426
43662CB00010B/1322